B Kroupa

An Artist's Tour

B Kroupa

An Artist's Tour

ISBN/EAN: 9783744723909

Printed in Europe, USA, Canada, Australia, Japan

Cover: Foto ©Andreas Hilbeck / pixelio.de

More available books at **www.hansebooks.com**

AN ARTIST'S TOUR

GLEANINGS AND IMPRESSIONS OF TRAVELS

IN NORTH AND CENTRAL AMERICA

AND THE SANDWICH ISLANDS

BY

B. KROUPA

WITH THIRTY-FOUR ILLUSTRATIONS BY THE AUTHOR

LONDON

WARD AND DOWNEY

12 YORK STREET, COVENT GARDEN, W.C.

1890

[*All Rights Reserved*]

PREFACE.

THE present volume contains the record of a prolonged expedition undertaken for the purpose of sketching. A few reflections, dotted down at intervals for my own amusement, have, after nine years of zig-zagging through America, grown into a book. Its contents are nearly all derived from personal impressions and real incidents of my travels. An apology, perhaps, is needed for introducing details which by some readers may be considered obsolete, or of minor and merely personal interest. With regard to the former of these objections, I must plead that in quick-moving America everything hurries with such amazing rapidity that it becomes antiquated in as many days as it takes years in other parts of the world, and as for the latter—the reader will kindly accept unwritten explanations and excuses. A few of the descriptions have already appeared in print, but these have been recast and put in a somewhat different, and I hope an improved, form. Thinking that a publication of these jottings in the form of a book might be acceptable, I offer them herewith to the kind consideration and judgment of the public.

CONTENTS.

CHAPTER I.

New York to Chicago—A Railway Smash-up to begin with—Omaha—By Emigrant Train Westward—My Fellow Passengers—A Disbeliever in the Rotundity of the Earth—Across the Prairies by Rail—Prairie-Dog Villages—Indians—The Church Buttes—The Thousand-Mile Tree. 1

CHAPTER II.

Ogden—Salt Lake City—A Wedding Ceremony at the Tabernacle—Promiscuous Kissing—A Trip to the Salt Lake—A Mormon "Outfit"—The Sequel of a Frugal Repast—A Funny Story—A Dangerous Ride—Jottings in Utah—Mormonism. 13

CHAPTER III.

Humboldt Sink—Virginia City—Sierra Nevada Mountains—City of Sacramento—Visit to a Chinese Joss House—Arrival at San Francisco—Its Sights—The Seal Rocks and Sea Lions—A Disappointing Fête Champêtre—A Visit on Board the *Friedrich*—Santa Rosa—A Social Excursion to the Redwood Forests—Californian Dust—Scenery on the Russian River—A Scare—Picnicking at Saucélito. 29

CHAPTER IV.

A Jaunt to the Calaveras Grove of Big Trees—A Bulky and Confident Fellow Passenger—An Accomplished Bird—A Great Natural Curiosity—Arrival at Murphy's Camp—The Big Tree Hotel—Sounds of the Forest—Discovery of the Mammoth Trees—The Calaveras Caves—Remnants of an Indian Battle. 47

CONTENTS.

CHAPTER V.

On the way to the Yo-Semité—The Town of Sonora—Garrote—The Watershed of the Tuolumne and Merced Rivers—Prospect Point—First Sight of the Yo-Semité—Descent—Rambles in a Wondrous Valley—The Bridal-Veil Fall—The Cathedral Spires—A Trio of Merry Scotchmen—Their Descent into the Valley........ 59

CHAPTER VI.

The Mirror Lake—Fellow Visitors—An Unbidden but Welcome Guest—Encamped for the Night—A Squabble—The Nevada and the Vernal Waterfalls—A Terrific Thunderstorm—Fording the River. 74

CHAPTER VII.

Joining the Mysterious Stranger—The Cap of Liberty—An Interesting Narrative—A Tender Romance—Our Excursions—Hunting and Mining Adventures—A Touching Story.......... 89

CHAPTER VIII.

Roughing it in the Sierras—A Weary Ride—Overcome by Fatigue—A Rough Climb—Sunrise—A Grand Outlook—Camping out—My Genial Friends—Our Parting............. 106

CHAPTER IX.

A Visit to a Chinese Restaurant and Opium Saloon—My Initiation into the Mysteries of Opium Smoking—Its Consequences—Celebration of the Chinese New Year—Chinese Joss Houses and Funerals—Domestic Arrangements and Habits of the Chinese—A Stroll through the Chinese Quarter of San Francisco......... 118

CHAPTER X.

An Excursion to the Sandwich Islands—Lovely Weather—Flying Fish—First Sight of Maui and Molokai—Oahu—Harbour and Town of Honolulu—Decrease of the Population and its Supposed Causes—Costumes of the Natives—Freedom of Hawaiian Life—Excursion to the "Pali"—An Amusing Incident........... 137

CONTENTS.

CHAPTER XI.

A Visit to the Island of Maui—On the Way to Waikapu—Heat, Dust, and Bloodthirsty Insects—Riding to Makawao—Centipedes—Ascending the Crater of Haleokala—Disturbed Night—Return to Maalea Bay—Sugar Making—Planters and the Native Labourers—Work on the Sugar-Cane Plantations. 152

CHAPTER XII.

A Garden under Water—A Beautiful Sight—Kawaihai—Landing at Hilo—A Ride to the Kilauea Crater—Painful Intensity of the Heat—On the Wrong Track—Descent into the Crater—A Boiling Inferno—Eruption of Mauna Loa in 1880—Attractiveness of Hilo—Return to Honolulu—Farewell to Hawaii—Return Voyage to San Francisco. 169

CHAPTER XIII.

The Town of San José—The "Lick Observatory"—On the Santa Cruz Mountains—Salubrity of their Climate—Los Angeles—San Diego—With a Mule-Train through Arizona—The Start—Difficulties of the Journey—Camp Life—Fort Yuma—Gila City—Arrival in a Mining Camp—Placer Mining—The Hydraulic Method of Mining—Arrival at Tucson. 185

CHAPTER XIV.

My Interpreter—An Unexpected Meeting—The Chief of the Indians—Distributing Presents—Dissatisfied "Bucks"—An Extemporaneous Interlude—A Sketching Séance—Parting—A Wild Ride—We Come up again with the Redskins—On the Trail—Our First Halt—Water Discovered—A Restless Night. 198

CHAPTER XV.

Life, Character and Customs of the Navajos—Indian Trading Stations—Language of the Parushapats—Their Clothing and Ornaments—Confirmed Smokers—Their Weapons—Indian Dogs—In Camp—Wigwams—Evening Amusements—War Dance—Courtship—The Medicine Men—Vigils by the Dead—Funeral Ceremonies—Methods of Burial—The Sun Dance—Self-inflicted Tortures—Their Religious Belief and Superstitions—A Doomed Race. . . . 206

CONTENTS.

CHAPTER XVI.

A Ride in Northern Mexico—With Indian Caravan through Sonora—Scouting—The Head-waters of the Rio San Ignacio—Aggressive Insects—Bathing and Toilet-Mending—Indian Trails Discovered—Unwelcome Visitors—Encamped on the Banks of the Rio Sonora—A Sad Incident—Mourning—Burial—Arrival at Ures—A Trying Journey—Scarcity of Water—Mexican Pedrigals and Vegas—A Dreary Region—Rio Yaqui—A Narrow Escape—A Timely Help—Leave-taking. 221

CHAPTER XVII.

Mirage on the Plains—A Welcome Sight—A Hospitable Hacienda—Our Next Halt—A Disreputable Company—Attack by Robbers—Fortunate in Misfortune—A Lassoing Scene—Arrival at Guaymas. 232

CHAPTER XVIII.

Along the West Coast of Mexico—Southward Bound—A Motley Company—Mazatlan—A Fight amongst Steerage Passengers—Manzanilla—Diving for Coins—A Curious Sight—An Alarming Incident—Acapulco—Bay of Panama. 241

CHAPTER XIX.

The City of Panama, Isthmus of Darien—A Stroll along the Coast—A Tropical Sunset—The Panama Railroad—Chagres River Scenery—Aspinwall—Voyage up the Chagres River—Alligators—A Hunting Expedition—In the Swamps of Gorgona—Tropical Vegetation—Look out for Alligators—A Capture—Camping out—Dismal Sounds—An Inquisitive and Distrustful Guide—Uncomfortable Night-quarters—Our Host and his Lady—The Usual Bill of Fare. 249

CHAPTER XX.

On the Way to Mount Ancon—The Natives and their Homes—A Weary Night—Birds and Insects—The Land and the People—Camping out—Mosquitoes and other Nuisances—Deadliness of the Climate—The Panama Fever. 271

CONTENTS.

CHAPTER XXI.

A Terrible Experience at Sea—The Lull before the Storm—Caught in a Cyclone—Man Overboard—The Steamer comes to Grief—Sad Incidents—We Arrive at Vera Cruz—Mexican Festivities and National Dances.................... 283

CHAPTER XXII.

Our Interrupted Voyage continued—We enter the Mouth of the Mississippi—Voyage up the River—Arrival at New Orleans—Its Sights—The Creole Women—I Engage Passage to Havana—Our Sail Down Stream—Disappointments—Nervous Forebodings—Sickness on Board—Quarantine—An Iliad of Woes—Yellow Fever—Its Horrors—Free Again—City of Havana....... 300

CHAPTER XXIII.

The Keys of Florida—Harpooning Turtles—City of Charleston, S.C.—Arrival at Jacksonville, Florida—An Excursion to St. Augustine—The Last of the Seminoles and Modocs—A Turtle-Breeding Establishment—A Sail on the St. John River—Lake Santa Fee—A Taciturn Lady Artist—The Journey Continued Northward—Lake Memphremagog—Its Scenery in Autumn......... 313

CHAPTER XXIV.

Arrival in Canada—Montreal—Christmas at Toronto—Niagara Falls in Winter—A Voyage down the St. Lawrence River—The Thousand Islands—Shooting the Rapids—Quebec—The Montmorency Falls—An Excursion to the Saguenay River—Gulf of St. Lawrence—Island of Anticosti—The Shores of Labrador—Homeward Bound—Conclusion...................... 325

LIST OF ILLUSTRATIONS.

ROUGHING IT IN THE SIERRAS—A DANGEROUS SCRAMBLE
(see page 109). . . . . *Frontispiece.*

	TO FACE PAGE
THE "CHURCH BUTTES," UNION PACIFIC RAILROAD.	10
A DANGEROUS RIDE.	23
A CHINESE JOSS HOUSE.	32
THE "SEAL ROCKS" AND SEA LIONS NEAR SAN FRANCISCO.	36
MAMMOTH TREE, "THE FATHER OF THE FOREST," CALAVERAS GROVE.	54
THE THREE BROTHERS (POMPOMPASUS), YO-SEMITÉ VALLEY.	68
THE BRIDAL-VEIL FALL (POHONÓ) YO-SEMITÉ VALLEY.	69
THE "MIRROR LAKE," YO-SEMITÉ VALLEY (*from a Photograph*).	75
THE DIVIDE OF THE MERCED GROUP OF THE SIERRA NEVADA MOUNTAINS.	93
OUR EXCURSIONS IN THE WOODS.	98
A CAÑON IN THE SIERRAS.	111
VIEW OF THE YO-SEMITÉ VALLEY FROM THE MARIPOSA TRAIL.	115
IN THE CHINESE QUARTER OF SAN FRANCISCO.	131
A CHINESE OPIUM DEN.	135

LIST OF ILLUSTRATIONS.

	TO FACE PAGE
THE ISLAND OF OAHU.	139
MAALEA BAY, ISLAND OF MAUI.	153
PART OF THE CRATER OF HALEOKALA.	160
THE BURNING LAVA LAKE IN THE CRATER OF KILAUEA.	177
"PRAIRIE SCHOONERS."	190
ON THE TRAIL.	203
ENCAMPMENT ON THE PLAINS.	210
EVENING AMUSEMENTS IN CAMP.—THE "TUGWEWAGUNT" (MEDICINE MAN) RECITING A LEGEND TO THE "BUCKS."	212
INDIAN CEMETERY.	215
ON THE RIO YAQUI. (THE WHIRLPOOL.)	228
A NARROW ESCAPE.	229
BAY OF PANAMA	248
A HUMMOCK OF PALMETTO TREES.	254
TROPICAL SWAMP VEGETATION.	258
A PANAMA SWAMP.	262
THE NATIVES AND THEIR HOMES: A PANAMA VILLAGE.	272
THE QUARANTINE SHIP (HAVANA).	306
THE "BRANDY POTS" ON THE RIVER ST. LAWRENCE.	333
COAST OF LABRADOR	335

AN ARTIST'S TOUR

AN ARTIST'S TOUR.

New York to Chicago—A Railway Smash-up to begin with—Omaha—By Emigrant Train Westward—My Fellow Passengers—A Disbeliever in the Rotundity of the Earth—Across the Prairies by Rail—Prairie-Dog Villages—Indians—The Church Buttes—The Thousand Mile Tree.

IT was, I believe, the late Rev. Henry Ward Beecher who made the highly diverting, but really well-grounded observation, "That there is a definite amount of the vagabond in almost every man, and that he must work it out in one way or another. Nothing is more fatal than to bottle it up. You may shut a man in, cork him up, put a seal upon him, but he will come out some day, unless you succeed in smothering him entirely, in which case the man is of no more account than stale ginger-pop."

The wit and truth of this utterance can scarcely be questioned. The love of a gipsy life is a fever too contagious to be resisted by any one predisposed to this failing, which the writer of these pages has the misfortune to own. From my earliest youth my thoughts and longings often carried me abroad, and in one of these restless moods I picked up my valise, determined to go and see that part of America which, according to the best geographers, is called California. Starting from New York on my journey to the much-vaunted West, I was soon across the Hudson river at Jersey City, and snugly seated in one of the Pennsylvania railroad cars.

Being somewhat behind time we were out like an arrow from the station, speeding over the States of New Jersey and Pennsylvania at the rate of twenty-five or thirty miles per hour until we reached Harrisburg. Whilst standing on the track our train had a smash-up which might have had more serious consequences. A heavy coal-train came rushing in, and nearly telescoped the last car of our train. Fortunately there was nobody hurt; but it was ludicrous to see the passengers, after they had recovered from the terrible crash, searching for their belongings in the wreck around. They rushed forward to the luggage-car which was smashed into matchwood, one grabbed one thing and one another, each trying to save and secure his property, though some left their own and took by mistake that which belonged to their neighbours, regardless of what was left behind. I stood mournfully amongst my fellow-passengers, who were uttering doleful lamentations, and looked around in agonised suspense. How could I hope that my only trunk with all my shirt-collars had escaped in the midst of such universal ruin? But to my astonishment and joy I found it undamaged. After we had changed the cars, I told the baggage-master that I would like to take my small trunk which had had such a narrow escape from destruction into the car with me so as to take care of it, and keep it under my own eyes. But that man—that ill-tempered man—turned on me disdainfully and thundered out that I ought to have been born an elephant for then I should have had my trunk under my eyes all the time. This was urbanity's self, and no one could have mistaken it, as he uttered these words in the presence of the bystanders. The sole aim and object of repeating this stale joke is to placard the stony heart of this fellow for public execration, and the incident gives a fair idea of the immeasurable politeness of many of the American railway employés towards passengers, whom they may for a moment find it in their power to snub and annoy.

Pittsburg, which is redolent with smoke and dust, yet a model of enterprise, and famous for its thriving iron and other manufactories, was the next town of note at which a stoppage was made. The town is like many a child we see that would be pretty if its face were washed, but to make up for this omission the country, surrounding the city, has many natural beauties. The bold bluffs of the Ohio river are softened with a tender leafage, and the view as one walks across the fine bridge to Alleghany City is very pleasing.

Reaching Chicago, I stayed there for several days, visiting the various galleries, libraries, parks and manufactories. Some people think Chicago a Pandemonium, but I have nothing but good to say of the city. Little more than half a century ago the spot where it now stands was inhabited only by wild animals, or occasionally by human beings apparently scarcely more civilized than their four-footed neighbours. The whole country around, being then covered with a dense forest, was the hunting grounds of the Indians, but through the agency of the hardy pioneers the forest-trees were felled, and rude huts and temporary houses erected, which have been superseded from time to time by more substantial buildings, until palaces have taken the place of hovels. Most of the houses at the present time are not only comfortable but beautiful buildings. The principal churches, institutions of learning, and large business warehouses are all built of stone. The avenues are most graceful, and seem to have no end, whilst gardens, adorned with trees and a great variety of shrubs and flowers, are attached to many of the residences. Amongst the many elegant hotels the Palmer House is one of the finest, and so is the Sherman House. These two hotels for a long time held undisputed sway, but they are now put into shade by the Grand Pacific. The largest and finest of the public parks— the Lincoln Park—stretches for a long distance along the shore of Lake Michigan, and contains, besides its nice walks, ponds, hothouses and pavilions, a menagerie of various beasts. The enormous stock-yards, and the beef-canning factories where the beeves are either speared or shot in the cattle-pens, are worth visiting, and the process of slaughtering, cutting-up, salting and packing the pigs in some of the large pork-factories is, if not exactly a pleasant, at all events a curious sight. Chicago transforms an enormous number of these squealing quadrupeds into hams and bacon for exportation. It would be tedious to say more about a city which has grown large and famous within our memory, and which so many visitors have described.

I left *viâ* the Chicago and Rockisland railroad. The line crosses the Mississippi between Rockisland and Davenport, and speeding onward through Iowa city, Des Moines, Council Bluffs, and over the great iron bridge across the Missouri, our train finally stopped at Omaha, Nebraska.

My first occupation on taking my seat in one of the cars of the Union Pacific Railroad at Omaha, was to survey the travelling companions I had to live with for several days, and it was therefore well to make friends with my neighbours, short or long. It did not take me a long time to find out the peculiarities of them all. There was a common purpose manifested by all, viz. to sleep, yet originality was clearly stamped on every one, for each tried to get into a more cork-screw position than his neighbour. Trying to sleep in the cars is rather a peculiar sensation, so after having my neck slightly wrenched, and my brains uncomfortably shaken about, I gave it up as a bad job and tried to enjoy a smoke. And so we went whirling for hundreds of miles in the valley of the Platte river which sneaks along between low banks like an assassin river going to drown somebody. It proffers fords and gives shifting sands, and has often in former times engulfed in its treacherous bottom horse, rider, waggon, herd, and all that was trusted to it. There was a great deal of raillery and banter going on in the car; each of the passengers became in turn the butt of the others. They derided and jeered at each other as if they were the worst sinners out of purgatory. One worthy citizen of Omaha was called an "Omahog" and quickly returned the compliment by calling his abuser a "Nebrascal." The conversation turned on the subject of transmigration after death. The Omahog was a firm believer in the doctrine and was expatiating largely upon its points. He was interrupted in his speech by the question: "What do you suppose youself to have been before you were born to your parents?" "I do not know," replied the Omahog, expectorating copiously at the same time. "I might have been a mule or a pig for aught I know." "Well," rejoined his interrogator, "you have not altered much, only got upon your hind legs." After this not very flattering remark, the Omahog bounded from his seat, and while I was lighting a cigar I felt a touch upon my shoulder—the Omahog asked me for a light. Accepting my cigar, he drove it into the bowl of his pipe; he quenched my cigar but got no light. After apologising he borrowed a match from a passenger in the further end of the car and after lighting his pipe he handed me the still blazing match and made the occurrence an excuse for dropping into the seat at my side. He had the aroma of a distillery in full blast floating around him, and spoke of the weather, the alkali-plains, the scenery, the mines, and various other things, and skilfully sandwiched his remarks with indirect inquiries as to my business, place of residence, point of stopping, and object in travelling. In fact he bore a striking likeness to the man who was accused of talking people to death, and I could not help being more and more impressed with the idea that he was a little mad, but he was none the less entertaining on that account. He questioned me as to where I came from, and I told him that I had sojourned in different parts of America, and spent the last few months in New York city, but that I hailed from a country where milk and honey flow in abundance, but unfortunately flow only into the throats of the rich and mighty. He seemed pleased to hear that I came from New York city, and said that his married daughter lived there. "Yas, sir, she's in New York, she went out there as soon as she was married. Her name is Simpkins, she is freckle-faced, maybe you've run across her out there?" I responded that I didn't think I had, but how delighted I should have been to meet her, and added: "New York is a very large city, you know." "Yas, so I hear," he went off again at full speed, "but you might have heard her hollering at her children—maybe you are a little deaf." Then he paid me a very flattering compliment by remarking that he knew at once I was a Scotchman; that he liked the Scotch because they are so gay, polite, and social. I am sure I should have felt deeply indebted for his good opinion, and indeed I was just going to apologise with a meek air for not being born in Scotland, when he spoiled the effect of his prattle by asking: "By the by haven't you got a cigar about you? I have forgotten to buy some." The Scotch proverb, "The souter gave the sow a kiss; humph! quo' she, it's a' for my birs,' came into my mind as I complied with his request. He was very profuse with thanks and brimful of promises, so full indeed, that he would not have had time enough during his life for fulfilment of half of them. He promised amongst other things to give me "heaps of cigars whenever we meet again." The majority of people are most generous when they have nothing to give. Our conversation quietly rippled on, but unfortunately most of his ideas did not accord with those entertained by the world at large; so for example, in his brains the idea of the rotundity of our planet was, as he termed it, "a pretended humbug. Now, to me," he ejaculated with emphasis, "and to every other man with a grain of sense in his head, it is as plain as a pikestaff that the world is as flat as the prairies of Nebraska." Feeling rather tired of his silly prattle, I left his side and crossing the car I sat down at an open window and tried to give a little attention to the landscape. We were all this time on the prairie along the slowly creeping river, cursed by its drifting sand, which whirls in eddies along the inlets, bends and curves of its shores. The clouds were hanging heavily around as we were approaching Cheyenne; the sky was as black as iron and seemed equally hard and pitiless. Later on, however, as the breeze freshened, the clouds rose gradually from the plains, and a shaft of light cast a brilliant glare over the grass and heather, and made the distance remarkably clear. Soon the sky became again a blue vault shading off into bright orange and crimson. The skies, though frequently overcast, clear readily, and a gleam of sunshine follows on the heels of every squall. The scenery around is not interesting, and much less enchanting, yet whatever else may be lacking on the prairies, the sunsets are magnificent. To be sure, the settlers thereabouts cannot be held responsible for that; if they could get at them, they would fry them.

Cheyenne is a most barren and uninviting place, and was noted for the great number of desperadoes who made this place their rendezvous after the U. P. R. R. had been built. Under the inspiration of a score of drinking saloons and dance-houses, they revelled in gold, whiskey, gambling, music and dancing, and occasionally in swearing, fighting, shooting and stabbing. They were such men as are so well described in Joaquin Miller's beautiful lines :

> "Men blown from any borderland,
> Men desperate and red of hand,
> And men in love, and men in debt,
> And men who lived but to forget,
> And men whose very hearts had died,
> Who only sought this land to hide
> Their wretchedness ―――"

Drunken brawls and murders were not infrequent, but as time went on things grew brighter until the better element of the community consigned the ruffians to a dark night of oblivion. When we were again on the move over the Laramie plains, there was plenty of room in the cars, and we were free to pick and choose our seats at leisure. After passing a sleepless night, I folded up my blankets and went into the smoking car at daylight to enjoy a smoke. The sun was rising from behind the barren plains, and its warm beams were sent through the windows of the car. Noticing a placard I stepped up and read the following "Warning. Passengers are hereby warned against playing games of chance with strangers, or betting on three-card monte, strap, or other games. You will surely be robbed if you do." While I was enjoying the warmth of the sunbeams the Omahog came in and shrank back in a corner. He looked somewhat subdued, but after a while he broke loose, and we were listening to his quaint talk. "Yas," he drawled, "I got enough of Cheyenne last night; it hain't no place for me nohow. It's a mighty hard place, Cheyenne is; an' a man don't want to git there more than onct. There came a feller on the car an' told me not to git my supper in the depot, but to go acrost the street to a cabin an' to git it there, an' I'd save a dollar. So I went acrost the street with the feller, an' I got enough of Cheyenne. Look hiar, don't you never stop at Cheyenne, go straight through, an' you'll save money on it. Yas, we went over to the cabin, an' there we've seen some fellers a playin' uv Injun cards. Did you ever see an Injun card? I've never seen one afore that. They hain't like the common cards with jacks, an' kings, an' queens, an' spots on 'em. There's only three Injun cards in a pack. One of 'em's got a woman on its face, another's got an eagle bird, an' the third's got something else. You hold on a minnit an' I'll show you the cards, I bought them from the fellers what got my money."

He searched himself high and low, but could not find the cards. Then he began looking over a pocket-book and while turning over the dirty leaves he came across them, tucked carefully away.

"There they are now, I knowed I couldn't have lost 'em; yaas, them's the very cards. You see there's the woman, an' there's the eagle-bird—dash the eagle-bird! that's the one I lost seventy-five dollars on. Well, those fellers they threw the cards around this way, an' that way (himself shuffling the cards in a very awkward manner) an' bet me I couldn't tell which was the eagle-bird. I bet several times on the eagle-bird, an' I knowed it was the card, for one of its corners was turned up an' I seen it, but I'm dratted if the scoundrel didn't slip the card afore my eyes, an' I lost my money. I kept a looking at the fellers chuckin' the cards until the cars nearly went off and left me. My old woman will be a hootin' when she hears of it.

Oh, Cheyenne's a great place for Injun cards. I got enough of Cheyenne. Anybody who wants can stay an' be bamboozled, but it ain't no place for me nohow."

We all laughed outright. It was evident to the whole company that the Omahog was very "green" and got fleeced.

We passed several prairie-dog villages, and a number of the little, harmless creatures balanced on their hind-legs and greeted us with their wheezy barking. These queer, squirrel-like animals sit watching by their holes, ready at a sign of danger to whisk their tails and rush off to their hiding-places. Each underground burrow is marked by a little heap of excavated earth, upon which they sit, and plunge head-foremost into their holes on the approach of any unfamiliar object. A bullet will seldom stop them. Some of the passengers were cracking away their pistols at them from the car-windows with the sole result that they saw the twinkle of their white feet and the comical jerk of their tails as they disappeared with lightning rapidity. We also saw several herds of antelopes in the distance.

We were now running down-hill at a great rate of speed, having crossed at Sherman station the summit of the Rocky Mountains, at an elevation of 8,242 feet above the sea.

Rushing at intervals through snow-sheds, some of which are hundreds of feet long, we arrived at Green River, Wyoming Territory, 845 miles distant from Omaha. There was a number of Indians squatted on the plaza in front of the station, as our train stopped. The men were fantastically painted, and their glossy hair was plaited all round their heads, which were adorned with feathers, and their necks and arms were encircled with rows of beads and brass-wire. Their faces were smeared over and the prevailing distribution of colours appeared to be red with long stripes of yellow and black along cheeks and chins. One stolid old man, who was probably the chief, was distinguished by a profuse display of trinkets and a huge necklace made of the claws of some wild animal. As to clothing, there were the usual oddities of costumes, but nearly every one had the same covering—a blanket and dirt. "Some were in rags, some in tags," with the addition that some wore instead "velvet gowns," soldiers' old uniforms, and strutted around in them with wonderful dignity. Disdain of the white strangers seemed to breathe from their persons, although they snatched with eagerness the cigars and tobacco that sympathising hands proffered them.

The dust and the blinding sun-glare from the parched-up plains rendered looking out from the car-windows very unpleasant, but nevertheless I was unwilling to miss a glimpse of the surrounding world of wonders. Rock-cuts become now very frequent and abrupt along the railway track, and sandstone buttes crowd thick for many miles around. As we neared "Bryan," the next station, the Uintah Mountains hove in sight, looking but a short distance to the south of us, but these sharp, clean-cut cones are in reality many miles away—so deceiving is the clearness of the air on the plains. Leaving Bryan with its few cottages, we passed up the Black Fork Valley, and presently crossed a little stream, and kept pretty closely beside its winding trail for the next twenty miles or more. On the opposite bank rose the long, solid lines of buttes, streaked with brown and tawny yellow, and a few low cotton-wood trees made a scattered fringe along the current's edge, and cast their shadows dimly on the water. As we passed through this valley the glow of sunset suffused the heavens with a subdued illumination, the buttes became more and more purple, and some owls, hooting on the opposite shore, added to the weirdness and gloominess of the scene. The sky changed gradually from orange to red with a few crimson-tipped clouds, while here and there a pale, little, trembling star came forth to watch the last faint crimson-streak fade from the west. The next morning we were still winding along through the bluffs with the Sentinel Domes of the Uintahs always in sight, until we arrived at Church-Buttes station.

The Church-Buttes are a curious range of steeply-sloping mounds, tipped and bordered with rocks which moisture, wind,

THE "CHURCH BUTTES;" UNION PACIFIC RAILROAD.

frost and heat—the sculptors of the earth's surface—have worn and hewn into all sorts of quaint and fantastic shapes. Turreted castles, battlements, buttresses, domes, spires, pillars and columns range and rise one above the other. The effect of these weirdly beautiful rocks, when the sunlight strikes aslant them, is very deceiving and puzzling to the mind of the traveller. He seems to be entering a cemetery of departed giants. The fantastic columns vary in pattern, and crowded as they are with fine traceries and figures they look like a freak of fancy on the part of some old-world sculptor. One cannot help wondering whether it was by the hand of man or of nature that all this was done. Over all this wilderness of bluffs and rocks is laid the warm, rich colour of the red-brown sandstone which glows in the sunlight against the background of sky. Some of the rocks are shaded by lighter and darker belts, and the dark pines which grow in the deep crevices and niches heighten and bring out the richness of their colouring. Towards the end of the buttes, the pillars dwindle somewhat in size and assume at a distance the likeness of rows of old, grim Egyptian sphinxes. This group of rocks is a part of the "Bad Land" and stands ten miles south from the station, which derives its name from it.

Leaving Church-Buttes Station we traversed a good stretch of hunting land stocked with deer, elk, bears, wolves and the detested coyotes. Sulphur and soda springs also abound. The track crawls, winding and doubling in and out around the spurs of the Uintah Mountains. The next station Piedmont is reached by a heavy up-grade. It is a wild, windy region, where the winter storms must rage fearfully. The white crests of the highest mountains crowd the southern horizon, and their cones of snow seem to chill the air. The snow-sheds and the drift-fences follow the track almost continuously, and at the summit of the divide comes the longest snow-shed of the Union Pacific Railroad, telling that the snow-drifts here must be mountains in themselves. The stony bluffs, which heave wildly all around the lonely little settlements near the railway track, are crossed and intersected with drift-fences, hinting strongly what the winters must be to the dwellers of this region. So far there was still some show of vegetation, however spare, of sage-brush in unvarying monotony, but leaving Piedmont we entered the "Bad Lands," passing through a most uninteresting country, a lifeless desert utterly devoid of vegetation. The irreclaimable waste stretches away for many a long mile to the south and west, without a single green thing to vary and enliven the scene. The surface of the ground is in many places encrusted with alkali, and a great number of little pools, only a few inches in depth, are scattered over the plain, the water of which is very bitter, pungent and unpalatable.

Before daylight the following morning we passed the far-famed "thousand mile tree," the only tree for hundreds of miles around. What there is to be seen of that curiosity I cannot say for two reasons, firstly because it was pitch-dark when we reached there, and secondly, being pretty well fagged out, I was partly asleep during our tedious ride.

CHAPTER II.

Ogden—Salt Lake City—A Wedding Ceremony at the Tabernacle—Promiscuous Kissing—A Trip to the Salt Lake—A Mormon "Outfit"—The Sequel of a Frugal Repast—A Funny Story—A Dangerous Ride—Jottings in Utah—Mormonism.

PROCEEDING westward, the Union Pacific Railroad enters Utah through a narrow pass called "Weber's Cañon," and sweeping through the "Devil's Gate" into the open valley, the fine view of Ogden, the first Mormon settlement, is a relief to the eye of the traveller, fatigued by the unvaried sameness of sage-brush and sand. It is a pretty place, smiling, sunny, and brilliant with light—an oasis in the surrounding inhospitable and dreary waste.

From Ogden I started south to Salt Lake City, forty miles distant. Having secured a room in one of the hotels, I sallied forth to take a general view of the town, resolved that I would look at everything, and scrutinise everybody. And now, even at the risk of being pelted with the sticks and stones of public opinion, and of drawing upon me the animosity and wrath of those folks who are never happy except when they are making themselves miserable over some imaginary grievance, and never satisfied but when they are meddling in other people's affairs, I am going, and deem it right, to state that my ideas of truth do not accord with those entertained by these people with reference to the customs and doings in Mormondom. I have heard many strange stories, and many writers upon this subject have certainly given great encouragement by their reports to others, who might feel inclined to follow their example, abusing these remarkable and much married people; but judging by what I saw with my own eyes and heard with my own ears, I could not fail to come to the conclusion that the general public seems to be far too sweeping in its condemning assertions respecting the moral state of the Mormons. Surely one advantage of travelling is that, while it removes much prejudice against strangers and their customs, it enlarges our sympathies, and intensifies our appreciation of the good traits and qualities of other people. Those who believe in the existence of good men and women can find them even in the less trodden regions of the world, beyond the boundaries of their own quarter of the globe. Now here, what wonderful progress I saw, notwithstanding all that is averred against the Saints. The virgin soil of untrodden wilderness and waste, which was reclaimed from nature, not many years ago, is dotted with pretty cottages, nestling amongst fruit-bearing trees—homes of industry, perseverance and affluence. Truly this is wonderful, and cannot be dismissed from one's attention with a cynical observation.

It chanced on my ramble through the town that my way led me past the great Mormon Tabernacle. I heard the buzz of many voices, and following the sound, I entered noiselessly with slightly nervous expectations. An Argus-eyed Cerberus motioned me to a seat, and I sat down quietly close to the barrier among the other spectators. A marriage ceremony was being performed. The contrast and glitter of attractive colours, and the graceful grouping of the fair assemblage formed altogether a scene of vivid beauty. All the resources of the place were expended in giving effect, and the result was a scene at once unique and brilliant. Festoons and garlands were suspended from the walls, and mirrors displayed the splendour of the spectacle with multiplied effect.

An avenue was left clear for the bridal procession. The notes of the organ pealing forth a wedding march, betokened the arrival of the bridal party, and in a few minutes, arrayed in white silk, and preceded by several bridesmaids, the bride and the bridal procession entered. They advanced slowly, and on reaching the front filed off on each side. The ceremony was the usual one, and was very short. After the quaint admonition: " . . . which God will that you receive, and wear from henceforth to His praise, and pleasure, and honour," &c., was pronounced, the procession was again formed, and marched with great pomp to strains of the organ, and faded away "like the baseless fabric of a vision," into the shadow. I followed the procession into the recesses of the vestry, and no one showed any wish to drive away the random visitor. There the bride was congratulated and kissed by scores of her relatives and friends, until a mania for kissing seemed most electrically to seize upon the whole company, for everybody was now laid hold of by every limb, and kissed and embraced by a score of people, the large majority of whom, I grieve to say, were the very hardest specimens of what is called the softer sex.

Well, I thought, "never miss a kiss, even if you should kiss a miss," as the old saying goes, and with great animation, though with something of excitement, I entered into the handshaking and kissing business. As the pump-handle method of expressing eternal friendship was put in operation, the eyes of the Cerberus were rolling upon my visage. My heart sank within me. Now the worst would come, thought I, if they find out that I am a bachelor, then I shall have to pay dearly for this; but I got out of the door unmolested. I never shook hands with a Mormon before; it feels odd, but it does not hurt.

Late at night, after writing the above in my diary, and when I set about the glorious task of laying my head on the pillows, I felt the proud consciousness of having vindicated a much-slandered reputation and said a good word for the much-abused saints; but I felt restless, notwithstanding, and could not sleep, so raising the blinds, I looked out upon the city. A fresh breeze blew in upon me through the open window.

In front, to right and left the streets presented the same appearance—deserted, silent, the dark shadows of night still hanging over them.

As daylight was making its first faint appearance, I could see that heavy clouds hid half the sky. After breakfast I went into the streets, although a drizzling rain fell, soaking the ground into the consistency of a dingy pudding, which is a rare sight in Salt Lake City. Mightily pleased with my first day's impressions, I went again to the Tabernacle. This time I was ciceroned by an elderly Mormon with whom I casually struck up acquaintance the previous evening. The old Cerberus, with his blear-eyes, was again moving about, either collecting money or showing people to their seats, whilst a stout man in a black coat, with blazing eyes, distended nostrils, trembling frame, and nervous hands, with his grey hair streaming in the air, was preaching. Mighty thoughts were surging and battling through his brains, and a torrent of eloquence was bursting from his throat and striking into the ears of his audience. He stood on the pulpit as if it were a quarter-deck, and every now and then he shook out the top-gallant sail of some bold utterance.

It was George Cannon, the most energetic and active of the apostles and leaders of the Mormons. As he concluded his sermon with a sigh, as if over the lost delights of bachelor life—well, far be it from me to speak slightingly of his matrimonial bliss—and left the pulpit, loving hands met his, and kind looks from gentle faces answered the listless gaze he threw around him.

Next morning, after the rain and dulness of the preceding day, the sun shone out clear again, and I started in a rumbling vehicle, into which I was basely inveigled by my casual acquaintance, to have a view of the surrounding country. It was certainly the most wretched-looking affair in the form of a "buggy," and the mustang turned out to be the most vicious animal in the shape of horseflesh I ever saw. We soon

found ourselves without the limits of the town, and for a mile
or two we passed holdings cultivated as market gardens, and
beyond these we drove over a plain, where deep waving fields
of ripening yellow corn lay extended in gay succession, with
gentle slopes and pastures between, meeting occasionally a
much-married citizen escorting his healthy-looking housewives
with a glad sense of undisputed ownership. A good many
horses and cattle were seen on the green meadows, in some of
which mowers were piling upon hay-waggons the sweet-scented
grasses for transport to the neighbouring stack-yards. Beyond
the river Jordan the road became very bad, and even dangerous,
as we were nearing the divide of the range of bluffs which
skirt the Salt Lake. Winding along the crest, we made ovals,
arcs, and half-circles in our serpentine course, and looked
upon huge boulders torn from the mountain-side, and upon
splintered rocks, deep gorges, and wild chasms. The horse
required something more than the volleys of oaths which were
showered upon him from time to time. He was vicious, shied
and stumbled, and my companion had to thwack him during
the whole ride. He gave as much trouble as possible. I
murmured secret prayers that I might never have the ill-luck
again to drive in a Mormon "outfit" (they call everything in
the Western States, from a single packhorse to the largest
freight-train, "an outfit") and behaved for a long time with
quite a monumental patience, but at last, after several unsuccessful attempts I made my companion hear, and he pulled
up to ask me what I wanted. "I can't go in this abominable
machine any longer," I said by way of opening a conversation.
"Why don't you people here have better roads and carriages,
or ride on asses as they did in olden Biblical time?"

He reflected for a moment and a thoughtful look filled his
eyes as he replied that, "There was not much travelling then,
nor were there any carriages in those days."

"Then how did the people get around to business?" I
asked.

"They rode on asses," he replied.

"Well then, are there not enough asses in your city?" I asked again, but seeing the withering look he turned on me, I hastened to change the subject of our conversation by asking him if he was married, and if his wife was still alive. This seemed to cheer him up.

"Yas, sir," he said, "I have a good wife an' children too."

"How many children have you?"

"Five, an' this reminds me that to day is the anniversary of one of my girls' birth."

"I suppose you gave her a present, a token of your fatherly love before you left?" I said.

"Oh, she gets presents enough of her young chap. You see, she's got a sweetheart, an' he takes her out to some dancing, an' stuffs her pockets with sweets, an' she eats up her share, an' it makes her sick."

"You should not begrudge her the joy she feels," I said.

"No one begrudges it, but her sickness costs me generally three dollars doctor's fee."

"What does she get from her sweetheart that it makes her sick."

"Wal, all sorts of things; generally a gingerbread heart, with 'Think of me,' or 'Forget me not,' or 'Remember me' on it; an' she remembers the derned thing for a week, I reckon. No, I don't think such presents are healthy."

"I don't know anything about the sanitary condition of gingerbread presents, but if they make her happy so much the better. Isn't she going any more with him?" I asked.

"I reckon if you ask her, you won't have to build a fire under her to get her started. I s'pose she's going whilst I am away, so I made her a present in advance."

"What was it?"

"I belted her before I left till she promised not to eat any of the derned stuff."

"Have you got any boys?"

"Yas, one little boy."

"How did he come out?"

"He got licked."

"What for, did he eat hearts too, with 'Think of me' on them?"

"No, he heard some of the boys a swearin', an' he allows himself sometimes to do the same."

"And you licked him for that, of course."

"No, not for swearin'," he broke in, "I do a little of that myself sometimes. I licked him because he torments the soul out of me. Every time I send him to fetch something he brings back something I didn't send him for. But it's of no use; his mother always shields him. Forgiveness for his errors is too easily obtained from the old woman. It is very disagreeable for a man to become a father, and suddenly find himself the parent of a boy whom he don't exactly feel at liberty to spank when he likes." He dwelt on the different sins and transgressions of his boy for a while longer, and then he in turn asked me, "How's your wife goin' on? How's your children?" But disregarding this question I surveyed the surrounding landscape until we came to a lonely spot, perched high above the lake, which lay outspread like a sheet of burnished glass, as far as the eye could reach. Its shores are rocky and rugged, but they present from sunrise to sunset a great variety of the most exquisite tints and shadows: and the distant arid plains and the sheltering Wahsatch mountains offer endless attractions.

"And far away, 'mid peaceful gleams
 Of flocks and herds and glistening streams,
 Rose, fair as aught that fancy paints,
 The wondrous city of the saints!"

On an open space, stretching ourselves on the grass, we took our frugal repast of choice pieces of antelope, while the horse that had brought us out in the family buggy grazed peacefully by. Liquid soon brought us to animation. "When I am at Rome I do as the Romans do," note all their ways, and eat what they've got in their shops, whether sausages, ham, antelope or pork chops, and drink what they drink; but unfortunately my Mormon friend seemed to entertain the very same opinion though in a highly exaggerated degree, for his every feeling and faculty was bent on the repast. The pampered greedy-gut swooped every now and then down upon the basket with the viands, and buried his talons deep in them, but still oftener he snatched at the Californian wine before us. It was vain to beg him to moderate his zeal, so I thought it better to remove the temptation from his side. "Hold on, hold on!" he shouted, "that hain't fair," and stared at it with bewilderment, but as for letting the eatables escape—ask a hungry lion if he feels disposed to part with an antelope which he has just met in an African jungle. Soon to my mind the idea that he was pretty "tight," as some people term it, was an undoubted fact. He began to be very communicative, and talked of human heads as if they were as many strawberry tarts. For a timid gentleman of quiet habits his society was not alluring. He poured into my ears a very queer story, and horrible to relate, whilst doing so, he took out from its socket one of his eyes. Now I noticed that there was something very strange in the expression of his visage, but I thought that maybe the Mormon creed produces such an effect upon the human countenance, and I had no idea that, his right eye being of glass, he had to look upon the beauties of nature only with his left. Answering my question as to how he came to lose his eye, there came such a tale of woe from his lips that it made my hair stand on end. He told me how he travelled with ox-teams across the plains; how his eye was popped out by Indians; how, hoping to make existence sweet by travelling, he joined hands with a circus-show in the western territories; how he succeeded in filling out the gaping vacuity of the socket with a glass eye, which matched his real eye; and how, depositing his eye in a glass of water upon retiring one night, he found the next morning when he awoke that one of the circus artists was gone, and so was his eye. He then borrowed a glass-eye from the leading lady equestrienne, the star of the company, who had a variety of them. But the borrowed eye was a bright blue eye, and his other eye was lustrously black. However, it was made to pass in the emergency, and in this guise he sought out the erring friend who stole his eye, and gave him a most tremendous cudgelling, which brought out the fact that he had sold the eye to an Indian squaw. Then he went after that squaw, gazed upon his eye which she wore amongst a string of beads as a necklace around her neck, and with rage in his real eye, he cut the false eye from the squaw's necklace with a knife, but alas! its luminous lustre was destroyed by having a hole cut through, and thus was he obliged to retain the services of the borrowed blue eye. And drawing himself up into an almost impossible attitude, he narrated another story: how a man once upon a time attempted to lick him, and how he got exasperated and relieved him of a part of his ugliness by gouging out one of his squinting eyes. I was also informed, whilst he cut another quid, that on several other occasions he had followed the scriptural injunction in relation to the teeth—"a tooth for a tooth," &c.

Finally, he began moaning and muttering to me in a kind of sing-song which it would have puzzled any one to tell the meaning of, and several times I had difficulty in escaping being embraced by his huge paws. I tried to console him by telling him that he was still very well off, and that he could see more than I could; that he could see both of my eyes, whereas I could only detect one of the orbs in his face. But, unheedful of my well-meaning consolations, he moaned that he looked back upon a cheerless life; that his misfortunes began at his birth; that no opportunity was given to him to display his numerous accomplishments and highly-prized qualities; that he was a good citizen, a dutiful husband, a loving father of several children, a good Christian, farmer, and harness-maker; that he was the man who treads the bellows or pedals of the great organ in the Tabernacle on festive occasions, gala, and holidays; and in fact that he was a genius. He concluded the recital of his wrongs by entreating me beseechingly, with a woe-begone face, to let him lie and fade in the grass amongst the flowers. I felt inclined to tell him that genius, as a witty Frenchman observed, is the capacity for making an ass of oneself at the unexpectedly right time, and that he either always had been or was a fool at the present moment; but as I was standing near a precipice, and had seen the gleams of fire flashing from his eye, and the dangers that lurked in the deep bosom of the lake, I thought it but common prudence not to say so.

At last he fell off into a tranquil sleep, and as it grew rather late, I nudged his ribs to apprise his brains of the fact, but all to no purpose. Getting at last excited, I called him every abusive name I could think of; but unheedful of all this, the good man slept tranquilly, and without even a snore, peacefully and contented. I am sure that this ridiculous episode would have amused me mightily, had it only occurred at a less unfavourable time and place. How long I sat sketching and waiting I do not know; suffice it to say that the surrounding landscape was blent with the rays of the setting sun as my companion awoke from his repose on the bosom of mother Earth; and that darkness was fast approaching as the horse was "fixed up" and the task of driving home over the rugged ridges had to be faced.

And here I come to the pith of my tale. Whilst we crossed the dangerous bluff the gentle pattering of rain began to fall upon our ears, and we were blanketless, having no covering save the cold and comfortless vault of heaven.

Soon the night became very dark, not a star venturing to show from behind the sable shroud that invested the firmament. The still distant thunder was heard gradually approaching, and I could think of nothing when I looked at the black heavens but the agony of my baffled and repentant soul, and the visions of domestic happiness which my companion had called up and which I had — escaped. Half-way down the steep, precipitous grade I felt a thrilling and creaking, and looking back behind us I saw the trigger of our vehicle lying broken on the ground. Then

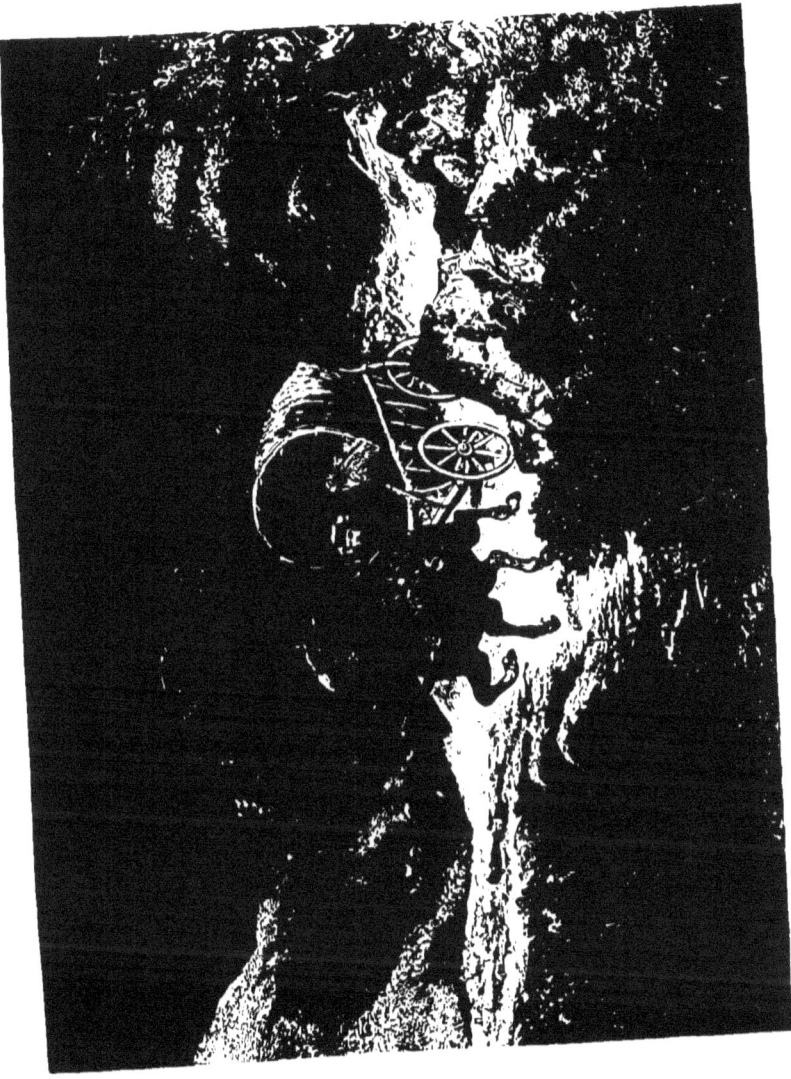

A DANGEROUS RIDE.

down the grade we thundered, sending the gravel and stones flying over the side of the precipice. I saw the danger, while again came the ominous rattle and cracking noise, and the horse snorted and otherwise betrayed great excitement.

> "Men sometimes, in certain situations,
> Derive a sort of courage from despair,
> And then perform, from downright desperation,
> Much more than many a bolder man would dare."

One glance more I gave around, then tearing the reins from the hands of my half-witted and silly driver, gathered them together, shouted at the top of my voice, and lashed the horse wildly, till it leaped and neighed in advance of the impending danger. Speed was our only chance. The horse's nostrils smoked; sparks snapt, crackled, and played around his hoofs, and every hair in his mane seemed a porcupine's quill.

It was a terrible drive; a single false step of the horse might have sent us rolling over, in which case, upon reaching the bottom, there was a fair chance that horse, buggy and its occupants would not be worth sixpence a bushel. We tore along beside the declivity, when suddenly the animal tripped over some obstacle in the dark, caught against the edges of the stones, snorted with fear, then laid back his ears, and made a final, desperate bound. By this unexpected shock my scared, and by this time thoroughly-sobered, partner flew from his seat, his nether extremities appearing where his bewildered head ought to have been, and then he was dashed to the ground; whilst horse, buggy, and I glided to the bottom, over the treacherous rockslide, coming down with a solid thump into a waste of sage-brush and sand.

I got up, fortunately not much hurt, and turned around to take in the situation. Stunned and bruised, my friend lay on the ground dumbfounded, but soon recovered sufficiently to call me and inquire if I was safe. He looked about him, and peeped, with a sheepish expression in his face, up the rugged bluff, over which the nag took that desperate slide—it was enough to make one's flesh creep.

In true Christian spirit I made to my blue-eyed companion, who had been smitten by his fall on the right cheek, the proposal to turn his left for a similar favour; but he indulged in some remarks which were not at all characterised by an unusual warmth of acknowledgment for my generous offer. We stripped a hickory-bough and patched up the badly-shattered vehicle as well as we could. Whilst we bound and tied the broken pieces together, my friend gave vent to his wrathful feelings, and looked as if just ready to snap the nag's head off. I gave him another dose of soothing consolations, and with them my warnings as to the dangers of enjoying with too much appetite antelope-steaks. But above all, I said, don't take too many drinks, then you will not feel oppressed, and if you should fall asleep, you will not sleep like a log. He answered with a grateful look, and the horse having recovered by this time from its trembling fit, we continued our homeward journey, and arrived again at Salt Lake City without further accident.

Salt Lake City is situated in a well-cultivated valley, which is surrounded by the Wahsatch mountains. Most of the farming is done by means of irrigation, and the fields bear evidence of efficient husbandry. The water for this purpose is obtained from the adjoining mountains. Some of the streams have been dammed along the uplands, and canals or ditches constructed, through which the water is conducted over the plains. The town is nicely laid out in squares, and contains some fine buildings. Picture to yourself on an undulating plain, walled from the world by barren and sterile deserts, a fine town with substantial, comfortable dwellings, and broad streets, lined on both sides with trees. There seems to be a plentiful supply of water, for in every street one can see a clear stream running along the gutters. Everywhere there are indications of an easy-going, contented life, and even in the poorest shanties cleanliness and neatness are displayed. And all this was done during the lifetime of one man. Walking along the streets of this Mormon town one can scarcely believe that the span of one human life could suffice to found and build up a city as large as this. The history of Utah is full of romantic and sad incidents; and how eventful was the progress of this town, yet so young! The first settlers of this district, which was at that time (1847) a Mexican dependency, were exclusively Mormons. Brigham Young came from the east at the head of his followers, and laid the basis of the prosperity and success of the country. It was on the 23rd of July, 1847, that Orson, Pratt, Milford, Woodruff and Brigham Young entered Utah with 146 men and three women, being chased out of Nauvoo on account of their Mormon proselytism. When they came to the place where Salt Lake City stands at the present moment, they determined to build there the "City of the Saints." Without delay they began the construction and erection of buildings, and the colonisation of the new country. Soon afterwards 16,000 emigrants arrived, and without much concern for the claims of the Mexican government, they founded a State, whose prosperity soon evoked astonishment and envy. They transformed the arid soil by cultivation into a condition that would do credit to the best agricultural community of any country, and made the wilderness around "blossom like a rose."

Years came and went, and the Mormons lived in their new homes separated from the whole world. No mail arrived, no news or information reached them, and they hardly caught the echoes, or felt a flutter of the outlying world. After the Mexican war, when the far West, to the shores of the Pacific, was ceded to the United States, the country was annexed as a territory, and Brigham Young was, in the year 1850, nominated by Congress as its first governor. His indomitable will and iron perseverance in the teeth of adverse circumstances, as well as his charitable and kind actions towards his grateful followers, together with the influence he exercised as the high-priest of Mormonism, were the causes to which the rapid rise and progress of the city is ascribed. Even to this day the life in a Mormon town or settlement is quite patriarchal, and its inhabitants enter but seldom into a law-suit, or commence an action in a law-court.

There are thirteen church-circuits at Salt Lake City, each under the charge and supervision of a bishop, two councillors and six teachers. These constitute the tribunal in a dispute or legal suit, and endeavour to reconcile the contesting parties. Only in very few cases is the protection of the Government-court sought, for even the " Gentiles " (as every non-Mormon is called by the Mormonites in Utah) have occasional recourse to the church-courts of Justice. When this tribunal is unable to end the case by a decision satisfactory to the parties, and they are still anxious or willing to seek right and justice before a higher Mormon tribunal, they can appeal to the " Court of the Seventy," composed of bishops, church-councillors, and teachers; and if even their verdict fails to pacify the disputants, there still remains the " Court of the twelve (so called) Apostles," whose decision is final. A Mormon, unwilling to submit to their final judgment, is expelled from their church; this however happens very seldom. Utah has at the present moment a population of about 145,000; of whom about 120,000 are Mormons.

The real originator and founder of the Mormon sect was a man named Rigdon, born in Pennsylvania, who was, in the year 1823, cast out of the Baptist community for being an eager adherent and defender of communism. Being ambitious and a good judge of human weakness, he knew well that the shortest and surest way for gaining influence, power and wealth, is to advocate and disseminate that religious superstition and bigoted intolerance, towards which so many people of the lower classes in America incline. As a prophet he began to preach some new doctrines, and one of his confiding disciples—Joe Smith—a youth full of enthusiasm, worthy of a better cause, became, after a short preliminary drill, the most eloquent and zealous preacher of the new creed. Having convinced himself that his new occupation of making converts was as easy as it was lucrative, he separated from his master after a short time, and became himself the leader of the sect. Pretending to have been inspired by a supernatural revelation, he proclaimed polygamy as advantageous and consistent with the teachings of Christianity, and plurality of wives was thereupon introduced as a lawful measure into the Church. Joe Smith became a second Mohammed. Adherents began to multiply, and proselytism flourished, until the violent death of the prophet, which made him in the eyes of his people a martyr, whose memory they honour and revere.

After Smith, Brigham Young took the leadership with remarkable success, having besides a good endowment of sagacity, courage and daring, a considerable talent of statesmanship. He it was who conceived the bold design of leading his believing flock to the then almost unknown West, in order to escape the oppression and harassing of their persecutors. After having suffered fearful privations and hardships on their long journey, they clung to their liberator from trouble and affliction with a slavish submissiveness, which he knew well how to make use of. Brigham Young died a few years ago, having left a fortune of three millions of dollars, and nineteen—presumably mourning—widows. The mantle of the prophet descended to the shoulders of John Taylor, but the Mormons possess since the death of Brigham Young no real leader. They are governed by twelve apostles, of whom Taylor is the president; but George Cannon, his best confidant and first counsellor is in reality their present head.

Polygamy is very expensive, and therefore only the church dignitaries, and wealthy members of the community are able to have more than one wife. Neither do many of the Mormon girls covet the questionable privilege of becoming the second or third wife of a husband. They prefer the undivided love of a man, be he ever so humble, to the decrepit affection of even a Mormon bishop or apostle. Besides, there are also secessionists, who repudiate plurality of wives. Joe Smith's own sons are such apostates. During the last years Mormonism has gained but few converts in America ; and the European immigrants are as a rule the poorest, most ignorant, and uneducated people, enrolled in Scandinavia, Germany, Ireland and Wales. It is therefore evident that Mormonism, as a religion, can still exist for years to come, but its whole principle and system has outlived its vitality, and its final collapse and dissolution cannot be far off.

The old Tabernacle, though outwardly very unpretending, has remarkable acoustic properties—a pin dropped on the floor at one end, can be heard at the other. Its great middle aisle is 450 feet long. The so-called Assembly Hall, which is used as a church in winter, is much smaller than the Tabernacle, but it contains a good many pictures referring to the Mormon creed. The new Tabernacle which is now, and has been for a good many years, in course of erection, will be a splendid structure, and undoubtedly eclipse all the other buildings in the town, when finished. As for means of amusement, Salt Lake City has two theatres, but they are almost exclusively frequented by the Gentiles.

CHAPTER III.

Humboldt Sink—Virginia City—Sierra Nevada Mountains—City of Sacramento—Visit to a Chinese Joss House—Arrival at San Francisco — Its Sights—The Seal Rocks and Sea Lions—A Disappointing Fête Champêtre—A Visit on Board the *Friedrich*—Santa Rosa—A Social Excursion to the Redwood Forests—Californian Dust—Scenery on the Russian River—A Scare—Picnicking at Saucélito.

BIDDING adieu to the City of the Saints, I resumed my journey westward, round the northern shore of the Salt Lake, which reflected the light like a great mirror. Angry clouds rose in the west, and soon a violent thunderstorm swept over the lake. As the storm receded we saw a double rainbow. The concentric circles were lace-like in their formation, and the colours clear and distinct; the arches were perfect, and their ends tinged the water with their brightness. The lake reflected the exquisite hues, and as they gradually faded, the passengers all declared that they had never witnessed anything more lovely. Only a muddy little fellow made the remark that he had seen something like it before, but he was obliged to take it back. Having obtained furtive snatches of sleep during the night we looked with curiosity at the surrounding country when daylight dawned upon us. We had now fairly entered the alkali plains, the great American desert, and a more desolate and barren region it would be difficult to imagine. This stretch of land offers larger and more favourable opportunities for successful starvation than any other section of America I had visited until then. It is indeed, one of the most distressful tracts of country that I ever set eyes on. The fine, penetrating alkali dust reduces everything to nearly the same tint. Most of the passengers were kept awake during the weary two days and nights of our journey through this desert by the overwhelming dust which made eyes and throats sore. Everybody was stretching, and gaping, and gazing out of the windows; and rough miners, emigrants, and bordermen sat side by side, and chatted, smoked or chewed with great gravity.

At last we came in sight of the "Humboldt Sink"—a large, lake-like expanse of water, into which the river of the same name flows and disappears, to gush forth again at another point. This is characteristic of several streams in the mountainous regions of Western America. But in the desert of Nevada there are no declivities to explain this disappearance and reappearance of the Humboldt.

Arriving at Reno, I took the stage for Virginia City, Nevada. The town is quite undermined, and I visited one of the Comstock-lode mines—the richest of all silver mines in the world. A shaft had been sunk down to a depth of 2,000 feet, and from it the miners have run drifts in every direction, and unearth large quantities of the precious ore. The most powerful machinery is employed to hoist the excavated rocks, which yield enormously. With such inducements to labour, it is not surprising that the days are devoted to hard work; but when at night the crowds of miners congregated at the gambling and drinking saloons, and music, liquors, and cards were all displayed in a most alluring guise, the scene resembled a pandemonium. The sign of the saloon projects over the streets with astonishing frequency, and it seems that gambling is openly indulged in without the interference of the law. There is a great mixture of races from every country in the world—Chinese, African, and Indian as well—uniting to form a strange contrast of manners, language and complexion, and giving the place a cosmopolitan character.

After many a weary hour of tiresome travelling some faint, blue outlines appeared on the horizon, as if nature had dipped her pencil in the faintest solution of ultramarine, and drawn it across the western sky with a hand tender as love's. We were approaching the Sierra Nevada mountains. They seemed to be made of air and the sunshine which showed them. We arrived at their summit the next morning, just as the east was beginning to flush with royal crimson and purple, and the earliest gleam of the morning sun was sprinkling its gold upon the tops of the tallest trees. The sunbeams broke through the floating clouds of mist, and enabled us to gaze into the tremendous abyss of the "Emigrants' Gap"; at the bottom of which the Trukee river foamed and glittered like a silvery thread. The mountain chain is cleft by several deep gorges, through which the waters of the rivers and lakes flow down into the plains of the valleys. There are some magnificent scenes of solemn grandeur along the railway track, but the numerous snow-sheds are a great nuisance, and spoil many of them. Through these we were now thundering, in semi-darkness, wrapped in the heavy black smoke-clouds from our engine.

After the summit is gained, the route leads down towards the Sacramento river, whose waters wind and stretch far away between the gently undulating slopes. Only within a comparatively recent period has this land been properly opened up to emigration, yet what wonderful progress we saw! To-day the hills and valleys are dotted thickly with settlers' homesteads, farm-buildings, cattle-ranches and fields of waving crops. In 1848 gold was first discovered by Captain Sutter at Coloma, about sixty miles from the spot where the city of Sacramento now stands, and thereupon crowds of people from all parts of the globe flocked to California to share the vast treasures of the new land of gold. The city of Sacramento is built on the left bank of the Sacramento river, and "J" and "K" streets (the thoroughfares are named after the letters of the alphabet) are its principal avenues of business. Here may be seen at all hours of the day almost every variety of vehicle and draught-animal, from the light buggy and pony, to the heavy freight-waggon and stolid ox-team ; the owners of which are busily engaged trading with the merchants, whose shops and stores line these thronged streets for several blocks.

I took a stroll through the Chinese quarter, and arriving at a " Joss-house " I stepped inside. On either side of the entrance stood two large figures, about twelve feet in height, tinselled and painted off in true Celestial art. The inside of the place looked very much like a curiosity shop, being filled with bronzes and china. Groups of wood-carvings were suspended from the ceiling, and about six feet from the floor were large glass-cases arranged upon shelves, in which all sorts of Chinese figures, ten to fifteen inches in height, were displayed. Still further back was the Celestial altar and throne, where the great Joss himself allowed the stream of bounty to flow upon his subjects and adorers, or turned it off as it pleased him. Nothing but the painted face of the great Joss could be seen peering between heavy curtain-folds, but the face possessed not a single Mongolian feature. It resembled more the general appearance of a Turk. An immense flowing beard and moustache covered the entire lower part of the face, and the complexion being florid was in striking contrast with the pallid and wax-like skins of the Chinese themselves. On a table in front of the idol there was a spread of what looked like roast chicken, pork, tea, &c., and on either side some wax candles were burning, and mingled their fumes with the sickening odour from numerous smouldering tapers and pastilles. I was very much pleased to make the acquaintance of the old gentleman, although he gazed down upon me with a frown from between the curtain-folds, and through the spectacles which straddled his nose, as if he wished to draw the unbidden guest's attention to the door. In one corner, quite by himself, sat a dwarf figure of a man of an enormous *embonpoint*, who had a more villainous countenance than any of the other idols. He seemed to have been held in high esteem by the Chinese in spite of the expression of almost fiendish malig-

A CHINESE JOSS HOUSE.

nity which rested upon his face, for a great number of peacock feathers—which are used as decorative indications of nobility and rank—were conspicuously disposed around him. The Chinese consider corpulence to be one of the most important qualifications, and regard it as a physical virtue which imparts dignity to the appearance. The most popular gods in the Chinese Pantheon are remarkable for their obesity. The stairs and the passage which I had to pass before I reached this "holy of holies" were dingy and dirty, indicating very little reverence on the part of the worshippers. No forms of etiquette, and no solemnity of demeanour are enjoined upon or expected of those who visit the Joss-houses. Shoes are not removed from the feet, the head is not even uncovered, nor are there the slightest signs of awe or reverence—in short, there seems to be very little religious zeal amongst them, and whatever may constitute the belief of the Chinese, they are certainly not enthusiastic or devout in the matter of religion.

Leaving Sacramento, I continued my journey to San Francisco on a steamer down the Sacramento river and the Suisun and San Pablo bays. The high hills which separate the bay of San Pablo, in the rear of Oakland, from the Pacific ocean, prevent the rush of the cool winds to the heated plains beyond the coast-mountains; but a very perceptible change in the temperature is felt when nearing breezy San Francisco. In passing up the Bay we experienced the full force of the air-current which passes very freely from the ocean through the Golden Gate. It was long past midnight, and the sky was studded with bright orbs of the most brilliant lustre as we crossed the beautiful bay of San Francisco. It was a gorgeous night of stars; Fort Alcatraz, and the spires and towers of the city stood out in clear outlines against the sky, and the burning lamps of the long rows of streets that run across the hills, blinked from afar their welcome to us.

My chief occupation during several weeks after my arrival at San Francisco was wandering through the streets to see its sights. What crowds of people one meets in the course of the afternoon promenades, for who can sit tamely down to work in such incomparably and intoxicatingly lovely weather as they enjoy there for about nine or ten months in the year. The city of San Francisco is not more than forty years old, yet it has many fine buildings, which in style, and beauty exceed those of the eastern cities. California does all on a large scale. A city of palaces has been built on a site which, thirty-five years ago, was distinguished from the surrounding wilderness of sand only by a Jesuit mission, a log-fort and a few canvas-tents of miners and miserable hovels of the Indians. To-day its streets are a perfect network of tram-lines; many of its houses, and some of the hotels especially, are very fine edifices, which are nowhere surpassed in the world. The Palace Hotel, for example, is a magnificent building, which covers an entire block, and is seven storeys high. Its court-yard is a general meeting place of the habitual *flâneurs* and fashionable promenaders—a band often discoursing music there in the evenings. Some of the tram-lines are being worked by an endless wire-rope, which is necessary, as some of the streets are very steep, especially California street, where are most of the swell mansions. The houses of the rich are most tastefully adorned, and surrounded by nice gardens, abounding in flowers, statuettes and fountains. San Francisco is a very breezy place; the wind sings at times a dismal wail down the chimneys, and whistles with energy through the key-holes and crevices of the wooden buildings. I very often stood wondering and musing while the boisterous zephyrs were indulging in their untutored gambols without let or hindrance. Hats bound and roll through the streets, while the crazy antics of their owners are, in some instances at least, comical and grotesque.

Towards the end of November we had the first rain, and parched-up nature accepted it as the first instalment of the showers which were expected by everybody very soon. That "it never rains but it pours" is a very good proverb, and nowhere better applicable than in California. The rain did fall like a second deluge, and after a few days of rainy weather the grasses spread stealthily over the gladdened soil, and the brown, sun-dried hill-sides were green again and glorious with their verdant pasture. All looked washed and refreshed, and even the birds wet their wings in the rills and pools, and burst into joyful twitter. Occasionally whilst the soft rain descended, the warm sunshine streamed through the clouds, and seemed to be playing a game of hide and seek with them, and sometimes there was an oasis of bright sunshine in the desert of rainy days; but at last the sun shone out again with its traditional splendour, and we could admire it to our hearts' content. The trees, lately so dusty and drooping their cheerless and dreary boughs, very soon felt the effect of the rain, and looked as if they were whispering blessings for it. The flowers and plants which bent their heads, dried up by the parching sun of the dry season, received new life, which they poured out in grateful fragrance. The very smell of the moist earth was delicious, as the first faint tinge of pale green was stealing over the bleak, sandy hill-sides, and every plant put forth a leaf here and there, wherever it could.

The beauty of these winter days (falsely so called) is indescribable, and as I breathed the fresh, clear, bracing air, and felt the blessed sunshine beat on me, I concluded that I had no cause to regret being in California. Incredible seemed the accounts which came to us in newspapers of heavy snow-falls, sunless days and intense cold on the other side of the Sierra mountains, and the Atlantic slope of the continent, whilst we looked on all the wealth of roses, fuchsias and geraniums.

One of the prettiest places in San Francisco is Woodward's Garden, with its numerous fountains and cascades, rare plants and shady nooks, its collection of living animals, huge sea-lions, bears, camels, tigers, and other beasts of prey; and above all its thousands of gorgeously-plumed birds, collected in large cages. There is also a large museum of Californian curiosities and stuffed animals, hot-houses full of beautiful plants, art-galleries, concert-hall, skating-rink, theatre, restaurant, &c., &c., attached to it. This garden is the daily resort of numbers of children with their attendants; and from the arcades in front of the restaurant one can watch the cease-less flow of visitors and promenaders outside. I often went there and stood looking at the open mouths of the baby-spectators, and listened to their shouts of joy before the seals' pond, the monkeys' cage, or in front of the inclosure where the bears were housed and made clumsy attempts to hoist themselves upon their hind-legs. They were as peaceful and playful as so many kittens; and one day I watched two charming young ladies, dressed in velvet and satin, feeding them with ginger-bread, until—although I dislike ginger-bread—I began to wish that I too were a bear, to receive cakes from such fair hands.

The Golden Gate Garden, San Francisco's public park, is many acres in extent, and contains some very nice walks and carriage drives. A short distance from the park is the Cliff House, where visitors can obtain accommodation and refreshments. There is an inclosed and covered piazza at the back of the house, high above the sea, which is a favourite resort of the guests to look at the Seal Rocks, which are about two or three hundred yards distant, right in front of the house, and swarm with seals and sea-lions. The cooling breezes come from the blue expanse of the Pacific, and as one sits nestled in the shade of the verandah, the view from it is charming. The rocks in the foreground make a striking picture when the surf comes rolling in, and dashes and surges and leaps against them, while every now and then a wave, larger and mightier than the others, hurls itself upon them and throws its

THE "SEAL ROCKS" AND SEA LIONS NEAR SAN FRANCISCO.

spray, like an immense glittering fountain, twenty or thirty feet high; or rushing between the rocks, sends a water-spout high into the air. The water boils and hisses around, and on the outlying, jagged cliffs the barking of the huge sea-lions, and the screeching of thousands of sea-fowl seem to testify to their thorough enjoyment of the tumult of the waves. A few hundred yards from the Cliff House is a smooth beach of white sand, where one may bathe with safety almost any day, for the surf is not very high along the beach, and the bathing is excellent.

On one fine day I took part in an excursion to Fort Point, and the Helmet Rocks, lying in the channel of the Golden Gate. This entrance to the bay of San Francisco is certainly not misnamed, for it is like a draught-channel through which the cooling winds and air-currents sweep inland from the ocean. The wind pours in with such violence that there is almost always a heavy swell in the channel, and small vessels roll and pitch as if there were a severe storm.

The day was sunny and the scene cheerful; the waves impelled by the wind, broke on the sands cheerily though somewhat briskly and roughly. We had sent some provisions in an express-waggon early in the morning to an appointed place on the shore to await our arrival, but when our large company, after a fatiguing tramp in the sand, reached the place, there was no sign or indication of the team having been there. After climbing the surrounding rocks and sand-hills till nearly noon, we at last detected the waggon, horses, coachman and provisions—stuck in the sand, and in a very sorry plight. The provisions were at once unpacked and carried to our chosen pic-nic ground, and not the children and ladies only, but the whole of the hungry and thirsty party together, who had been long searching and watching for their appearance, praised the kind heavens, and called them blessed. There were many happy hearts to testify to the yearnings of very vigorous appetites. The gentlemen tried first to appease the hunger of the children and ladies, but unfortunately our caterer had invested the funds, intrusted to his own good judgment, in a multitude of slippery sausages of a pale complexion, such that no man could guess whether they were steamed, boiled, fried or baked. Their dry and hard surface resisted defiantly all our efforts to soak and parboil them in hot water—it was of no use, they remained like grindstones. They had probably been used as a sign in the show-window of an ancestral butcher, and had descended to us in their old age, bleached by the sun and flavourless. The sausages were certainly a failure; but then, there were cakes and pies—pies indeed, but as ancient as the sausages, yet they were as manna fallen upon the earth, and were eaten by the children and ladies with a humble and pious offering of thanks to heaven. What a mingling of mirth, fun and disappointment do such occurrences on such occasions yield!

The Austrian frigate *Friedrich* was lying at anchor, at the time I am writing of, in the bay of San Francisco. Having hired a row-boat, in company of some friends, I paid a visit to the man-of-war, and passed some very pleasant hours on board the ship. Before leaving we arranged with some of the officers of the frigate to go on a social excursion to the red-wood forests on the Russian river, in Sonoma county. Taking the steamboat to Donahue's Landing, and the railway thence to Santa Rosa, we arrived at that lovely little town in the evening, and remained there over-night. Santa Rosa lies on a rich and fertile plain which is in a high state of cultivation. All the semi-tropical fruits grow there, and the grapes are of the finest varieties, and the most luscious I ever tasted. There are many wonders in California which have never attained a celebrity beyond their vicinity, and so this little town of Santa Rosa is blessed with one of the largest rose-trees in California, which spreads over one entire side of a large wooden house and climbs up to its roof. It bears white and red roses on the same trunk. Though it had plenty of roses of both these colours on its boughs at the time when we saw it, people told us that its appearance then could not be compared to its richness when in full bloom. Then the roses literally hide from sight the whole top of the house and present the picture of a colossal bouquet of beauty and fragrance. Looking at it, one was reminded of some of the old English ballads, like—

> "There grew out of the earth a red, red rose,
> And out of her a briar—
> They grew and they grew to the church-steeple top,
> Till they couldn't grow any higher."

The beautiful and poetic idea of immortality, which is embodied in these images, and is so conspicuous in love-legends of the Merry Isle, is strengthened in one's imagination in a land where the orange grows, and the olive thrives, and gardens are gay with rose-blooms in mid-winter. Great numbers of these delightful flowers are brought daily to market, and sold in the streets of San Francisco. Poor flowers! though in your beauty you presume to breathe the perfume of spring, you may be cropt at any hour, and

> "Though it may then your fortune be to rest
> On the soft pillow of a fair maid's breast,"

you must wither, and be thrown away, for it is your doom! I will not further attempt to describe the wealth of the fruit, and the beauty of the flowers; of the fuchsias climbing to the house-tops, with their gorgeous effect when in full bloom; and the geraniums growing to the height of a man's head.

As we were galloping, the following morning, in an open buggy over a bad and broken road, we got a foretaste of what Californian dust means. If any one wishes to know what dust really is, let him go to California, and he will get the desired information. During the dry summer months, the dust whirls and dances along, powdering everything, so that there is a strange uniformity of colour given to every object. The shrubs by the dusty road, dusty themselves, grey-green and draggled, and every place, cottage and tree resemble each other in a remarkable degree. Arrived at Korbel's mills, our destination, we went straight to the Russian river, only a few yards distant, and having plunged into its water, we felt once more in our right minds.

Sonoma is one of the most fertile counties of California ; it has a glorious climate, and is blessed with rich harvests of manifold crops. This county has played a very important part in the history of California, and among other remarkable events, the American war against the oppression of Mexico broke out there. Its southern part, the so called valley of Sonoma, is well known to every inhabitant of San Francisco, as the place where the best American vine grows.

In the year 1812 some hundred Russians with about the same number of natives of the Aleutian islands landed at the mouth of the river which bears now their name, founded Fort Ross (Russ?) hoisted the Russian flag, and dwelt there till the year 1841. Some of them travelled, traded, and lived with the Indians, and by intermarriage with them became the ancestors of the half-breeds of Russian and Indian blood, some of whom are still to be met with in the county. Others of them sowed wheat and corn, or busied themselves with cattle-breeding, fishing, hunting and trapping, especially of otters, which at that time were very numerous along the rivershores. Often have the Californian governors protested against the settling and colonising of the Northern barbarians in this territory, which was first claimed by Spain and afterwards by the Mexican republic. In the year 1823, General Vallejo as commandante della linia del Norte, established a military garrison at Sonoma, having received special instructions to keep a sharp eye on the Russians ; but the latter abandoned their settlement in 1841, and sold all their property and belongings— the fort as well as the guns included—to Captain Sutter, the subsequent discoverer of gold in California.

On the Russian river begin those proud red-wood forests (redwood = sandal or Brazilian wood) which supply San Francisco with fuel and building material. They spread northward along the coast to Mendocino, and the only access to many parts of them is by ascending the river-beds of the numerous coast-streams and creeks. Daring lumbermen load their ships during tidal time, and thus transmit the lumber from the northern saw-mills to the harbour of San Francisco; but the forests along the Russian river are already intersected by a railroad. Korbel's mills are in the midst of this majestic forest, whose trees are noble and graceful in form and stature. Their sturdy majesty is almost oppressive to a human being; they rear their colossal forms as straight as ships'-masts into the air, and the river glides like a harmless serpent amongst them, so softly as to cause no ripple. They stand guard around, and the wind is never permitted by these pensive guardians to disturb the calm of its waters. They perform this service most disinterestedly, for in return they scarcely ask to have their classic features mirrored on the river's gem-like surface. Yet the waters kindly reflect their images towards the serene sky, but they never behold them, and so do not err in vanity. Majestic as they are, they bear the neighbourhood of lesser trees, and the yews and aspens that stand near the margin of the river, peer into the smooth water to catch their own reflection, while the madronas stand near them with a well-affected nonchalance, derived from a legitimate consciousness of their beauty.

The banks of the Russian river are encircled by a multitude of these giant red-wood trees. There, the soil being deep, rich and humid, they flourish most, and attain to the full pitch of life. They tend, however, to become extinct, and seem to be murmuring anathemas on the human pigmies, the sound of whose axe and saw mingles with the voices of these monarchs of the forest, while they shake their heads above the scene as though in sorrowful protest. The whistle of the locomotive now desecrates the solemn dignity of the place. Those colossal red-woods (*Sequoia sempervirens*) are next in size to the Mariposa and Calaveras big trees. They are from 200 to 300 feet in height, and from ten to twenty feet in diameter. On a space of about one acre we counted more than eighty of these giants, and one of them, which had been felled in our presence, furnished material—according to the approximative appraisement of the lumbermen—for the fabulous quantity of 500,000 shingles. In another we saw a cavity, which was spacious enough to offer shelter to a score of people. What immense trouble and labour is required to dig up and exterminate the stumps of the felled trees, may be imagined from the fact that,—blasting powder being often found ineffectual,— coal-oil has to be poured over and firewood piled around them, and the mass being set on fire, they are burned out. In this way a good number of acres had been cleared, to fit them for fields and plantations.

We used boats as well as horses on our daily excursions. The wood-paths were all alike; a short distance from the mills we were in the densest forest. Some of the old trees along the banks of the river have been dead many a long year, and in many cases their topmost boughs have blossomed into a new life of green mosses and glistening lichens. They looked like phantoms, and it struck me that to gain a realistic idea of Hades one needed only embark in a slight craft and glide along the smooth river among these ghastly shapes. Their white arms were like those of skeletons, and they moaned and whispered gusts of sorrow over the silent waters that washed their feet. The mosses were like the memory of olden sins fastened in their marrow, as remorse feeds upon the soul, and the mistletoe and the vines and creepers that climbed up their old hoary stems, were their only joy—a reminiscence of childhood—the verdure that will never spring and bloom again!

My three companions from the Austrian frigate left me after a few days; their short leave of absence passed too quickly. I had been sketching very industriously, and every day found some new charms and beauties in the woods. The ground was covered in many places by a dense growth of brambles, vines and thorns, and I often lost myself as I scrambled among them. My heart was awed within me when I thought of the silent and perpetual work of creation around me—finished, yet renewed for ever. The process by which an accumulation of vegetable matter is constantly produced so as to render the soil fertile, is in itself very interesting. Nature sows first furze, briars and thorns, the leaves of which annually die and shed. Thus a vegetable mould is prepared for larger plants and shrubs, which again in time decay and perish and help to prepare a bed of soil deep enough to bear trees. The process of nature acquires accelerated force as it advances, and plants, bushes and trees continue to be produced and decomposed, for :—

> " Lo !
> All, all grow old and die—but see again,
> How on the faltering footsteps of decay
> Youth presses; ever gay and beautiful youth,
> In all its beautiful forms. These lofty trees
> Wave not less proudly that their ancestors
> Moulder beneath them. Oh, there is not lost
> One of earth's charms; upon her bosom yet,
> After the flight of untold centuries,
> The freshness of her far beginning lies,
> And yet shall lie. Life mocks the idle hate
> Of his arch-enemy Death—yea, seats himself
> Upon the tyrant's throne—the sepulchre,
> And of the triumphs of his ghastly foe
> Makes his own nourishment."

The poet who wrote the above lines, which often came quite vividly to my mind whilst I was roaming through these forests, had certainly communed closely with nature, and his soul had truthfully caught the meaning of her miracles.

My favourite retreat was a deep, shadowy gulch, called

Elliot's cañon, in the midst of which stood a rough, deserted lumbermen's shanty, shaded by the most enormous red-wood trees that I had up to that time seen. A heavy atmosphere of dampness and gloom brooded over it, and there was a suggestion of the sinister presence of all sorts of slimy creatures lurking in the furthest secluded nooks and chasms, which might dart out and devour any unfortunate being, should fate cause his foot to slip, when gazing at those tangled masses of vegetation. But I had grown too much accustomed by that time to the various inhabitants of the forest, to experience any shudder and creeping of the flesh even at the awakening of moccasins and vipers from their torpid repose, although I must confess they never impressed me very agreeably.

I did get rather a fright one day. In a gloomy nook a singular, silent shape burst suddenly on my view as I was sketching in the cañon. It stood quite still and so fixed and immovable—glaring at me with large eyes through the twisted boughs of the bushes—that I could not realise at first whether it was living or not. My eyes started from their sockets with superstitious alarm, but as I approached the solitary presence, the combined effects of light and shade grew more distinct, and I found it was—a strayed cow. I gave a lively chase, caught and tied her with my horse's bridle to a tree, and drove her in the evening in triumph to the mills.

Having swallowed again an enormous dose of dust on my homeward trip, I arrived safely back at Santa Rosa. This county-town has a population of about 3,000, and is the centre of one of the most productive districts of California. From the top of its principal hotel can be obtained a charming and extensive view of the surrounding vine-clad country. To the north-west rises the Geyser peak, and to the north-east Mount St. Helena rears its lofty crest.

We were a merry pic-nic party one lovely morning shortly after my return to San Francisco, steaming out to the beautiful grove of Saucélito, which lies on the northern shore of the bay.

We had a delightful sail. The broad-winged barks of commerce were passing in and out of port, and the bay was full of sails, white and brown. Yerba Buena Island, Fort Alcatraz, Oakland, Angel Island and Saucélito, all appeared successively in view— so picturesque and all so rich in never-to-be-forgotten reminiscences. Saucélito—what memories does not that dear little place recall! This sunny sea-front village, which lies so beautiful, so quaint on the mountains' slope, is blest with a green crown of laurels and live-oaks, and charms by its picturesque beauty. It lies high, and its air is remarkably bracing and breezy. From the top of the hill, on the slope of which the neat cottages are erected, the view on all sides is charming. Above our heads was a sky that would not disgrace Italy, and below the scene was scarcely less enchanting. Before us smiled a bright little valley, dotted with huts, and gleaming with snug villas; and at the foot of the hill was the sparkling water of the bay which laves the base of this quiet village, just rippling into a kind of languid animation under the influence of a balmy wind; and on its surface floated boats, packets, vessels and steamers, beating the waves through the Golden Gate to the Pacific ocean, or making their way to Oakland on the opposite shore. We strolled among the country lanes, human voices made the solitude musical, and the air responded in glad echoes. I was listening to the shouts of joy and mirth, but I was in no mood for badinage. The thought that I had to leave San Francisco in a few days and all the kind friends perhaps for ever, tuned me to sadness. There are moments when the mirth of others only saddens us and jars on our own mood. The young girls laughed, and sang, and romped, picked roses and put them to their pouting lips, and with their tender, purpled fingers wove wreaths of flowers in their flowing hair and looked so pretty. One of the young ladies—a sweet child-face—picked a rose with her lily hand, and gave it to me in memory of that far-off ramble. Alas! her kindness was worse than cruelty.

Late in the evening as soft breezes bore our ship slowly towards our homes, we sat on deck, and one of the ladies favoured us with a song. Her whole frame seemed to thrill with ecstasy and joy as she sang in a sweet, musical voice, which was quite in keeping with the ruby lips from which it proceeded. The day's outing was thoroughly enjoyed by all.

CHAPTER IV.

A Jaunt to the Calaveras Grove of Big Trees—A Bulky and Confident Fellow-Passenger—An Accomplished Bird—A Great Natural Curiosity—Arrival at Murphy's Camp—The Big Tree Hotel—Sounds of the Forest — Discovery of the Mammoth Trees—The Calaveras Caves—Remnants of an Indian Battle.

THE wind seemed softest and the sunlight brightest as the steamer bore me away from San Francisco out into the beautiful waters of the Suisun bay. Winding through the tortuous, and, in some places, narrow San Joaquin river, along whose banks extensive gold-washing operations were formerly carried on, our steamer reached Stockton late at night, and the coach for Murphy's Camp was to start at 6 A.M.

Trying to "fix a bite" before starting, I was rather late in the morning, and on arriving found the coach crammed full with a motley crowd of passengers. I surveyed the company. On the top of the coach was squatted a small colony of cackling Chinamen, and in the inside were several men, but none of them friendly-faced, besides a robust woman surrounded by baskets, bundles, boxes, and a large cage housing a parrot. I was at a loss to find a place where to squeeze myself in, but the driver urged me rather impatiently to take my seat inside. I told him that I had a prejudice against being smothered to death, and that I did not want to go inside at all. "But you have to; there's no other place," replied the driver. Reluctantly I shoved myself in, hoping that at one of the next stations there might be a vacant seat on the outside; and wedged myself in between a broad-shouldered man, the bulky woman, a bundle of wearing apparel, and the cage with the parrot. The feathered biped greeted the featherless one, *i.e.* myself, with a *pot-pourri* of screams and cries of a deafening description—objurgatory, angry and defiant. This frightening welcome from the angry parrot was soon answered by chuckles, squalls, crows and cackles from chickens, geese, turkeys, ducks and other animals, which were aroused from their sleep in an adjoining poultry-yard. It will always remain an open question as to the dignity or good taste of the parrot in starting this competitive exhibition of the strength and volume of the various throats, and methods of crowing and cackling at six o'clock in the morning.

I was told by my neighbour of the coarser sex to think myself lucky in having secured a seat among such a select company, and at the side of such a fair neighbour. Indeed, considering how all public conveyances are now being used by the "coloured gentry," and the troops of the pig-tailed celestials the steamers are bringing to California without cessation, it is creditable to the authorities and managers of rail-roads, steamboats, and stages that they should be able, and deign to contrive any arrangements for the conveyance of ordinary Christian travellers. The parrot could not be reconciled. He made forcible complaints and gave tongue to his indignation in piercing cries at being pushed unceremoniously under the dark seat, but his screeches were carried to the most extravagant point as we started, drawn by six horses in a brisk trot. In spite of being crammed and jolted over an execrable road, I was surprised to see the perfect confidence towards me which the woman displayed in resting her wearied head on my shoulder, of which free and easy conduct and the suffocating feelings which followed I shall ever retain a lively remembrance.

"Does your parrot talk, mum?" asked the broad-shouldered neighbour of the woman, who was enjoying the comforts of sweet repose on my shoulder.

"Not that I know of," replied the woman; "why do you ask?"

"Well I thought you bought him at Flaherty's auction in Stockton yesterday."

"No; was there an auction yesterday?"

"Yes, didn't you know Pat Flaherty, who died a short time ago in Hornitas?"

My attention and curiosity being aroused, I asked who Pat Flaherty was, and what his exploits were before he left for the "undiscovered country, from whose bourn no traveller returns."

"Well, sir, Pat was a square, honest chap, but he had, like most people have, a hobby—he used to have all kinds of animals around his place. I met him the first time in the placer-minings, it must have been more'n twenty years ago, I reckon. Even at that time when he was gold-washing, or prospecting, he always used to have some sort of animal with him—a monkey, a cat, or dog, or a bird, an' we used to have heaps of fun with him. There was something or other sure to come off wherever Pat was. He was a favourite with every one of 'em chaps, though he exhibited sometimes a striking amount of perfect cussedness; but then you must understand that at them early times in Californy, he who could display the most of dare-devil cussedness was thought the most of. He had been in this country for a good many years, and was one of the pioneers, led a most adventurous life, met with ups and downs, but like a cat always fell on his feet, and always seemed to get ahead in spite of fortune's frowns. For the last few years he settled on a small farm, and collected quite a menagerie on his place, and when he died, his widow sent all the derned brutes left after him to Stockton to be sold at auction. I was there yesterday. The monkeys brought from one to three dollars; a big bear was knocked down at fifteen dollars, but the auctioneer made a great hit with a parrot, just like yours is, mum.

"'Now gents,' he said, 'here is one of the finest parrots on

E

the American continent ; he swears like a Barbary-coast pirate, and can sing the tral-la-loo like Adelina Patti—how much am I offered for 'm—five cents ? guess you don't know what ye'r buying, gents—ten do I hear ? He talks better'n some of your congressmen and ministers—ten cents I'm offered—why, gents, he knows Tennyson all by heart, and 'll outswear any man in the crowd ; just the thing for little children ; an' only ten cents I 'm offered.' Here the auctioneer stopped to take breath, and looked reproachfully upon the crowd. The accomplished bird was finally knocked down to a preacher who came in just in time to hear that the parrot could sing all of Watts' hymns."
...The old gentleman started out highly elated with his prize, but when the disreputable bird told him to go to—not to heaven, he went back to the auctioneer and wanted to swap for an orang-outang, or something that didn't talk."

Whilst the interest of the narrative was culminating, the good woman fell asleep, and unheedful of profane observation was slumbering profoundly on my shoulder. If modesty is a quality which highly adorns a woman, as the ancient saying runs, I failed to discover it in her. Subsequently a little shift gave me the full force of the pressure of her, I grieve to say, very heavy and bulky form. At the first station, when the horses were being watered, I pleasantly bowed myself out of the woman's warm embrace, and got up on the box-seat beside the driver. The former occupant of the place, an almond-eyed celestial, gaped at me gaggling and gibbering, but as the stage was going to start, he crowded into the coach to the utter dislike of the bulky woman and her olfactory organ.

The driver was a most excellent whip. He handled the ribbons with admirable skill and boldness ; in fact most of the Californian stage-drivers are noted for their clever management of the horses. They are a singularly fine race of men, possessed of great shrewdness, and inured to hard work, as they were formerly exposed to constant danger from the border-ruffians who poured into California, and from the Indians. They are very civil, obliging and communicative. The country around

Stockton is for a considerable distance rather flat and dotted with oaks and other trees, which give it a park-like character, like to the valley of San José. We rode in merry mood through leafy avenues, among oaks, tall pines and firs; across grassy glades; and later on we skirted deep gulches and climbed uphill and down dale, but not for a moment slackening from the sharp, brisk trot. It was really remarkable to see the skill, ease and mastery, with which our driver governed the six spirited horses over a road which seemed occasionally almost impassable.

Arrived at a station we took our breakfast, and had about half-an-hour left to look about the place. Wandering through the streets hard by, I came to the post-office and saw the following—" Notice to the Public," which adorned its rural walls: " Straid or Stole a large red Kow. It belongs to a widow, eight or nine years old, with yaller specs on her off-side, and a short tail."—" Well," said·I to myself, "that beats everything that Barnum has ever shown·to the public. How many people there are who would be glad to see such a great natural curiosity—an interesting widow of eight or nine summers! How this remarkable lady would adorn high society, and make drawing-rooms that are dull with rich dowagers blazing with the diamonds of Golconda and the gold of Ophir, gay and picturesque with her 'yaller specs and'—well, truly—'There are more things in heaven and earth, Horatio, than are dreamt of in your philosophy.'"

We had to mourn at this station the loss of the bulky woman, who was sitting in the midst of her chattels as we drove off; but I was not rewarded like my companions with smiles, or even an acknowledgment of the comforts which she had experienced on my shoulder. A gentleman with a sanctimonious countenance took the vacant seat in the coach, but I fancied that he must have feared to turn heathen in this heathenish company, for after a short while the driver had to pull up, and he requested us to make a little room for him on the outside. No wonder, for the heathenish influence began to tell upon us, in the form of invisible aromatic vapours, in spite of the clerical fellow-traveller, whom I supposed to stand between us and perdition.

Our drive was beautiful, as at times we had magnificent views over valleys, and far away over the plains to the mountains. The entire road opened up a series of charming landscapes in thousand varieties, from the utmost ruggedness of outline to a delicate one of grace. We arrived at Murphy's shortly after 6 P.M. and the air being pure and keen, enabled us to do ample justice to the excellent repast furnished. The famous big trees of Calaveras were my next object of inspection. Saying adieu to my fellow-travellers, who continued their travel to Sonora, soon after ten o'clock the next morning I set out on horseback for the grove of mammoth trees about fifteen miles distant, in company of a young guide. We soon entered a narrow valley and commenced ascending the cañon of a small stream; scrambling up a steep and rugged trail to the height of several hundreds of feet, occasionally getting glimpses of deep, wooded hollows, overhung by rocks and cliffs. Proceeding farther—what a glorious forest of pines we rode through—many of them from ten to twenty feet in diameter and towering up as straight as liberty poles for 250 feet or more, and without a branch for 100! Such a ride alone compensates one for the trip. These giant pines stand widely apart, and being free of underwood, and branchless up to a great height, one can see under the shade of their sombre foliage to a great distance. Unconsciously the fancy grows that one is gazing through the proud gothic arches of a mediaeval cathedral. The surface of the ground rises in swells and elevations so smooth and rounded that a carriage could almost be driven amongst the lordly trees. About noon we reached an eminence and began descending into a sheltered valley. The hills on all sides were densely covered with pines and spruces, the shadow became more dense; and passing on our way, we reached one or two enormous trunks which rose above the sea of forest high into the air.

We dismounted at the door of the Big Tree Hotel; a comfortable frame building, surrounded by the shadows of one of the most magnificent forests known on earth. The valley, in which the hotel stands, is situated between the slopes in a depression of the mountains, at an elevation of 4,370 feet above sea level; thus the grove is sheltered on all sides, and has a very deep and moist soil. The first of the great trees that claimed my attention is at the side of the hotel, and lies prostrate upon the ground. It was cut down about six feet above its roots. This operation employed five men for three weeks, and pump-augers were used for boring through it. The stump was smoothed level and now forms the floor of a handsome pavilion connected with the house. The solid wood of the stump is twenty-five feet in diameter, and adding the thickness of the bark, the whole diameter is about twenty-eight feet. Lower down on the ground it is about thirty-three feet. I took up my quarters in the pleasant, clean hotel, and wandering for several days from tree to tree, I never became weary of admiring them. It was only after the glóaming, when afraid that night would overtake me in the depth of the forest, that I reluctantly quitted a scene fraught with such interest. When returning towards the hotel in the waning light, I was more than ever impressed with the grandeur of these forests. During my excursions on the Russian river in the preceding year, I was overawed by the enormous size of the trees there, yet they were mere saplings, not half arrived at the maturity of tree-hood compared with these. There are several groves of these remarkable trees in California, but none are so celebrated and widely known as those of Calaveras and Mariposa, which rank first in point of height and girth. They are always found in groups, and are the hugest mammoth trees known up to the present time in the world. They have rivals in the eucalyptus trees, which grow in Australia and attain even more than 400 feet in height, but the largest do not exceed the girth of eighty feet. There is again another big tree which exceeds the Californian giants in thickness—the baobab; but this species although swelling out at the base, is of a low growth, never exceeding seventy feet in height. If therefore both thickness and height of the great trees of the Pacific slope be taken into consideration, they stand as yet without a known rival. The highest tree now standing in the Calaveras grove is the "Keystone State"; it measures 102 feet in girth, and its height is said to be 386 feet. "He is monarch of all he surveys—his right there is none to dispute." For comparison's sake I may mention that the height of St. Paul's Cathedral in London is 360 feet, and of the Capitol in Washington 288 feet. The age of this tree is estimated at 3,500 years. It spread abroad its branches in the very pride of prosperity of the mysterious Egyptian Empire. In the grove, the big trees number ninety-three; of those more than eighty feet in circumference however there appears to be only about twenty. These possess as yet the undisputed sovereignty of the primeval wilderness.

The principal trees have received fanciful names, such as Beauty of the Forest; Pioneer's Cabin; Three Sisters; Husband and Wife; Hermit; Pride of the Forest; Hercules, etc. The Father of the Forest lies prone on the ground, and near by stands, or stood at the time of my visit there, the Mother of the Forest, more lucky in her fate than her venerable consort, though her bark had been stripped off to the height of 116 feet from the ground and sent to England as a visible representation of a mammoth tree. Relics undergo sometimes strange transpositions—the Obelisk of Luxor from the burning sands of the Nile to the centre of the Place de la Concorde in bustling Paris; the frescoes from silent Pompeii to bright and sunny Naples; the monuments of Nineveh from Assyria to the British Museum, and Cleopatra's Needle from Egypt to the Thames Embankment—all these are odd changes, but not much behind them seems to me the removal of this bark from the mystic solitudes of the primeval forests of California to the crowded galleries of the Crystal Palace at Sydenham. It was put together and exhibited there, but unfortunately it was destroyed by fire in 1866. The dimensions of the Husband and Wife are nearly equal. They

MAMMOTH TREE, "THE FATHER OF THE FOREST," CALAVERAS GROVE.

stand in seemingly affectionate nearness to one another, yet they must have indulged occasionally in a little matrimonial squabble, as some of their limbs are broken and deformed. Many of the big trees have unfortunately been touched by fire, the ruthless work of Indians and hunters in former years, and several have fallen since the grove was discovered. A trunk lying prone on the ground has been hollowed out by repeated burnings, and before the lower part became filled up by earth and stones, washed in by a brook, two men, it is said, could ride through it abreast on horseback. The tree is much charred and decayed. Another of the trees is half embedded in the soil, but as he clutches the earth is grand in his decay, and worthy of his brotherhood. Royalty was with these trees before the historic ages; they were in existence hundreds of years before the Star of Bethlehem had risen in the East, and before great Caesar died; yet some of these grisly giants look as if rejuvenated and metamorphosed into youth. Their proud trunks clothed in rich, odorous robes of resinous bark seem to swell with a fine consciousness of dignity and glory, while the wind sings to them under its breath of infinity inconceivable. The age of these trees has been computed at from 2,500 to 3,000 years, but it is almost impossible even to arrive at an approximation. As is the case with other trees, it is supposed that each concentric circle of about two inches in diameter, represents the growth of one year, and as nearly three thousand of those circles can be counted in the trunks of the fallen trees, the conclusion seems inevitable that they were in existence three thousand years ago—or eleven hundred years before the birth of Christ, and spread shade over many feet of ground when the Egyptians were toiling and carving on their pyramids and obelisks. How many generations of the human race have been born and vanished in the chaos and storms of these centuries! The climate of the Pacific slope seems to be wonderfully preservative for trees, for no tree could ever live that long in another climate. These olden trees are religion carven into trunks and branches; they chant the mysteries which wound our souls with bitter doubts and appalling speculations, and which our impious will tries to penetrate. They indeed preach an eloquent sermon, which in its very nature has a moving pathos in it, and ever are they echoing to our thoughts piteous prayers and expressions of their yearning for eternity. They are as Joaquin Miller sings of the old Druid oaks of Ayr:—

> " Precepts! Poems! Pages!
> Lessons! Leaves and Volumes!
> Arches! Pillars! Columns
> In corridors of ages!
> Grand Patriarchal sages
> Lifting palms in prayer!"

Theirs is the unapproachable majesty; they signify the mystery of that repose which comes only from tested power and seasoned strength. They are like a congregation of worshippers who have hidden themselves deep in the woody wilderness, and have given their lives to thoughts and prayers till they have outlived the generation born with them. They tend to elevate the mind, and turn it towards the Great Power which has fashioned with equal care and wisdom the tiny blade of grass and these giants of the forest. There is sometimes a strange tone about their sobs and sighs, and when night falls, tiny fire-flies float in the atmosphere with the brilliancy of a spark, and the whole forest becomes full of the sights and sounds of life and motion. The impenetrable mass of verdure, which arches over all, appears to be enchanted, and sounds seem to proceed from all parts of the woods. One's ear listens with rapt attention to this wonderful harmony—now and then soft and sweet like the mysterious accents of an unknown tongue; and the eye questions the darkness to discover the beings who thus manifest their existence. One seems to detect life in all things around, and the hum is like a thousand gentle whispers celebrating in a universal concert the coolness and magnificence of the night. Altogether the place is one of solemn beauty, heightened by the solitude and seclusion, and appealing with irresistible force to a sensitive mind.

The Calaveras mammoth trees were discovered in 1852 by a hunter who was employed to supply a mining-camp with fresh meat. While pursuing a bear he suddenly found himself in sight of these colossal trees. On returning to the camp he related what he had seen, but found incredulous ears, and his big-tree story was ridiculed and laughed at by the miners. Guiding them to the grove, he convinced them however of the truth of his statement. The new species of trees, of which soon more or less accurate descriptions in various newspapers and magazines appeared, was named by an English botanist *Wellingtonia gigantea;* but the Americans had certainly justice on their side when they complained of this want of courtesy to them, in naming an American tree after an English hero. As these trees grow only upon American soil, good taste might have suggested the name *Washingtonia.* The Americans adopted the name *Sequoia gigantea* received from a French botanist, who visited and described these trees as early as 1854. The name is derived from a famous half-blood Cherokee Indian, whose name was Sequioyah. (In Catlin's *American Indians,* and Appleton's *American Encyclopaedia* may be found the particulars of an alphabet which this Indian chief, whose anglicised name was George Guest, invented. It consists of eighty characters, and is said to be the most complete alphabet of any language in the known world.)

I was off at daylight one day to see the Calaveras caves, situated on a small stream called M'Kenney's Humbug. What wonderful names the early explorers and settlers gave to some places and rivers! A supply of good names was evidently wanting when these Western places were christened, and their sponsors plainly lacked imagination — Fiddletown, Poverty Bar, Screech-Owl-Flat, You Bet, &c. They are in strange contrast with the Spanish names of some places in California, which sound like music to the ear ı Modesto, Sonora, Amador, Vallejo,

Purissima, Eldorado, Aurora, Eleanor, Alameda, Calistoga, Rio Vista, San Leandro, Benicia, Los Angelos, Mariposa, Huerfano, and many more.

There are several caves which bear as many different names : Council-chamber, Cathedral, Music Hall, Bishop's Palace, &c. Their interior reminded me strongly of the Peak and Blue John caverns in Peakdale by Castleton in England. After seeing the latter it is to see them again, under, perhaps, a slightly different aspect. All their sights are too numerous to mention in detail, but the most beautiful amongst them is the Bridal-chamber, with pillars and curtain-like stalactites hanging from its ceiling, which look like the handiwork of a sculptor. They form most weird groups, and the effect which the burning fagots and candles produce as they throw their light upon the capriciously decorated rocky walls, is highly impressive. Many Indian relics, arrow-heads, perforated sea-shells, and many human skulls and bones were found at different times in the caves. It is stated by the Indians of this neighbourhood that long before white men were seen in California, the Northern Indians came down to this valley and met their ancestors in battle ; and such a great number was killed on both sides that it was impossible to bury the bodies of all the slain, so they were thrown headlong into the mouth of the cave. There they were sleeping the long sleep of death, and were never disturbed afterwards, until the pale faces came who did not hesitate to desecrate the defenceless dead. Whether this is the true account of the accumulation of these remains, or not, it is impossible to say.

I had been several hours underground, crawling and creeping on hands and knees, had lost the whole day—a day with its joyous morning, noon and sunset of crimson and gold, and had gained—well, some more sublime memories. No doubt the caves are a great natural curiosity.

CHAPTER V.

On the Way to the Yo-Semité—The Town of Sonora—Garrote—The Watershed of the Tuolumne and Merced Rivers—Prospect Point—First Sight of the Yo-Semité—Descent—Rambles in a Wondrous Valley—The Bridal Veil Fall—The Cathedral Spires—A Trio of Merry Scotchmen—Their Descent into the Valley.

IT chanced that several visitors were staying at the Big Tree Hotel besides myself. Having become acquainted with two of them, I found we had many objects of common interest, and as my plans suited theirs we resolved to proceed together to the Yo-Semité valley. Our arrangements being completed we took leave of our friendly host, and early one morning mounted the mustangs, rather in a hurry to be at Murphy's in time to catch the stage. While the dwellers in cities were still asleep our little cavalcade was *en route*. After casting a last farewell look at the old, hoary trees, we set out at a brisk trot. Ahead rode our guide and we were caracoling merrily in single file behind. The ride through the magnificent forest was beautiful. As we wound our way along the side of the precipitous hill overlooking the valley, we caught from time to time exquisite views of dreamy distances, chequered with light and gloomy, tangled shadow, and now and then some monarch of the forest, craning his long neck above the other trees, had his lofty top wrapped in the delicate embrace of thin, white vapour. Rapid little brooks came rushing down across the narrow trail, struggling, jostling and interlacing, as they dashed steadily down the incline to mingle their waters with those of the placid stream which flows slowly and smoothly on through the valley with a never-ceasing murmur towards the sea. I was struck with the beauty of the picture which changed at each turn in the trail. What a perfect summer retreat! What breezy mornings, when the mists fly away from the deep ravines, and shadow and sun play hide and seek among the dense foliage of the haughty trees, whose odorous boughs brush against the clouds.

Arriving at Murphy's Camp, which is a ranche, but has been fitted up for the accommodation of tourists, the pleasant clean house was none too large to accommodate our merry cavalcade, and the numerous tourists, who poured in at the arrival of the stage. The old man in his mountain-home was as simple and courteous in his demeanour as he possibly could be. All the guests sat down to the breakfast-table, and as regards the good fare, the same may be remarked of the various inns all along the route to the Yo-Semité valley. The owners are generally intelligent, well informed and industrious, apparently superior in many respects to the same class in other out-of-the-way places.

Fresh horses having been hitched to the stage-coach, we started once more on our journey, traversing an open undulating country, containing few shrubs and trees, but plenty of wild flowers and dust. On the road we passed several places celebrated for their diggings in earlier days, but now only worked by a few Chinamen. The coach was happily not overcrowded, as a number of tourists left it at Murphy's to go to Calaveras, yet we had one of the hottest, dustiest, and most jolty rides I ever experienced. The heat and dust were almost too painful to be endured, so we were not sorry when we arrived at the little town of Sonora.

The hills around Sonora are literally honeycombed by the gold-washing, which was carried on there formerly, but only a small number of Chinamen now remain of the mining host of the once prosperous times. This was a tract of land, perhaps the most prolific in purest gold of any other Californian mining district. The surface has been all dug over and well washed by hydraulic power, and the once so noisy and boisterous place, echoing from the bacchanalian revels and bloody feuds of the gambling miners, where so many scenes of violence and murder were enacted, is now a quiet and orderly community. By nine or ten o'clock at night there is scarcely a light in the town. No whirr of wheels of the quartz-crushing mills—all is played out; the mills have come to a standstill. Only a few country-stores, a cozy little inn nestling under the shade of a large tree, and an old wooden church perched on a hill with a cemetery around, where some of the daring miners who were driven by murderous hands into a premature grave, lie at rest—that is all that remains of Sonora, once the liveliest of Californian mining-towns. We started off again, the driver blowing a cheerful melody through his horn, and rode on by the banks of a creek which rippled merrily over a pebbly bottom, and climbing to a well-wooded table-land we reached and drove briskly through Chinese Camp without stopping. We now began the ascent of the mountains. The country here, and henceforward, was of the wildest and most romantic character; the road grew narrower and rockier, the air was cooler and purer, but the views more charming. The shadows were creeping over the hills as we clambered across the wooded slopes, and just at sunset we arrived at our night quarters in Garrote, where, after an excellent supper in the Washington Hotel, we retired to enjoy such a sleep as a long ride in a pure and bracing air always insures. The distance from Murphy's to Garrote is thirty-eight miles; so we had travelled since early morning, counting the fifteen miles on horseback, fifty-three miles.

At dawn of next day, after an early breakfast we again started and plunged into the woods; our route winding through a magnificent pine and cedar forest interspersed with evergreen oaks and flowering shrubs. The ground was perfectly enamelled with wild flowers, some of them very beautiful. This day's journey was but a succession of grand panoramic views of valley and hill; the landscape ever changing in character. We rode for a considerable distance along a path cut out of a mountain's steep side, and hundreds of feet below us we saw the tops of tall pines and spruces. No farmhouses or villages were to be seen; there was no sign of life save when a wild rabbit sprang across the track. Then we again descended into a valley through which a foaming brook flowed, finding its outlet between two hills in the background. Near Crane's Flat the road leads past some mammoth trees, two of which, named the Siamese Twins, grow from the same root, but divide into two separate trees, and attain an altitude of over 325 feet. They measure near the ground 114 feet in circumference.

Whilst we halted for a while to contemplate these giant twins, a peal of thunder warned us that a storm was at hand. The gathering gale blew on the surrounding hills a hollow, threatening wail, and then the brooding tempest quickly burst upon us. A blinding rain descended in torrents, the lightning flashed, and the thunder boomed and made the earth tremble, as it echoed through the vale from peak to peak. Fortunately the storm lasted only a very short time, and passed over as rapidly as it burst upon us. The heavy rain-clouds lifted and disappeared behind the mountains; the sky became clear, and nature assumed again a calm splendour. The whole landscape had after the heavy shower an indescribable freshness about it.

Passing in due succession several ranches, and Hardin's and Hodgeden's mills, we reached at last the watershed of the Tuolumne and Merced rivers, which, dividing here, pour their waters in opposite directions. We hastened on to the rim of the basin, and stood silently gazing upon the surpassing majesty of a landscape which none could contemplate unmoved; and as the exceeding beauty of the scene ripened in our souls, we involuntarily bowed our heads in reverence. The whole reminded me irresistibly of that gorgeous passage of descriptive poetry in the *Lady of the Lake* where Sir Walter Scott paints for us in glowing colours the dark ravines, the rocky "thunder-splintered pinnacles," the mossy glades, the flowery dells, the luxuriant foliage and flowering bushes of the Trossachs—

"So wondrous wild, the whole might seem
The scenery of a fairy dream."

We mounted again, and at Tamarack Flat began the descent, which from this point is 4,000 feet to the valley. Perpendicular precipices, thousands of feet in height, heave their unwieldy forms along the side of the trail, which makes several winding inflections in its descent. It is by no means an easy descent over the steep and sharp declivity of the downward track, for frequently huge boulders, presenting themselves in front, threaten opposition to all further progress. Now and then the trail seemed blocked up a short distance before us, and we wondered how we should proceed, but an unexpected turn always solved the problem. At one of these sudden turns, whilst crossing a rough wooden bridge, a most beautiful view of the Cascade Creek was unexpectedly thrown upon our eyes, refreshing them with its rich beauty and variety.

The guides led us to another rocky elevation called Prospect Point, and approaching a projecting crag over which a fresh breeze blew, the valley burst suddenly upon us in all its rare and undefinable sublimity and grandeur. The peaceful and luxuriant vale has a very impressive effect contrasted with the vast rocks of gleaming granite that environ it. Various lesser vales open into it and through its depth flows the meandering Merced river, several thousands of feet below the general level of the surrounding country. I contemplated the scene with worshipping admiration, and could hardly take in the separate details of the landscape before us, my eyes and attention being so arrested by the novelty and beauty which surrounded us everywhere. It was like looking down from a balloon. Would I had but the power to describe this vale of wild enchantment! Fantastic crags leaped into the air and seemed to hang suspended as if by some magic, and in the rocky chasm yawning below our feet, extended in all its magnificence—like a dreamy glimpse of fairyland, or a vision of Paradise itself—the valley of the Yo-Semité!

Above us was a lustrous sunshine with a sky deliciously blue, and far away, many miles off, rising into the crystalline air and piercing the horizon, the snow-capped mountains of the Sierra Nevada reared their lofty summits and peaks till they were blent in the distant sky. As far as eye could reach rose a multitude of sharply-defined blue and purple peaks and crags; the valleys between filled with frightful ravines, seeming the merest gullies on the earth's surface. To the south Mount Starr King, to the east and north-east densely-wooded hills, cleft in two, through which runs the Merced river. Farther off rose the dim outlines of Mount Hoffman, lonely and superb, with a cloud-wreath about his brow, and many other snow-clad mountains of the Sierras, some of them thirteen to fourteen thousand feet above the level of the sea. And far, far beneath our feet slept in sylvan and graceful beauty the Yo-Semité valley, hemmed in on every side by giant cliffs and rocks.

In all my wanderings round this world I never conceived the idea of grandeur and sublimity to a fuller extent; the whole conjured up some fairy scene as memory recalls many a tale of childhood, where imprisoned princesses and huge giants had their dwelling in some such impenetrable spot, and imagination found a parallel here in these Titan rocks. The whole was beautiful, and the mind became almost enrapt as the eye wandered towards the cliffs, and savage crags and precipices; for there the great good Spirit of the Indians might be fancied sitting on the very verge, absorbed in the mournful contemplation of its grandeur. Then imagination would figure the fantastic scenes of former Indian life, when the solemn silence of these mountains, forests and cañons was broken but by the roar of the torrents that leap the rocks, and the savage yells of the wild, free children of the woods. My mind's eye would see the steel of their tomahawks and scalping knives glittering in the sun, and all those imaginary things to which the fertile brains of poets and story-tellers have given an existence, and which will end only with mortality.

And now let us go, and follow the trail. Beneath our feet our eyes caught now and then the flash of the spray of the Cascade creek which pours its water, in a succession of hissing and seething falls, into the abyss. We heard the whirr and clash of its ceaseless progress, and cautiously made our way down the sheer declivity in Indian file. After a ride of several hundred yards through a pleasant grass-grown space, we came to the hill's abrupt side, broken by ledges and clothed with tangled vines and underwood. A tiny and scarcely perceptible trail led along the dizzy height. To the right was a ledge a hundred feet high, down which trailed moss and vines, and along which grew tiny white blossoms in dense masses. Sometimes the path was so steep that we preferred to dismount, and lead our horses rather than take the risk of being pitched over their heads. Half-way down the mountain we could hear the sound of the waterfalls, which was borne to our ears like the distant echo of the rush of a railway train, and sometimes through an opening in the trees we caught a glimpse of their white foam as it poured over the rocks. Finally we came to a plateau covered with laurel bushes and rhododendron thickets. Masses of their stout bushes hung along our path, and showered their fragile pink and scarlet blossoms upon us as we pushed through. By a gradual descent we reached the level; the dangerous scramble was accomplished in safety. As we jogged silently along through the valley, the murmur of waters and the whispering of the evening wind filled the air, mingled with the drowsy hum of insects, and the plaintive song of birds which flit from tree to tree. The brooks never rippled so musically to my ears, and the perfume of flowers seemed sweeter to me than it had ever been before.

As we came into the open space in front of Black's Hotel, just opposite the great Yo-Semité Fall, its majestic voice broke on our ears with increased strength. All drew rein, and gazed silently up to the seething waters, flashing and glistening in the rays of the setting sun. The lurid reddening of the sun had vanished and the valley was beginning to be steeped in gloom, ere we turned from the fascinating scene to wend our way to our night quarters.

Making an early rise next morning I set off for the valley on foot and quite alone. The other tourists went in groups to different points of attraction ; I let them go, as I preferred to be alone and stroll and admire at my pleasure without the hindrance of hearing other people's opinions and criticisms. I made up my mind to have a general view of the whole valley before studying the separate objects of wonder and interest.

The valley is about seven miles long, with a width of from half a mile to a mile. It is almost level, and seems to have been formed by a sudden subsidence of the earth. The rocks on either side rise like granite walls from four to six thousand feet in height. The valley lies nearly due east, and about 150 miles, as the crow flies, from San Francisco, in the lap of the Merced group of the great Sierra Nevada range of mountains, and the Merced becomes a stream in its bosom, taking its rise higher up in the mountains. It was first discovered in 1851 by an officer of the United States army, when in pursuit of some predatory Indians, but only within the last fifteen years has it been accessible, except to a few hardy pioneers. Now the difficulties are easily overcome, each year renders the facilities of travel greater, and alas! it is even proposed to carry a railway into the valley, which is accessible only by two entrances—the one by way of the Mariposa trail, and the other at the opposite end—the one our party had taken. There are at present three hotels in the valley where the fare is good and accommodation clean, a large drinking saloon has also been recently erected, with hot, cold, and Turkish baths attached; and a laundry and a photographic studio. What next, I wonder! A railroad, a newspaper and a printing-office, then a pawnbroker's shop and—the majesty and beauty of the valley will be spoiled.

I now began my explorations of the valley. I contemplated for some time the exquisite view of the Yo-Semité Falls (the meaning of the Indian word Yo-Semité is grizzly bear) whose descent is arrested three times by projecting ledges of rock, upon which the water crashes with the noise of thunder. First the stream, shooting downwards from on high in a magnificent cascade, precipitates itself 1600 feet on a broad ledge projecting from the smooth cliff, and again, beaten into foam takes a leap of 434, and finally by a third bound of 600 feet reaches the valley, there to be lost in the waters of the Merced river. Fancy, a cascade of a perpendicular silvery sheet of over 2,600 feet high! Fourteen times higher than the Niagara Falls. Of course it is not more than a glittering thread when compared to the enormous magnitude and volume of the latter; although some of the guides who have ascended the mountain over which the falls take their headlong leap declare that they are fully forty feet wide at the summit, and that in spring-time they are a hundred times more majestic when the snow in the mountains is rapidly melting under the sun's rays. This I can readily believe to be the truth.

Crossing the main stream I continued along its bank, walking under the canopy of shady oak, pine and maple trees, round which seemed to breathe a perpetual spring, so fresh and luxuriant did they appear, every one more and more beautiful. Penetrating the valley, the river, which is about forty feet wide, flows slowly and smoothly between thickly-wooded banks, and glides now placid and silent, now garrulous and foaming over shelves and slabs of sand and rock, which stretch across from side to side of its channel. But huge cliffs are piled up here and there beside its course, rising almost perpendicularly from the tiny stretches of sand at the water's edge; and in these places the stream, impeded and checked by driftwood and rocks, grows turbulent and rebellious. Thence it rushes and hurries hissing and seething, and dashes into breakers and swirls—a mass of white foam—and the impetuous motion of its current is grand and effective as it beats against the myriads of rocks set in the channel-bed. One of the wonders of this valley is that it seems to have been cultivated for centuries, so beautiful are the vines trailing over the rocks and trees, and the luxuriant foliage of the shrubs and willows fringing the channels through which the streams and brooks wander.

The Indians gave soft poetic names to the hills and streams and cliffs of this valley, through which I now made my way. Some of these have been retained and are still in use, but in many cases they have been cast away, and the unmeaning and hackneyed commonplaces of the rude days of early explorers and pioneer-settlers have superseded the expressive appellations of the Indian language. How bold and grand Tutockahnulah looked, the great chief and guardian of the valley, beetling 3,300 feet over the gorge! Adjoining him Pompompasus (mountains playing at leap-frog) resting one upon the other, ponderous and grand. Their English name is Three Brothers. They face the Three Graces (Kosookong) of softer beauty; and the lonely Sentinel Rock, Loya, on whose crest so often blazed the watch-fires of the Indians. Beyond stand the Cathedral Rock and the Cathedral Spires (Pooseenuchucka).

I followed the current of the stream over a rich carpet of green. The water was sometimes deeply dark in colour, now and then faintly blue or purple as the sunshine played upon it through the thickets; and everywhere amidst the crystal ripples, which seemed to be racing each other, danced flitting reflections of the glowing sky and lovely foliage. Here and there I came to a place where the river expanded into a little bay, or to lawns and blooming meadows dotted with hickories, pines and oaks, and where clusters of rhododendrons, laurels and azaleas grew over old, fallen trees. By and by a soft melodious sound, only faintly audible like the sweep of a light breeze, was borne to my ears, and the murmurous pines around

THE THREE BROTHERS (POMPOMPASUS), YO-SEMITÉ VALLEY.

THE BRIDAL VEIL FALL (POHONÓ) YO-SEMITÉ VALLEY.

joined in the plaint. It was the voice of the Bridal-veil Fall, called by the Indians Pohonó, meaning Spirit of the evil wind. Diverging slightly by pushing through a pine and laurel thicket, I got close to it. A perfect cloud of spray enveloped me, but as the wind presently drove it aside I had a fine view of the fall amidst the roar of its waters. The thunder of the cataract almost deafened me. Amongst the huge masses of rocks that are scattered at the foot of the fall, the noise seems to come from the very ground under one's feet. A gap in the mountain high up is pierced by a rapidly flowing stream, which lets itself down from the brink of the cliff without encountering opposition, and bursts with majestic fury upon a mass of gigantic boulders, foaming round them with eddies and swirls. With what rage it rushes down! The fall is 940 feet in height and forty feet wide. Soon after taking its wild leap over the precipice, the stream loses its massive unity, and spreads out in its descent like a gigantic piece of lacework against the black rocks in the background, till it resembles a bridal-veil. It rushes with such violence from the dizzy height that the water is projected far from the rock, and the sheets of dazzling spray dependent from the hoary walls of the chasm, are hundreds of feet long. The water, boiling into whitest foam, pours down the sides of the great boulders which jut out at the base of the cliff, making minor bubbling and seething cascades and rivulets which unite lower down into one current, swift, strong, and musical. The noise and perpetual tumult of the falling torrents awe one's soul in this veritable dungeon of inaccessible rocks, from which there is seemingly no outlet. The pines and spruces, many of them more than a hundred feet high, which grow by the side of the immense wall closing around, seem but saplings, and lean over the huge precipice as if awed by its depth. Frail rainbows hover at times above the rocks, and then the light in the chasm, when seen through the transparent veil of the spray, is almost supernatural. One's eyes are blinded by the brilliant colours which cast a fantastic glare over every minute object, and even the pebbles grasses, and ferns amongst the rocks over which the water pours, are within the magical influence of the lovely light. No wretched huckster has yet obtruded his vulgar advertisements upon the virgin rocks of this sublime region, nor disfigured the impressive grandeur of their solitude. According to Mr. Hutchings's excellent book, *Wonders of California*, this waterfall was held by the Indians in great fear, and Pohonó, from whom the stream received its musical name, was in their belief an evil spirit who worked his deadly spells with malice and mysterious power, and was consequently dreaded and shunned by them. They were cautious not to be near the fall late at night—they fancied, in truth, that the dead who have been drowned in the stream came up and kept strange revels, and that they could hear their voices perpetually warning them to shun Pohonó.

Continuing my walk along the course of the tumbling river I was aroused from my reverie by finding myself at the base of two stupendous cliffs, very picturesque and suggestive in their outline. The Cathedral-Spires, the name given to these jagged stone monuments, rise to a height of 3,000 feet in the air, serene and titanic, while the racing river frisks and gambols at their base. They bear the aspect of the oldest stage of nature, and form a most imposing remnant of primeval architecture. Their rugged sides are here and there stained like the walls of some old towers, and it is not difficult to imagine that one is beholding the ruins of a huge castle. Hundreds, nay thousands of fragments of almost every shape and form lie scattered below, as though hurled down by an avalanche; and swarms of birds hover and fly in and out among the crags. Adjoining them stands the Cathedral Rock, a gigantic pile of solid stone with its foot planted among the thickets, and its brow upwards of 3,000 feet in height and almost perpendicular. Tutockahnulah loomed up like ramparts in the background, and the sun tinged the sky above him with crimson and purple. The sunshine played upon his walls which were at times of dazzling whiteness. His sheer fall seems to continue to the very level of the valley, though broken in many places by projecting ledges. At the summit can be traced the profile of a human face, looking, as it were, across the valley in the fixedness of eternal contemplation, and tradition connects this rude resemblance with the demi-god whose name the rock bears, rising from the depth of the cañon to draw across the entrance to the valley the luminous veil of Pohonó, torn away since by the ruthless invaders.

Evening closed silently around, the shades gathered, and the low murmur of the water drifted on the calm air as I strolled homeward by the edge of the stream. The evening was still and warm, only the cheery halloo was heard of some mountaineers descending into the valley, and the answering echo borne back along the ravines and crags. Everything around seemed to keep time with the refrain to which all nature was tuned. I felt rather tired with my long walk when I had returned, and sat for a while in front of the hotel, gazing and watching the eddying wind bending into wavy lines the snowy veil of the Yo-Semité Falls, until the welcome sound of the supper-bell called me inside.

During our supper I listened to the gossip and descriptions of the scenes which the other tourists had visited that day—and how thankful I felt that I had not accompanied them! Sometimes it is interesting to see and hear the modern tourist. For one moment they criticise, or point out the beauty of a fascinating object in nature, the next moment they talk about church-meetings or parties, and wonder if anything could exceed the graces and beauty of the figure of Miss So-and-So, and the sweet expression of her face, and at the same time throw out a shadowy indication that she wears false teeth and shoes No. 9. Their travels are nothing but modern masquerading and a matter of mere foppery.

Late at night there arrived a trio of merry Scotchmen in the hotel. They came without guides and climbed the fearful trail down to the valley in the dusk and shadow of the evening. They amused us with their tale of adventure. They were tall, powerful men, clad in rough costumes, with the omnipresent broad-rimmed, grey slouch-hats down over their foreheads. One of them had only one arm, and he, seating himself with admirable carelessness before the fireplace, warming his only hand by the gleaming ashes, and smoking his corn-cob pipe, courteously told us how they scrambled over the rocks in coming down to the valley that evening. " I never want to come here in the night again;" he said, " we lost the trail, and had to search for it, and came to rocks over which we were compelled to crawl and drop cautiously into black-looking rocky crevices, out of which we had to scramble as best we could. However we toiled on and clambered over large boulders, clinging sometimes to roots, sometimes to frail and yielding tufts of grass and ferns, until everything was hidden in such darkness that we could hardly see our hands before our faces. Passing a slippery rock we sat down, stretching our feet carelessly, and listened intently a minute to some kind of noise that drifted to our ears. Luckily enough we didn't move, we were mighty still for we were tired, but pretty soon the chilly night-air crept right smartly into our bones. I placed my hand to my ear, and thought that the noise must come from the hotels in the valley, and that they could not be far from that spot. Cold comfort, but no alternative. We set fire to a bundle of dry sprigs, and as the flame blazed up—good heavens! if we weren't perched on the very outer edge of a rock, and two inches between us and about twelve hundred feet of sheer fall.

" I flattened myself against the rock and threw the burning fagots down the abyss, and could see the tree-tops far below me in the valley. I did not look twice at the fall, I can tell you." " Yes," confirmed his friends, "he seemed to have seen spectres."

One of them after a while struck up, *My Heart's in the Highlands*, and all were able to chime in. They sang a great many songs to tunes which are so often heard in the Scotch Highlands. The echoes of the songs died away in the stillness of the night, and most of the guests retired to their night-berths.

"What do you think?" said one of the Scotchmen, turning to his companions, "had we not better take a night-cap before going to bed?" How many "night-caps" they drank I don't know, but there came long after midnight a faint echo from that room which sounded like "'n other."

CHAPTER VI.

The Mirror Lake—Fellow Visitors—An Unbidden but Welcome Guest—
Encamped for the Night—A Squabble—The Nevada and the Vernal
Waterfalls—A Terrific Thunderstorm—Fording the River.

AT early dawn next morning we were on our way to the Mirror Lake to see the reflections before its surface was ruffled by the breeze. The cheery voices of our united party, led by the merry halloo of a guide, were heard every moment, for the loveliest phases of nature gave us their inspiration. Dozens of foamy rivulets, overhung with vines and rich foliage, were pouring and leaping over the cliffs and rocks, and my eyes fed lightly on the fascinating vistas afforded by every turn we made. As we wound through the narrow pathway under the shade of lofty pines, the three Scotchmen appeared in a very tame guise, looking rather sorry for themselves. "Water, it seems, is the only thing here that continues to fall; everything else is rising," remarked one of them in my hearing as we were in full view of a waterfall. "Yes, the atmosphere is highly charged," observed the other. "And the hotel-charges and other things in proportion," added the third dreamily. The secret of their bad humour was out, they were evidently overcharged in the hotel. Having had some slight misgivings that possibly an enervating requisition might be attempted on my own purse, I asked about the matter, and one of the Scotchmen said fiercely: "Why, sir, is it not a reg'lar swindle to charge us ten dollars for our accommodation and the little drinking we did last night? Poor sort of luck for us!"

Another hour of floundering, and then coming through a

THE "MIRROR LAKE;" YO-SEMITÉ VALLEY.

clearing we suddenly saw above us the fantastic rock-piles of the South and North Domes piercing the clouds, and between them in a wealth of loveliness lay extended the placid lake like a sheet of glass, with the forest like a frame around a mirror. Not a ripple disturbed its surface, and in its pure depth the fleecy clouds, reflected, sailed slowly by, and each peak, ridge, tree, crag and shade, even every tiny twig and leaf of the surrounding shrubs was so faithfully reflected that it was difficult to discover where substance ended and shadow began. The illusion was perfect, the blending exquisite. The rocks and hills around are lovely, but the view of them mirrored in the lake is lovelier still. It is only a small sheet of water, but its remarkable translucency makes it appear much larger. The banks of the lake are fringed with noble trees and covered with the rarest flowers, amongst which bloom clusters of fragrant violets. It is one of the loveliest spots in the valley, and the Indians called it reverently Awyah—beautiful.

The lake lies near the head of the valley between the South Dome, Tissaack, on the one side and the North Dome, Tokoyoe, and Washington Tower on the other ; whilst on the north-east a deep cañon affords an exit to the Merced river, which supplies the lake, and is nowhere more beautiful than within a few hundred yards of this nook. Tokoyoe rises to a height of 3,725 feet. Its summit is destitute of shrubs or trees, and the bare granite on its top glistens in the sun like a bald man's shining poll. For about two thousand feet from its base its rocky sides are absolutely perpendicular. Tissaack, the goddess of the valley, rearing her mighty head to a height of six thousand feet, is one of grandest natural monuments in the valley, although its mammoth skeleton has been broken by some terrible convulsion, and the shattered fragments of rocks and boulders lie scattered in huge piles at its base. At times the valley is literally shaken by the shock of falling cliffs, thundering down the dizzy height, loosened and rent off by the floods of a heavy rain, snapping the great trees as if they were reeds. Evidence of the terrific power of these rock-slips is afforded by the large number of broken trees, nearly all dead, which stand like skeletons, their stems and branches bare and gaunt, while those still alive are stunted and gnarled. Many of them are clothed in a hoary garment of mosses, which, being alive, yet have the aspect of death. The mighty summit of the South Dome has never been ascended, and the Indians gazed upon the mysterious mountain, towering above all its compeers, with the fervent belief that it was the abode of the good spirit of the valley, the goddess Tissaack, who could see her lovely image mirrored in the azure of the lake beneath her feet.

Rambling around the lake, our little company came soon to the edge of a steep bank leading into the gorge through which the Merced flows. Its waters seem angry at being pent up among the cliffs, and fret and chafe against the obstructions. How the river dances between the granite shores and leaps along the stony bed! Its voice is always heard crying among the rocks, moaning and sighing as it laps the banks in the narrow gorge. A solemn silence fell on all as we entered the aisles of the cañon and climbed the knolls and boulders, which rose everywhere, clad in the sombre garb of the balsam. Beetling crags almost shut out the light and the stone colossus leaned towards the stream's edge as if just about to topple down. All around, the rocks towered up, and miniature torrents ran down their sides, rippling between the boulders into the river, upon whose farther bank there was no refuge whatever, only the sheer rock with its spare coating of foliage and the stream piercing its way between the stones, which seem as though they had been pounded by some titanic hammer into multitudinous fragments. Returning towards the Mirror Lake, an opportune ford allowed us to wade through the wavelets which caressed the overhanging willows, and crossing safely we came to a beautiful grove of balsam trees. The haughty balsam is emphatically a recluse among trees, consorting only with the proud rhododendron, whose scarlet bloom was the object of the Indian's most passionate adoration. The delicious aroma was almost too strong, and was perceptible a long way off. Here we stopped to lie on the turf beside the cool stream, and to drink in at every inspiration the pure mountain-air. Above us in the clear, bright sunshine loomed the mountain-peaks, so high, so beautiful, that our souls were lifted at the very sight of them. The forms of the distant rocks, over which pines lean and straggle in wildest confusion, and every projection, every vine and shrub on their surface stood out with startling clearness against the heavens. They looked so near at hand that by merely extending one's arm one seemed able to touch them, whereas in reality they were far, far away.

The afternoon was waning as we came back to the lake, where our little party was increased by the arrival of several visitors from the other hotels, who came to talk with us for a while. One of them, a young, sickly-looking personage was (the guide whispered in my ear) a German count. He was evidently just from his mother's apron-strings, yet now and then he tried to put on an air of that quality which overturns thrones and supplants dynasties. Feeling the exhilarating effects of the keen, rarified air peculiar to these regions, we partook of a sumptuous lunch which we had brought with us from the hotel, and which was disposed of in a most satisfactory manner, highly creditable to all concerned. Everybody was pleased, charmed and delighted with the scenery and the excursion generally. Just as we were in the middle of the feast, a queer sort of fellow suddenly burst upon us from among the surrounding bushes and trees. "Well, boys, have you got enough to eat? How are you anyhow?" This was his salutation on reaching us, which was in striking contrast with the artificial phrases of the German count, and the honest German who accompanied him. The peremptory inquiry was answered in pretty much the same tone by one of the Scotchmen, and a hospitable welcome to partake of our meal followed. Straightway without any bashfulness or hesitation he accepted the invitation, and leaning his double-barrelled gun against a tree, and throwing his blankets and himself on the ground, he helped himself to biscuits, cold meat, butter, cheese and bread, and dispatched the food quite unceremoniously. He attracted my attention. There was none of the modern conventionalities of dress visible about him. The man was cavalier enough with his woollen shirt without a collar, and his breeches fixed on his hips by a well-worn strap. His trousers ends were thrust into his boots, his slouch-hat cocked on his head with bravado air, and—to adopt a hackneyed phrase—a daredevil swagger was in his gait, and an " I'm as good as you" glance in his eye. I can imagine how disgusted the German count must have been at the utter lack of pomp and decorum, and at the simplicity displayed in the manners and cheap clothing of the fellow opposite him. The count's attendant was straight and tall as a poplar tree—he was indeed of such an unusual height that, when he complained that he had got his feet wet, and had a very severe cold in his head, the impudent fellow said that he must have got them wet a year ago, as the cold would require that long to travel from his heels to his head. The professor made a feeble attempt to tell a funny story, and I am sure we should have laughed consummately to please him, only when he came to the point, he had forgotten it. He promised to tell it when we met again, and by this time he has probably gone home to look for it.

The Germans no doubt marvelled at the queer people they had got amongst, as they shortly afterwards took leave of us, and returned to the hotel. " Each of the tall fellow's spindle-shanks would make a good handle for a broom," observed the impudent varlet, as the German party faded from our sight.

I told him that altogether his treatment of the count and his companion was a serious affair, and should not be attempted in such a light spirit of enterprise. "You have to consider and call to mind all the social prerogatives of the person you are addressing. No such slipshod, easy familiarity as 'Say, young chap,' or 'old fellow,' can be tolerated, with which you snubbed them. What you are, and what you have, is the matter to be considered."

"Bravo! that was a capital sermon," shouted the company; but the strange fellow, taking me by the shoulders, turned me round with no gentle hand, and surveying me from head to foot, exclaimed, "Why, that was very smart what you've said, though I know you don't mean it, but,"—he added with a scornful laugh of derision and disdain, "A count! reckon, I've seen enough of them in my mighty fine country."

"Are you not an American?" I asked.

"Sacred the secrets of every one," he answered with a touch of sadness in his voice, which was scarcely audible.

Sunset came and gilded the mountain-peaks and rugged crags, whose reflected outlines in the water looked most delightful. The frogs and crickets waked up their lonesome refrain, and fire-flies twinkled brightly among the bushes and trees. We were very reluctant to leave this wonderful spot and return to the hotel.

"Gentlemen!" said the stranger, "new pleasures await you if you will share them with me."

"What's that?" we exclaimed.

"Camp here overnight, and you will find ample compensation for the lost comforts of a soft bed."

All accepted with a joyful countenance. Sending our guide to the hotel with directions to meet us at this point again the next morning with provisions and horses, we began to build up a fire around which we could sit in the evening. It was fast growing dark, and sitting in a semi-circle, we ate the remainders of our lunch, and our mysterious friend manufactured whisky "cock-tails," which were pretty quickly annihilated by one or other of my companions.

"I've had four already," quoth one of them, "each better than the other. Do let me have another thimbleful." Raising the glass, he drained it to the bottom, smacking his lips. After a pause he observed with a touch of sadness, "Oh,

Heavens, what a drink! But five are enough." The consequences were charming, delightful; ay, and a step beyond. I cannot recall half the funny things that were said—I would not repeat them if I could. The confidence of such jolly and unguarded moments should be inviolate. Besides, many a savoury dish is relished warm which, if served cold, might be the very reverse of pleasant.

Whilst the others were thus engaged, I strolled along the lake shore and came to a spot where a musical echo was heard. I shouted, and the sound was prolonged for some seconds and repeated several times, dying gradually away in a most melodious cadence. The lake shone like a polished mirror, as clear as the fabled mirrors in the halls of the fairies, and the moon rose grandly above the rocks and flooded the whole weirdly impressive landscape with a stream of silver light. Profoundest quiet reigned. No sound broke the calm, holy silence of the wooded banks; no breath of wind ruffled the perfectly smooth surface of the water, in which the rocks, the brilliant moon and the glittering stars were all reflected with wonderful distinctness, more perfect than anything of the kind I ever saw. The surface-reflections dulled even the dazzling, moonlit whiteness of the South Dome, and my eyes were spell-bound by the contrast of this seemingly impossible effect. The fire-flies too, glittered and danced on every side, leaving traces of the phosphoric light on the leaves as they passed. The night was beautiful—what a host of starry splendours thronged above our heads! High up the Pleiades and Hyades were prominent objects in the sky, below them the great constellation of Orion was seen in all its majesty, while still lower down Sirius trembled and twinkled in lovely radiance, paling all the other stars. There was not an orb so small but shed its glory freely along the arch of heaven, so serene, so unfading, so far away—so very far that I could but gaze at the light celestial orbs and glorify the night.

Our company consisted of six persons. Beside those already named, there was a gentleman from Boston, who accompanied us from the hotel and remained with us. He was a figure of fine proportions, and a portly frame, dressed in a somewhat eccentric garb. He must have been an object of curiosity even in this mountainous part of the country which was probably his chief aim in life. In a belt girded tightly round his waist, he had a small arsenal of revolvers. With these he was more than amply garnished. Such a store, indeed, it has never been my fortune to see carried by one man. He was genial and friendly, but unfortunately he was a braggadocio who talked with the air of a millionaire in possession of wealth untold. He had always seen more and better things than anybody else, was quick and decided in opinion, and spoke of all and everything as if he held undisputed authority over all. He had the requisite consummate cheek, and many people, I am sure, thought him smart. Such a fellow gets the name, and those who are shy and humble will be elbowed aside in the race of life. Modesty often ruins a man. Such were my thoughts. The attraction of the valley and its surrounding mountains was most naturally the topic of our conversation. The mysterious stranger, who was acting as our cicerone, knew every foot of the country for miles around, and volunteered much interesting information in a frank, genuine, and unconstrained manner so that we felt convinced that he had seen and knew what he said. The Bostonian, as a matter of course, said that he had seen similar, or even finer scenery in the White Mountains, Adirondacks, or Catskill Mountains in the Eastern States. We did not remonstrate with him, for such a character is best seen and enjoyed while pouring forth unchecked the feelings of his heart. The stranger observed calmly that the eastern mountains are nothing but ant-hills, when compared with the Sierras. After casting his eyes critically over the traducer, the Bostonian asked him with the air of a grand seigneur, "Did you ever see the Catskill Mountains?"

"No, sir, but I've seen them kill mice," was the quick reply. A roar of laughter burst forth from the whole company at this funny answer. The Bostonian took unmistakable pleasure in exhibiting his armoury, in which he felt an evident pride. From the tales of his exploits in the last great war of secession, with which he regaled us, he must have been a dangerous foe to encounter. He drew forth a revolver for our gratification, and regarding it with undisguised satisfaction, said that he had killed a number of rebels with it. We may have looked a little incredulous, for the idea that he might be testing our powers of belief occurred very strongly to us at first; but he handled the revolver with a freedom of action that was not very pleasing, while its muzzle was pointed at our heads, and all the barrels charged, as he observed. Indeed, I fancied that he would not have objected, in a thorough feeling of *bonne camaraderie*, to prove the truth of his remarks upon his listeners. He requested me to handle the revolver to see how light and well poised it was. The stranger who sat next to me took it from my hand, examined it, and giving it back to me said that it was quite a new revolver. The interest with which I examined it, probably induced the Bostonian to show me another truly alarming weapon—a large double-edged knife, as sharp as a razor. He said that it was "just a little guardian in his adventures in the less favoured quarters of America," and added with a tone of bravado, "It would be very handy to scalp some rascally Indians." I asked him if the cock-tails had kindled his bloodthirsty hatred against the Indians, but he assured me that his skill as a marksman was in no way inferior to his dexterity in a hand-to-hand combat with the cherished knife.

The mysterious stranger asked him if he meant a hand-to-hand combat with a cheese, which seemed to nettle the Bostonian very much, for he got mad as a hornet and told him to mind his own business, and "advertise for sealed proposals for cleaning his finger-nails." Now, a cross word is a little thing, but it is what stirs up even an elephant. Drawing himself up, the stranger gave his antagonist a lesson which, if not very complimentary, might do him good in the future, just as it did our hearts good to see the extraordinary ease and rapidity with which he infused complaisance and tameness into the Bostonian. "My hands," he said, "may be hard and soiled, because they are not inclosed in the now for me unfamiliar casing of a pair of gloves. I will not dwell upon that, but drop a few remarks about the Indians, of whom you speak like one who sees only their faults, and studies the history of their barbarities and crimes as they have been recorded by people who—just as ignorant and prejudiced as yourself—were perhaps never within hearing distance of the whoops and yells of the red man, or saw the glittering steel of his tomahawk and scalping knife. Even among the Indians good and bad qualities are strangely mixed together; they have all their own dragging poverty and you, sir, you have none of their uprising wealth of spirit. You would be mean enough to throw a stone at a poor man because he is poorly dressed—the very whelp to kick a child because it is dirty. And as for your bragging—it's all nonsense and trash. Before people who know you, you wouldn't try to boast, and when at home you probably haven't the spunk of a hungry old mouse—now, get up and spin to your wonderful city you vaunt of—blast you, and your brag."

That was a piece of refreshing impertinence, and in my mind I was shaking hands with him. The Bostonian looked surprised, as if he had been struck in the back of his neck with a club. He evidently felt that he had whetted his tongue on the wrong person this time, but despite his bombastic assertions he accepted the terrible philippic with submission and good temper.

"Don't let us have the evening spoiled with ill feeling; let's be jolly!" exclaimed one of the Scotchmen.

"With all my heart, I did not intend to offend; my offer was well meant," said the stranger.

It was a memorable night I passed with my newly-made friends—one filled with rare and delightful enjoyments of nature's sweetest charms, and with quite a medley of eccentric doings and sayings. Each narrator tried to cap the comments which preceded his, and much of the playful badinage and good natured raillery was directed at the Bostonian and the *bêtise* of his behaviour. He, however, took the banter in very good humour. It was already dawning as we wrapped ourselves into the blankets to enjoy a few hours of sleep. Our lullaby that night was the cry of the night-birds and the murmur of the river, singing in our ears its delicious song of unrest and impatience at its mountain-bounds. I recollect that day as one of unalloyed content.

It was not without difficulty that our party got up in the morning as the guide arrived with fresh provisions and the horses.

The stranger and the guide made some excellent coffee for our breakfast in a very short time, after which we were in the saddle *en route* for the Nevada Fall. Our group of horsemen wound up a zig-zag path, now and then getting a glimpse of the glittering lake we had left behind. We crept skyward up the steep bank until we reached a wooded and rocky bluff over whose precipitous declivity we were compelled to clamber. We should soon have lost the track, which curved snake-like upon the slope of the bluff, but for our leader, who easily kept in its trace. The horses hobbled and stumbled up the ascent, so that we had to cling to their manes, but reaching the top where trees and plants sent forth a strong perfume, we could already catch a glimpse of the Nevada Fall. Leaving the horses with the guide, we scrambled into the bushes, and stooping worked our way to a cliff from whence we could overlook the abyss into which the Merced sends its leaping waters. We came out upon a very narrow ledge, running along the very side of the cliff, as if cut in its ribs. The ledge or path is at its beginning about three feet wide, but as it nears the precipice over which the water takes its fearful leap it is not more than two feet in width. We continued along the giddy path, hugging the wall, and fairly flattening ourselves against it, with frequently not a foot between us and the deep abyss. Cautiously creeping forward, sometimes clambering on all fours over the wet stones, we reached at last the corner of the ledge projecting directly under the shadow of the fall. The rock seemed to have no support above or below, as if suspended in the air, and I was giddy each time I looked over. Yawning below us was the dangerous precipice beneath which the torrent roared like thunder. With reluctant glances we gazed at the sublime and imposing spectacle of the smooth rock encircled by the mist and spray, and the dizzy chasm in whose depth the water is lost. We noted the changing gleams of the sunshine as they played on the immense mass of foam suspended between earth and sky. The sun, shining on the glittering spray, produced a most perfect and magnificent rainbow which appeared to envelop us. The brilliancy of the prismatic colouring was beautiful. The stream before throwing itself into the abyss seems to clutch passionately at the rocks, and then with a tremendous power and deafening roar dashes 700 feet in one unbroken leap into a chaos of rocks and stones, which are huddled together at the fall's bottom, and which have withstood the fearful shock of the whirling water hundreds of years. Having gazed at the magnificent spectacle for a short time we returned. The clouds of spray blown across the pass rendered it exceedingly slippery, so that great care had to be taken.

The coming down was a task even more hazardous than climbing up the ledge, as the sun was shining in our faces, and we were dazzled now and then by the blinding spray. Breathlessly we trod the path; our leader striding coolly forward and the rest of us following cautiously behind him, we reached the plateau in safety. In some places Indian ladders—rude steps cut into the rocks—are found, indicating that the Indians must have frequently visited this fall, and the tradition that it was the scene of some of their superstitious rites seems well authenticated. The Nevada Fall, called Yowiye by the Indians, although not as high as the other waterfalls in the valley, contains a far greater volume of water, as the main body of the Merced river descends through its channel. Mounting our horses we rode forward to see the second fall. Passing a house of refreshment, built on a rocky plateau close under the Cap of Liberty (a cone rising two thousand feet above the falls and four thousand above the plain) our party drew rein, and stopped to feed the weary horses, and to partake of some refreshments. Then climbing for some time between huge boulders and gnarled trees, we came to a narrow pass full of stones and knobs, where we were compelled to leave the horses again, and climb the remaining distance on foot. We soon came in sight of the Vernal Fall, named Piwyack, or cataract of diamonds, by the Indians. Seeing the water thundering through a rugged gorge and lit up with sparkling flashes as it pours down into a depth of 350 feet, one feels how faithfully the Indian name describes the cataract, much better than its unmeaning English appellation. We descended to the base of the fall by a series of ladders. A single false step or a failing of the nerves might have been fatal, and would have precipitated any one of us into the foaming torrent beneath. At this point, some years ago, the dead body of a stranger was found at the bottom of the waterfall, who had probably fallen from the ladder.

In addition to the famous waterfall we enjoyed an extempore water-*fête* in the shape of a tremendous shower of rain. Whilst we contemplated the noisy, boiling and foaming water, which becomes smooth a short distance lower down, only to break up anew into sparkling cascades, we scarcely noticed that dark clouds had crept up above and hung in ominous grandeur over our heads. Soon a storm burst over the valley with great violence. The thunder rumbled along the sky, the lightning flashed, and then the lowering clouds were suddenly rent asunder, and discharged their moisture in torrents. Silver-white rivulets rushed from the hill-sides and rocks with velocity and noise into the river, and spread their froth upon its surface. We sought shelter under the trees, and as we listened resignedly to the rolling and growling of the thunder, gave ourselves completely up to the grandeur of the occasion.

The storm was mighty, and we stood mute before the terrific fury of the battling elements. A storm amongst mountains is always effective, but a storm in this valley is an experience which gives an enlarged idea of the powers of nature. The sky was luminous, and crashes of thunder, whose reverberations were heard even in greater magnitude than the claps themselves, followed rapidly one another. The turmoil and mutiny around us were quite alarming; the very ground shook under our feet. The hurricane was accompanied by forked lightning of great intensity, which illuminated in vivid flashes the surrounding precipices and rocks, playing, as it were, hide and seek amongst their crevices and cracks. The wind swept down in overpowering gusts, bending the tall pines like reeds, and the terrible downpour of rain mixed with hailstones boded havoc to the vegetation. The storm at last abated. The clouds rolled gradually away scattering their last lingering drops; the rills babbled merrily, and everything around sparkled with an enchanting freshness.

What our fate would have been if caught by the storm whilst on the narrow ledge above the Nevada Fall, we trembled to think of. On resuming our homeward way we saw an old tree thrown on the ground through which the flaming sword of heaven had crashed. The stem was broken across the middle, the place around being littered with its scattered branches and leaves. Pursuing our ride we found that the clear and transparent stream, which we forded in the morning, was a yellow, turbid, dashing torrent, whose roar we could hear from a good distance. All the water collecting from the slopes rushed into the river, and we hesitated to descend into this chaos; but on the one side was the prospect of a cold and dreary bivouac, on the other shelter, warmth, and food in the hotel. The stranger took the lead, and divesting himself of his upper garments, and examining well the girths of the horses, showed his excellent horsemanship by plunging boldly down the steep bank. Whilst struggling in the water he turned to whoop at us to follow, for which we inwardly did not bless him. We looked at each other with joyless countenances, each anxious to leave the honour of precedence to his neighbour. Our courageous friend, who meanwhile had crossed the stream, seemed wonderfully amused at our discomfiture. Presently he beckoned us to ride a few yards lower down the bank, and pointed out a narrow sloping shelf by which we could descend to the stream. With an echoing halloo one of the Scotchmen launched himself boldly forward and we, with the exception of the Bostonian and the guide, followed and reached the opposite bank in safety, although at one moment my horse lost his footing and I made myself ready to slide, if necessary from his back, and swim to shore. In the meantime the guide was looking for some other way by which the Bostonian could cross, but a long halloo, strengthened by a pithy oath from the stranger, soon made them descend. The impetuous current carried their horses for some distance down the leaping stream before they drifted to the opposite shore, wet and bedraggled. We arrived at the hotel, and hastened to dry ourselves before a crackling fire.

CHAPTER VII.

Joining the Mysterious Stranger—The Cap of Liberty—An Interesting Narrative — A Tender Romance — Our Excursions — Hunting and Mining Adventures—A Touching Story.

THE next morning we parted with reluctance from our most amusing friends, the Scotchmen. They left with the heartiest and the kindliest of wishes for our welfare. They went to see the Pohonó, El Capitan, and the Cathedral Spires, which I had previously visited. They lamented greatly that we were not going their way; but fate had set our lines in opposite directions, and we never met again. They told us before they left that they had been sheep-farmers in Australia for several years, and having sold out their business they were then making their way towards their homes in Scotland, and *en passant* were visiting the points of attraction in California. They were good companions and enthusiastic admirers of nature; had none of the artificial manners of town, none of their guile. Their language was peculiar, but their manners, although awkward and rough, were always courteous. They presented the stranger with several San Francisco newspapers, which he gladly accepted, as he had heard nothing from the outside world for a long time. The Bostonian was sorry that he had not a Boston paper to offer him. We were not as deeply affected when the gallant Bostonian expressed his intention of accompanying the Scotchmen, and gracing their company with his presence. "Our stay with you," the Scotchmen said, as they pressed our hands on parting, "has been so pleasant, and you fellows so companionable, that no amount of good luck can obliterate the remembrance we will hold you in."

Left with the stranger, I inquired in what direction he was going. He answered with an invitation to go with him to the Cap of Liberty, for which he was just about to start. I gladly consented, as he told me to walk with him to the log-house of a friend of his, where I could hire a horse for less than half the amount I had to pay in the valley.

"Do you think of staying here long?" he asked.

"I should like to stay here as long as my purse will allow me," I answered.

Then looking significantly at me, he said, "You had better go then to some other quarters, where you can find ample grub and shelter for less money."

"I would feel very thankful if you would show me where."

"Come along, then," he said.

My strange friend was a good specimen of those who, with a love of solitary adventure, combine that rare quality of intelligence, which does not generally characterise the restless spirits who stray beyond the extreme limits of civilisation. I put my entire confidence in him, and the longer I was in his company the more opportunities I had to thank the good luck which had thrown a man across my path of such sterling qualities and such an enviable familiarity with all the secrets and vicissitudes of mountain life. Our route lay along unused pathways, constantly ascending, through forests, over rocks fringed with trees and overhanging vines and creepers. Still we went on, climbing up and up until we could see in every direction the blue stretch of far-away hills, or the shadow of luxuriant forests. Occasionally we stopped to look back on the glorious views which different points revealed. Tissaack was visible in the west, Tokoyoc and Washington Tower rose in the north, and the crests of Pompompasus were piled one above the other in the far background. It was indeed a lovely view, and I gazed with delight upon the panorama, and feasted my eyes upon the scenery, which was most varied and beautiful. The woods with their various shades of green mingling with the pink azaleas and white-flowering shrubs were most charming. A flash of sunlight played on the roofs of the hotels in the valley, and beyond in a nook lay the placid lake with the mountains near it mirrored in its unrippled breast. The rare atmosphere of these high regions gave new zest to our journey, and we hardly knew that we had travelled several miles when we reached a lonely log-cabin on a beautiful mountain-side.

"Halloa, Bob! how're you?"

"Right well, I reckon," a loud voice cried.

The owner of the voice came presently up through a small field, climbed over a low fence, and invited us to come into the cabin. Then he turned to both of us, and asked in the friendliest way possible: "How're you, Fred? How're you, stranger?"

That was the first time I heard my mysterious friend's name mentioned.

"Here's a fellow," he said, introducing me, "coming from somewhere near Hindustan, and I want you, Bob, to let him have the use of one of your nags. Just gird the saddle on; we are going to the Cap of Liberty. Hurry up; we haven't much time to spare."

The man secured at once a restive mustang that was looking over the low fence, and threw a Mexican saddle on its back. I surveyed meanwhile the interior of the cabin. Very humble and simple were the appointments of this home; everything however was clean. Coming back, the man offered us milk, butter, bread, and some fruit.

"Where's my nag?" asked my companion of the man.

"Guess in the corral—I ketch him—wait a minnit," said the man.

I went with my friend to the corral, and opening a little kennel he showed me his hounds, which greeted us with a cheery bay; then as we entered the corral a fine-looking mustang cocked his ears ominously at our approach, and stood still.

"That's my horse," he said.

"Do you live here?" I queried.

"Well, if I am not camping out, I do. Bob is a good chap, and I like to be with him sometimes. He is one of the guides to the valley, and you would be just as safe here under his roof as anywhere else. He can make a snug berth for you too— unless you are accustomed to napkins and silver spoons."

"Bob!" said my companion, whilst we were partaking of the offered food, "we might be late in the evening, and maybe not come back to-night at all, so you'd better put something to eat in our saddle-bags." After doing this, the man greeted us civilly as we mounted the horses, and leaning on the fence looked after us for several moments as we left. My friend cantered on, sitting gracefully in his saddle, and the dogs following us, made the woods ring with their yelping as we rode through a dense growth of laurels, vines and wild-rose bushes. We made our way through this tangled mass with difficulty, and it was curious to observe the knowledge which my friend displayed; there was not a trail he did not know, and every gulch and rock seemed familiar to him. After crossing a bottom with open glades, we wound our way along the side of a precipitous hill overlooking a valley densely wooded with a magnificent pine-forest. The track growing steeper, our horses worked and toiled upwards till at last we were on the top of the large buttress, hob-nobbing with the clouds. The Nevada Fall was just in the foreground, and we could hear the fearful roar of the tremendous headlong plunge of 700 feet into the gorge below. Farther in the distance, dimly shadowed near the point where the valley was lost in the breast of the hills, the majestic Yo-Semité falls flashed and glistened in the rays of the sun, and other streams at various points poured over the cliffs in sheets of dazzling foam.

The regal Tissaack, and far beyond, fading away into the distant blue, Mount Starr King, and a legion of lofty peaks saluted us.

THE DIVIDE OF THE MERCED GROUP OF THE SIERRA NEVADA MOUNTAINS.

Seen from a distance the Sierra Mountains seem always bathed in a mellow haze, like that distinguishing the atmosphere of an Indian summer. We looked down upon the tops of mighty forests, magnificent waterfalls, tremendous abysses, and a wild grandeur of passes through which the Merced and a number of streams wind their course like silvery threads. Having bestowed a sufficient amount of admiration on the fascinating scenery, we sat down under a sheltering rock and ate our luncheon. Pointing to a wall of gleaming granite which rose almost perpendicularly from beneath our feet, my friend said : " I got a fall from that rock once. I shot a large bird early one morning, and hunting for it in the bushes I strayed over the precipice, which was hidden in a dense mist, and rolled down and struck on a projecting rock. Clutching the stones on the edge of the cliff I hung in the air, and in trying to catch a foothold I sent some loose stones rolling down, and the thundering sound as they struck from rock to rock, growing fainter and fainter, made me guess the stupendous depth below my feet. Hanging by my hands I swung to a ledge many feet below me, but I miscalculated the distance in the dim light, and leaping to it, did not reach it with my feet. Whirling through space I landed on another projecting ledge, but broke my right leg above the ankle and otherwise bruised and tore my limbs fearfully. Having somewhat recovered after a while from the stunning fall, I set to work in spite of the excruciating pain, digging out footholds in the crevices of the rocky wall from point to point, and thus descended the perpendicular rock until I struck a trail. It took me a good hour of laborious and painful scrambling and when I came to the bottom I was quite exhausted from excitement and hard work. I reached my home with the greatest difficulty, where my wife tenderly cared for me during a long illness. Having recovered sufficiently, though wasted to a skeleton, I used to go out with my wife, who carried my gun in one hand, and with the other supported my tottering steps in our mountain rambles. In these walks an abundance of game was killed, and by that skill known to a good housewife she prepared it nicely for my then fastidious appetite. Living out-of-doors in the balmy air on these mountains during the summer months, basking in the blessed sunshine, and strengthened by nutritious food, I improved rapidly every day until I became again stout and well."

" You must have had some fearful adventures and hairbreadth escapes on these mountains."

" Time was when I took my life in my hands daily, and the war-whoop of the Indian was a familiar sound to my ears. When I first came to this region, it was almost unknown, except to Indians, and adventurous scouts in search of silver and gold. These soon vulgarized the sacred spot reverenced by the Indian, who lavishes on nature a wealth of affection he never feels for man. I have witnessed many of their boisterous festivals, and sometimes after a successful raid on the pale faces the dance and pow-wow were carried to most extravagant points by the delighted warriors. The stream was lined with wigwams of the different bands, and the scenes often there enacted will long be remembered by those who have been fortunate enough to be near. Tom-toms were loudly beaten by the squaws, and the savage yells and whoops could be heard for miles, and when an unusually terrific burst came from one band, it was almost instantly echoed by a perfect din in the same strain from another band far below. Many savages were dancing round the fires, and others flitting to and fro like so many evil spirits among the shadows of the wigwams; and, to make the scene still more lively, some of the bucks in their obstreperous mirth, imitated the howling of wolves, the hooting of owls, or cawing of crows. Add to this the barking, snarling, yelping and baying of all the dogs in the various camps which were startled by the noise, and the terrible hubbub may be better imagined than described. The poor Indians have almost all been chased away from the places of their most sacred memories, and the greedy rock-hunters too have left, but alas! another sort of people, even more unheedful of preserving the chaste grandeur of this region, is beginning to flock in. I hope and trust that I may not see the day, which seems not to be far away, when these lovely forests will be penetrated by carriage-roads, and steps cut along the ribs of these stupendous rocks." And pointing to the valley, on whose lovely face the evening-sun was shining in splendour, my enthusiastic friend exclaimed bitterly, " Look at the valley—it will before long be penetrated by a railroad, and the eternal voice of the falling waters outcried by the locomotive."

Then for a long while we sat silently, and drank in the wonderful view from the bold peak, and gazed upward towards the snow-clad summits of the lofty Sierras, which loomed up in the distance so solemn and so grand.

The sunny slopes of the surrounding mountains all green and covered with flowers, the murmuring pines and whispering laurels about us, the lovely valley below, the grand heights and glistening snows above, and the day just warm enough, just cool enough, balmy, beautiful, benignant, perfect—one of God's own days! To sit there like this and listen to hunting and mining adventures and Indian stories, which were the real thing and no make-believes—ah, that was enjoyment! I sat and pictured to myself a life in this far land, in the midst of the solitude and tranquillity of nature, far from the hum and stir of cities, and gazed, and gazed until my vision drifted into dreamland and the cliffs appeared a long bank of purple clouds piled from the horizon high into heaven. Thus was I dreaming till my heart was full of peace and joy in this calm hour.

The great sun was slowly descending behind the crags, and the valley began to be steeped in solemn obscurity. The dry wind rustled among the trees and mingled its notes with the restless, shrunken leaves on the ground as we rode homeward through the forest in the evening, and wild pheasants strutted across our path, and swarms of fire-flies frolicked in the shadows all around us—flashing and waning. My genial friend burst now and then into a song, now roystering, now tender, and the dogs joined in with their barking and baying. My friend possessed a rich mine of humour, and at the same time showed often glimpses of a deep, sensitive mind. A joyous outburst of a crazy ditty was succeeded very quickly by a sad and tender song. A melancholy gloom seemed to fall upon him as he sang in a low tone,

> "By the lake where drooped the willow,
> Long time ago,
> Lived a maiden, and I loved her,
> Pure as the snow."

It was like an earnest and fervid prayer. He bowed his head, and we rode silently on through the depth of the forest. By this time it was quite dark, and the rustling of the leaves and the occasional barking of our dogs were the only audible sounds I did not know then of the tender romance which was woven with the history of his past life.

Bob welcomed us home with a friendly face, and after the horses had been housed and cared for, and after our frugal supper was over, we sat, according to the custom of the country, on the Mexican saddles, and had a talk and a smoke. Both the men asked me many questions of the outer world, and talked with a frankness and unaffectedness which is not quite common and conspicuous even in large cities. They had been isolated on their lonely hillside amongst mountains for a great number of years; they had no neighbours and lived miles away from any human habitation, yet they were equal if not superior in politeness and knowledge to many who move in more civilised places. They propounded and explained their views in such a clear and unconstrained way that I was quite surprised to hear them. Even Bob, educated as he was only by the free influences of nature, had to the full a certain knowledge too uncommon amongst men in his rank of life. The mysterious Fred being absent for a few minutes in the corral to look after his pet-dogs and the horses, I took advantage of the opportunity to ask Bob a few questions about him.

"He's an Englishman," Bob said, "of a family of high

standing. He is very well educated, but having had a squabble with his folks at home when quite a boy, he left and came over to California in '49. He became infatuated with a prominent young lady of the theatrical profession, and she followed him to this country, and indeed, on all his round-about trips to the mining camps and hunting grounds. I didn't know her; she died I s'ppose about ten years ago—it'll be so long, as I've known Fred for about that time, I reckon, and when I first met him, he was alone."

" Where did she die ? " I asked.

" She died here. She must have been a brick of a woman—very high-minded—quite a lady; the mountaineers learned to worship her. She grew to love these rocks very much, and spent weeks in wandering with Fred, or alone among them. She became as skilful a shot as any of them, and when she died all the mountaineers mourned her loss bitterly, and Fred carried her remains to a mountain-top not far away from here, and there placed her in a grave among the rocks and balsam-trees she had loved so well. Fred is one of those men who take a pride in being Englishmen, yet unlike almost all others is too proud ever to return. He enlisted also with Walker, the filibuster, and displayed rare courage and bravery in Nicaragua, but after the death of the daring leader he returned to California. He has been in the wilds for a good many years, but he had travelled much before he left England. He had visited the chief capitals of Europe, and speaks Spanish as well as English; even a little German and French—for Paris was one of his experiences."

We sat long chatting and smoking, and then reposed on deer and bear skins spread on the plank-floor, whilst timid bats flitted silently to and fro, and little mice slipped trippingly in and out through the crevices between the planks and the chinks of the walls, and nibbled at the crumbs on the floor.

The following days I was always in the company of my friend, strolling up and down in the marvellous forests, or, mounting the horses, we ascended one of the crests where we could obtain a view of the distant mountains. A ride to one of the summit-ridges, or one of the superb falls was a sufficient work for one day, especially with a sketchbook in hand. "Clouds' Rest, Sentinel Dome, Mount Beatitude, the Glacier and Inspiration Points," &c., we visited successively, always returning at night to Bob's hospitable roof. The most exquisite view of the whole valley, whose upper end is shut in by the towering masses of the South and North Domes, is in my opinion from the Inspiration Point. Happy was the imagination that first suggested that name; for, wild as the massive rocks and hills are which nature here presents, they seem but the gates and portals to an enchanted valley, murmurous with the soft, low music of falling waters. On either hand one contemplates a scenery almost unrivalled in stern and commanding beauty, in loveliness expanding into grandeur. At the summit of Mount Beatitude the most conspicuous object, which is for ever stamped upon the memory of the beholder, is the Ribbon Fall, "Lungootookoya" (meaning long and slender, in the Indian tongue). The gleaming streamlet, piercing its way athwart the beetling crags, descends from a height of 3300 feet in a sparkling shower which, as it reaches the bottom, dissolves into fine spray and rain. It is the loftiest cascade in the valley, and most probably in the world. The "Pohonó" is to be seen on the other side of the beholder, while the "Three Graces" (Kosokong) tower up in the background to a height of 3600 feet.

But for a complete and unbroken view of the ocean of snow-tipped Sierra mountains, I prefer the noble crest of the Sentinel Dome " Loya," which includes quite a panorama. As one looks forward, bald summits, heaped against and over one another, rise lofty and sublime into the air, and one's mind is receiving manifold impressions of the grand scenery with its fanciful forms, the depth of its gloomy recesses, and its mountain

OUR EXCURSIONS IN THE WOODS.

streams thundering down the abysses with incessant roar. Mount Lyell, Mount Dana, the fantastic Mount Starr King, Mount Hoffman, the Castle Peak, Gothic Rock, and the Cathedral Peak, most of them above twelve thousand feet high, bare their proud cones and point into the sky like gigantic towers. A surprising number of other butts and domes rise thousands of feet above the level of the surrounding country, whilst the huge and thunder-split bulks of the South and North Domes (Tissaak and Tokoyoe) and the various waterfalls in the valley make a splendid foreground to the distant sweep of the horizon. Parallel with the great mountain-range run the foot-hills, a chain of lower mountains broken by cañons and gorges in the rocks, in which there is much scenery of a striking and majestic character.

The purity of the air on these mountains is most remarkable. It is so clear that it permits small objects to be distinctly seen at great distances, and mountains eight or ten miles away appear close at hand. Stones and rocks are often imagined to be of immense size and far away, whilst they are in reality small and near by. The air also appears to produce a wonderful effect in colouring the ranges of distant mountains. The tints which they assume are beautifully clear in the far distance, a deep blue is most common, but all shades of purple, violet, and even rose are seen. I never anywhere else saw in such perfection those beautiful colours which constitute the charm of mountain scenery. The transparency of the air becomes very evident at night when the stars shine out with all the splendour which they have in the clear nights of mid-winter in other countries.

One of the chief delights of travelling in the woods and wilds of the vast American continent, is to light upon one of those strange and quaint retailers of traditional lore in the shape of a backwoodsman, trapper, or miner, who can beguile the hours of repose with anecdotes and recollections of his past adventurous life. There is a tinge of old-world chivalry in the character of most of the men who came in early days to California, and less of the snob in them than in any man in the world.

Sitting under a spreading oak one evening, my genial friend regaled me with stories of early Californian life: "When I came to California in '49 I went first to mining in a tract two miles above Sonora. I laboured during several months with varied success, some days obtaining but a few dollars' worth of gold, but after several weeks of hard work and unremunerative pay, I one day 'struck a lead' and in two hours took out more than five hundred dollars' worth of gold. The same day, within stone-throw of me, two Mexicans unearthed two thousand two hundred dollars, while an eager crowd that soon collected around us got, some forty, some fifty dollars' worth of gold. This was my most successful day. At the time I am describing," continued my friend—"crowds of gamblers and roughs from the Eastern States, dangerous criminals of Great Britain, runaway sailors from American sea-ports, and all sorts of villains of the blackest dye from the Continent of Europe and from Sydney's Botany Bay, began to arrive among the peaceable and industrious men, and curse the Californian mines with their hateful presence. The result was that the previous security gave place to nightly loss of tools, and almost daily assassinations of the most bloody and cruel character. The bad element soon became so powerful that lawless men bade defiance to every law and order, and began to rob in gangs, roaming from camp to camp, and assaulting and murdering those who ventured to oppose them. The Sonorarian Camp, two miles below me, was one of the most insecure and dangerous of the Californian mines. It was a place in which immorality and crime of the worst description was rampant, and in which decent people were in constant danger of loss of property and life. There were congregated at that time the most lovely and bewitching importations of the female sex—Kanaka beauties from the Sandwich Islands; the dusky belles from Valparaiso; the fairest girls from Chili and Peru, with any quantity of vice and loveliness combined, from Mazatlan and China. It was undoubtedly the gayest and richest region of this golden land, for there had been taken out those twenty-five pound lumps of pure gold, whose discovery electrified the whole world. Many murders were committed there for which no one was punished. I was present one night in the large gambling tent at Sonora, curiously watching several of the 'big games,' when an altercation took place between a monte-dealer and a New York bully, and before the crowd could interfere the Mexican monte-dealer drew his revolver and shot his opponent through the head; the broken pieces of skull and portions of the brain being spattered over my gay Mexican serape, then much in vogue at the gold mines. On that same Saturday night, in that same tent, another man was stabbed through the heart. The next Sabbath morning I strolled through that tent where the two stabbed and riddled bodies lay stark and stiff upon two monte-tables, while a game was being played upon another close at hand. Such scenes were quite common in the mines during the early years of Californian mining, and I began to grow disgusted with the character of my surroundings, and finally left for the mountains, where I lived by trapping and hunting."

Such were his stories, and many more he related, but I will not make any more attempts to harrow up feelings by blood-curdling stories and hair-breadth escapes from horrible death.

A strange attachment grew up between Fred and me. He was a large-hearted man, with nothing small or mean in his whole composition, and often showed glimpses of such a generous nature, and such a refined and enthusiastic feeling that I could not help liking to be in his company. By our mutual intercourse I gained the conviction that the real education of an individual does not consist in the mere acquisition of a certain kind of polish, nor in the dull and pompous platitudes of modern society, but in the ennobling influences which mould his whole youth and manhood, and fit him for general contact with the dangers and vicissitudes of life.

On one occasion, whilst riding along through a beautiful grove on the crest of a hill, my friend said musingly: "I want you to come and see the grave of my poor wife."

I had been expecting this for several days, and though I longed to hear from Fred's own lips the mournful tale, yet I had feared to ask him, and respected his silence upon this point. After a short ride through thickets of rhododendrons and balsam trees, Fred alighted; I followed his example; and straightway he led me to a large spreading oak-tree, whose trunk was nearly hidden by creepers and bushes of pink and scarlet rhododendrons and white azaleas, emitting a strong delicious aroma; and in the midst of which nestled a little mound covered with timorous, tiny white blossoms of a multitude of flowers. Every breath of wind that whispered through the trees scattered a heap of odorous blossoms on the grave.

"Here rests my poor wife," said Fred, as we stood with bared heads before the grave. So we stood for several minutes silently; neither of us could find words to express his feelings. I broke the silence at last, and pressing his hand, I said: "Fred, this is a beautiful spot, but it must be a harrowing sight for you—let's go."

"Oh, no; I have spent many an hour here; let's sit down." And anticipating my desire as if he divined what was passing in my mind, he simply, yet with a touching eloquence, told me how she died.

"Beneath these leafy trees I often used to stray with Alice, and under this great oak we often sat. I was scarcely more than a boy when I wooed her in the old country, and finally succeeded in gaining her hand. If I had been content in this critical epoch of my life to let things run their usual course—but partly from the hope of pushing our fortune in America, and partly from a love of adventure, I sailed with her from home. The gold-fever lured me to California. She followed me over seas and mountains, and, sharing all my fortune's failures, she clung to me with pure sincerity and trust. She was like a sunbeam that ever shone through the gloom, and her affection for me had grown so strong and deep that no ill-luck could discourage her ardent soul. But sometimes, when looking in her face half hidden in her loosened hair, and meeting her look of tenderness and sorrow, I grieved to think of her passing her life thus separated from all her friends. So several years went by which wrought on her face a tender grace of melancholy and grief, and in spite of all my loving care she pined away, musing, as was her wont, on—I know not what. The cheeks that used to be so flushed became now deadly pale, and her eyes gradually assumed a dreamy, vague expression, as though she were quite forgetful of her surroundings. At intervals she brightened up, but soon her mind wandered again. Thus lingered she on for months, then took to bed and never arose from it after. One day I was sitting by her bed—she was dying. Her spirit was gradually sinking, and gently passing into the care of angels. At one moment she roused from her stupor, stretched her hand tenderly towards me, whilst her lips quivered as if blessings were passing over them, then a bright light came into her dim eyes, and calmly and quietly she breathed her last. I was quite numb with grief, and a thrilling pain went through my heart, such as nothing in all my previous life had ever equalled. My conscience reproached me that I had drawn her away from her friends, and late—oh, late in anguish I learnt bitterly to regret. Lying before me motionless and cold, with her thin hands folded over her pulseless heart, she seemed as if she were sleeping, and her face was lighted up with a peaceful smile. I buried all that remained of that pure being here amidst the old trees where we so often tarried in the summer glow, and spent so many happy hours together. I still often keep my tryst alone and weave strange garlands now amongst the withering leaves of the reminiscences of those days when by her side I stood. The earth closed over all that was dearest to me, but her memory clings about me like the scent of flowers, and thrills me now though many years have flown since. Her lips will never lisp to me again, and the eyes from which love's sweetest radiance shone, are now closed for ever. With her every blossom of my life lies dead. Sometimes my thoughts wander backward through the misty region of the past, and my wasted years for ever gone, vex me with their weary spell. I compare the picture of the present with the visions I once made for myself of the future, and, discouraged and wrecked, I starve on pride. Listen, how mournfully the leaves are rustling over her grave!"

I was deeply moved. Mounting our horses we rode silently through the forest for a long while. I could not say a word —what, indeed, could I say? Words are too stale, and have no comforting and soothing power for a mind so deeply wounded. The silence grew painful. It seemed so odd to me that I should try to cheer up and comfort a man, broad-built and wrought like a Hercules; yet riding up close to him, I said: "Fred, you may be sure that I deeply sympathize with your sorrow; but brace up; yield not to what you know cannot be undone. Hope for brighter days."

"My youth's bright hopes are shattered; they have vanished like shadows with the light of day," he answered.

"Wouldn't it be better for you," I continued after a while, "to leave this country, to which such painful reminiscences are attached, and, instead of taking your misfortune so to heart and fostering your grief, return to your friends?"

"My friends?" he said gravely. "Solitude is infinitely preferable to uncongeniality and incompatibility—they have no love for poverty. When she whose loss I mourn became my wife, they urged me to let her go, to let her perish. And as I spurned the thought of deceiving her, and stood by her who stood faithfully by me, and quite alone, they cast me off. Do you see the motive? Because no threat could shake my faith in her, and all their schemes were in vain, they thrust me on the world without my name. They thought that I should soon come back when left to pinching want; but they will have to wait a long time yet. No, I'll not pick their crumbs!"

And the bold and honest fellow raised himself up in the saddle, and we rode on silently until we reached our low-roofed night-quarters.

CHAPTER VIII.

Roughing it in the Sierras—A Weary Ride—Overcome by Fatigue—A Rough Climb—Sunrise—A Grand Outlook—Camping out—My Genial Friends—Our Parting.

WE determined one day to make a longer trip to the mountains. After careful preparation, which consisted in putting supplies of flour, biscuits, tea, coffee, sugar, dried meat, salt, &c., into bags, and taking an extra packhorse for carrying our supplies, we bid adieu to Bob, and started on our difficult trip. We decided to pay a visit to Mount Hoffman, 13,870 feet high. Knowing that we had a long journey before us, we started at sunrise on a lovely autumn morning. First we passed through a beautiful belt of forest land, then descending into a valley we rode several hours toilsomely over rocks of basalt and sand, after which we traversed a country broken up by knolls and ravines which were beset with dead and fallen timber, and thickly covered with undergrowth and brushwood. The farther we advanced the more the difficulties seemed to increase; obstacles of various kinds impeded our progress—fallen trees with their branches tangled and matted together; rocks and deep ravines; holes in the ground, and other difficulties over which our horses had to climb without the possibility of avoiding them. The horses made but slow and painful progress, and very soon I felt the effect of the weary ride in the hard, wooden Mexican saddle. In the evening, having travelled more than thirty miles, we reached the base of the mountain, and finding a cool spring amongst the wild rocks, we halted, and prepared to spend the night on this spot. I was very tired and fearfully sore from the long ride. I felt the warm blood oozing down my legs, and pulling down my nether garments, I tore long shreds of my skin along with them, which had dried and adhered to them. After bathing the bleeding sores, my friend rubbed a strong solution of salt upon them, which made me howl and jump high into the air with agonizing pain. To make our bivouac still more cheerless it began to drop with rain, which increased in time to a shower. We took refuge in a cleft among the rocks, listening resignedly to the monotonous pattering of the rain, and observed quietly the increasing darkness. Our poor animals also sought shelter against the rain that swept by in great splashes, and stood shivering by the fire of pine-logs and boughs which we kindled, but which the pelting shower half extinguished. The clouds had driven in on all sides, and only a faint streak of yellow still lingered in the Western horizon. Thus patiently we watched for several hours, until from sheer exhaustion and weakness I sank down on the wet, cold rock and fell asleep whilst my good-hearted friend covered me up with all the blankets, and built over me a roof of boughs covering them with the saddles and provision-bags. Sitting in the storm and rain, my friend smoked calmly by my side, and rubbed brandy from time to time on my throbbing temples, and tended the fire the whole night through without a moment's sleep. I felt ashamed of my weakness when I was awakened to an early breakfast by the good man. I shall never forget that morning. Benumbed with cold, I felt so faint and feeble that, as I put my foot into the stirrup to mount my horse, my legs refused their service; my strength failed me, and my friend had to lift me into the saddle. "You'll be all right when your blood comes into circulation," he said, and with many a jest and jocund remark decoyed me to good humour.

We made a steep ascent, all round us being enshrouded in deep gloom and looking mysterious and ghostly in the dim dawn of the early morning. The valley was filled with a dense and cold mist, which covered the trees around us with hoar frost, and out of the fog the adjacent rocks and crags rose like islands in a sea; but occasionally thick waves of mist came rolling on and tossed across them like ocean-surges, hiding them completely, and even the ground below our feet. It was a gruesome ride. Our cautious mountain horses walked with the greatest difficulty as we ascended the steep zig-zag path of intermingled flinty rock and friable slate, which wound up the side of the mountain. I soon discovered that an attempt to guide my horse was worse than useless, so I dropped the rein upon the animal's neck, and allowed him to take his own course, and kept as quiet as possible in the saddle. We needed all our strength for the later work, and could not spare our horses which suffered terribly until, coming to the most rugged and steepest part of the trail, we thought it safer to alight, and then leading the animals we proceeded—a dangerous precipice on one side and a rocky wall on the other. The wall on our right was almost perpendicular; and passing along the giddy verge of the abyss our horses paused from time to time as if in mute despair, for they could scarcely obtain a footing, and started every now and then the loose, broken stones which rolled from under their hoofs, and over the cliff they went thundering down. We could hear them strike with a dull leaden sound on the broken rocks below, and the sound aroused a thousand slumbering echoes, which rolled like a low thunder-peal from one mountain to another, reverberating fainter and fainter until they were lost in the stilly silence which they had so suddenly disturbed. This was the roughest part of a rough scramble and tried our horses terribly. I was very much afraid lest one of the animals should lose its footing and fall down from the rock; and I could not forbear starting occasionally when my horse's hoofs struck against a stone. A false step would have occasioned grief, and the least awkward movement might have cost us dearly, but fortunately the nags were surefooted. Once my horse slipped on a smooth stone and recovered himself only by a desperate effort; then he stood still and trembled for a moment. Thus we passed over some terrible-looking places, until after a long and fatiguing scramble we came to a huge mass of black, jaggedly-projecting rocks, where the ledge widened and was covered with dead and gnarled tree-trunks. Here we tied up our horses, and climbed for about half an hour to the topmost height of the rugged ledge. The climb was a hard task, for here and there were scattered heaps of loose stones, which seemed to have broken from the cliffs above, and over which we frequently had to crawl on hands and knees for a long distance. My friend helped me over the most dangerous part, and when we had reached a considerable altitude farther progress was impossible.

The light increased by that time, and from the brink of the overhanging rock we looked down sheer into an almost fathomless abyss. A single glance downwards was enough to make one dizzy. Prompted by curiosity I flattened myself on the cliff and bent over its edge to look down, but overcome by a sudden fit of giddiness I shrank back, digging my fingers into the crevices of the rock. My friend, however, held me fast in his iron grasp. All reckoning of distance was lost, as the mists, surging up, deepened still more by their veil the dizzy fall that yawned under our feet. The forms below were half obscured, and the eye could scarcely distinguish them through the vast depth. My friend said that it was more than five thousand feet; it seemed ten thousand feet—ten miles—any distance imagination might have made it. Above us towered a tremendous height, whose rugged sides seemed interminable, and in whose gaps and gulches the snow was glittering through the fog. The more distant peaks and crags looked like dark, jagged silhouettes thrown up against the sky, and a pale mist rolled slowly over them. By degrees—a good while before the sun himself rose—came the yellow hue of sunrise and covered almost the whole sky. Then almost on a sudden a rift was made in the fog, and the first gleam of the sun burst forth through the billowy, curling, and wreathing vapour, and illumined the hill-tops. The dazzling light—a very delicate saffron in hue—blazing upward in widening lines, seemed to rend the mist in twain. Enchanted with the scene we stood silently watching the fleecy clouds dashing and rolling tumultuously between the cliffs, but at the moment of the first break of sunshine through the noiseless, white sea of vapour, which gave us a glimpse of the far-distant mountains, a cry of enthusiastic delight burst from our lips. That view fully compensated for all the toil and fatigue we had to endure. The breaking up of the hazy, purple-gray fog-clouds had a peculiarly beautiful effect.

Later on a gentle breeze thinned away the mist in front of us, the remaining stars disappeared before the advancing light, and at last we saluted the sun from the beetling rock. The rim of the solar disc mounted slowly above the far-away mountains, growing larger and larger, a moment more and—behold!—the glorious sun in all its splendour.

Its rays shot upwards and outwards on either side of its centre, and a flood of light like liquid gold was streaming over the sky. The effect was grand. Above, more towards the zenith, wreaths of gold-edged vapour, which here and there shaded into a flush of pink, floated like so many islands in a pale greenish-blue sky, while below us the mists rose solemnly and slowly, revealing gradually to our admiring gaze the beauty and grandeur of the surrounding landscape. Peak after peak was unveiled; precipices and gloomy recesses, one by one dawned upon us; earth and sky glowed as if they had been set on fire. Hundreds of crags were shooting skyward brushing with their brows against the clouds, and beyond and beyond peaks and peaks and ravines and ravines!

When the view at last became entirely unobstructed, and the whole heaven was clad in pure azure, there lay rolled out before us the most glorious and unspeakably beautiful panorama of the valley, with the hoary mountains towering in the background, whose glittering, snow-clad peaks shot up into the blue expanse of heaven. The purity of the sunlight and the delicious blueness of the shadows gave a wonderful

A CAÑON IN THE SIERRAS.

effect of brilliancy to the scene. What a view it was! I was lost in admiration and felt such a sense of pleasure that I could not give utterance to my thoughts. Far above where we stood—higher than the eagles' flight—soared the summit of Mount Hoffman, flooded with the glory of morning; and sheer below us—far, far beneath, lay the winding valley burning in one ray of liquid light, and beyond the ridges rose and fell in endless succession like waves of a sea. All around lay a dizzy view of the world below, and against the mysterious vastness stood the outlines of our horses on the ledge of the projecting rock in the foreground, as if in trackless space. The bright sun mirrored himself in the dew-drops which still clung to the stones and mosses around, and the distant hills and mountains were of a heavenly blue. Crystal cascades, that looked like milk-white ribbons, came shooting down the manifold rocks and mountain-sides in dazzling sheets, and each of the ravines and rocky gulches was a scene of enchanting beauty. We could distinguish every object in the far distance; every detail of the wrinkled landscape beneath us. The rocks and forests, backed by the snowy peaks of the distant mountains, seemed to be creeping upwards, and everything seemed insignificant below in the valley. The tall trees were dwarfed to the size of shrubs; the belts of dark-green forest-land, lying almost two miles beneath us, looked like beautiful green oases, and the glistening streams were reduced to mere silvery threads. The scenery which we witnessed that day was the grandest my eyes ever rested upon, and no effect of nature ever impressed me more deeply than this grand outlook on mountains and dales. It was worthy of an artist's brush, but his hand would be cunning indeed that could picture its grace and animation. This was the best though most fatiguing of all our numerous mountain-scrambles, and my enjoyment was only dimmed in my mind by the reflection that it was of too short a duration. I felt quite sorry to leave, but we had to retrace our steps to see after our horses.

I am weary of description; I feel the hopeless task of expressing in words the solemn magnitude of these mountains. Into this vast upheaval of majestic rocks we now daily made our way, and the impressions of these wanderings are among the most vivid of my travels. What quiet rippling of gentle brooks and solemn roar of magnificent water-falls! I have never since seen so much of sublime grandeur, relieved by so much beauty, as I have witnessed during these days. Up at dawn and away over hill and dale, now clambering among rocks or riding through forests for miles, now stirring the reins and spurring our horses to reach shelter long after night had shrouded the landscape in darkness. Sometimes we slept in a lowly cabin and shared the simple fare of the stalwart lumbermen ; but oftener, wrapt in blankets, we stretched ourselves on the ground under a sheltering rock or a rustling tree, and with the saddles for our pillows, we gazed through the boughs at the far-off stars, until the deep, soothing music of the pines—the Eolian harps of the forest—mingled with our dreams. Although there are vast stretches of nothing but pine-woods, yet the tapering pines and firs have a beauty of their own. Prolific nature clothes these wildernesses with berry-bearing plants and shrubs of all kinds, while mosses of every hue, wild flowers of the richest colours, and tall and graceful ferns and grasses diversify the scenery.

In the mid-day siesta, whilst our animals grazed on the luxuriant grass, we used to lie in the shade, and gaze upward towards the snow-tipped summits of the Sierras, whose grandeur and majesty must be seen to be felt—they cannot be described. There, in solitary repose, where no busy steps tread the crisp grass and only beasts claim dominion, is Nature's chaste beauty displayed and creation's wildest charms are lavished in profusion. The lover of the picturesque may revel in the sight of towering rocks and cliffs, and the sportsman finds no lack of game on these mountains. They are the happy hunting-ground for those who enjoy shooting, fishing, and "roughing it," for they are the home of the lynx, the badger, and the wild cat; foxes are also numerous; and pumas (mountain lions generally called there) are frequently to be seen. Among the thickets, in the deep ravines which furrow the sides of the mountains, hides the timid roe, and many other species of deer can readily be found. The streams are full of all kinds of fish; wild geese and ducks are plentiful, and eagles almost at any time during the day may be seen soaring majestically in circles above the valleys. Grizzly bears are not so often met with as formerly. I was shown, however, a place where a man was severely wounded by one only a short time before our arrival on the spot.

Some of our experiences of mountain climbing and forest rides were exhausting and even dangerous, but the delights of the scenery and the healthy and invigorating outdoor life were ample amends. Sometimes when returning from an adventurous scramble, weary and sore, my friend very often put me to shame, always meeting me with a jest and unvarying courtesy.

His temper was even and placid, but when occasion required he could speak a bit of his mind in a style which was not easily forgotten by him who provoked the controversy. However, I have never heard him speak ill of any one, and only once did I hear him give vent to anything like wrathful feelings; that was when being gruffly snubbed by the "civilized" Bostonian. There was a dash of the filibuster still in him—the erect, proud port, and above all a calm sense, never disturbed by weather or the rude inconveniences of travel, which no discomfort could ruffle or difficulty daunt. The reason of this could be found perhaps in the fact that he had lived the greater part of his life, I may say, within himself, and amidst nature in her sublimity and wildness. Beneath the seemingly hard crust which years of a half-savage life had wrapped round it, there beat a true, a tender, and essentially noble heart. Combining as he did with these excellent qualities a warm and devoted companionship, and an enthusiastic fellow-admiration for lovely scenery, which largely increased the pleasure of our rambles, I am not saying too much when I assert that Fred was a "brick"— to use a Californian expression. A man unbiassed by mercenary selfishness, or petty and mean considerations and prejudices; unassuming yet clever, stern yet tender as a maiden—a marvellous combination he was of opposite extremes. He was a jovial and maybe a reckless and devil-may-care fellow, but withal he was manly and unselfish in supporting what he thought right, and as fearless of what others might think, or of what they might do. A nature of such a quick and sensitive fibre like Fred's required another treatment than he had received amongst his surroundings at home. Such a noble-minded fellow, though sullied and dishonoured by craven kin is still "a man for a' that;" aye, and of the best mettle too. "Many a fine-toned instrument never gives expression to the music that lies in it for lack of a hand to touch the keys."

But time is inexorable, and sped on till the day came when I had to tear myself from my friends and all the peaceful surroundings which had become so dear to me. I left my kind hosts, whose attentions had made their humble and lonely cabin a pleasant *séjour* to me, with sincerest regret. Fred and Bob accompanied me to the valley one afternoon where I wished to spend the last few hours, and upon my pressing invitation remained with me in the hotel over night. We had a good supper, but somehow or other our conversation was very scant; we could not manage our usual hilarity that evening. Many were the mutual expressions of regret at my early departure that passed between us, for I felt that nothing could have exceeded the hospitality and kindness shown by my two friends.

"Reckon you ought to leave us one of your pictures to remind us of you," said Bob, with a cunning smile.

"With all my heart, Bob," said I; and handing him my portfolio, I told him to take whichever he liked. It was

VIEW OF THE YO-SEMITÉ VALLEY FROM THE MARIPOSA TRAIL.

amusing to see him scrutinise the sketches with the most comical of grave faces.

"Well, which do you think you would like best?" I asked.

"It hain't no easy matter, nohow—derned thing! If I take the one where Pohonó or the Yo-Semité Fall is pictured, there isn't Tissaack to be seen, nor El Capitan and the other rocks; and if I take one with the rocks on it, I lose the Falls." And with a delightful bashfulness he selected one where his log cabin was depicted with the low and dilapidated fence, and the beautiful mountain-side for a background.

"Where will you hang it up, Bob?—if it's a fair question," asked Fred laughing—"I suppose in the front parlour behind the chimney."

"You bet!" exclaimed Bob, "when I ride to Sonora I buy a frame, and have it fixed up."

It was a chilly November morning as I started on my return journey by the Coulterville route. Fred volunteered to be my guide. Passing down the valley for about a mile we crossed the Merced, and continued along its bank close to the base of El Capitan. Here we halted to say good-bye to Bob, when many a kind word and wish for my welfare and prosperity I did hear. The wishes were reciprocal. We then took a steep trail upon the mountain-side. A tremulous mist hung about us, the clouds now and then shut the valley from our view, but having gained the ridge a burst of lustrous sunshine lent its cheering rays to relieve the sadness which clung to my heart as I took the last, fond, lingering look of the valley and the far-off mountains reposing in their blueness, and bade the beautiful vision in all its greatest glory, farewell.

O ye lofty mountains piled upon mountains in countless succession, elevating your huge bulks and rocky summits to the sun—unmoved, unchanged, defying the clouds and the storms! Thou, Tissaack, venerable hill, looking down from thy dizzy height; thou, Tutochahnulah; thou Mount Starr King; Mount Hoffman, and all ye others—you stand sole monarchs in your broad magnificence and giant superiority to the surrounding country. You often soothed and softened my unsatisfied feelings when a wild and restless longing overpowered my heart. From you I learnt to be grateful for the beauty of the earth; you revealed to me the splendours of the setting sun. Ye gloomy forests! Beneath the shade and amidst the melody of your rustling branches I have spent many an hour; your paths were my favourite walks; you were a breathing creation whose mysterious accents I could syllable. In your utter solitude I was taught to comprehend the low hushing and sighing of the pines and firs, to admire the gentle swaying of their tops, and love their sweet breath, when along your woodland paths I used to trace my way. Sublime visions hovered over my soul in the depth of your overarching aisles—oh, gentle, saintly dreams, why did you pass so soon away?

Pursuing our journey we had at times beautiful views over the valleys and the distant chain of mountains. My eyes followed the successive transformations of the scenery—the dim, blue, mystic peaks and crests marked on the horizon, and the lovely interfusions of colours which rested, faded, and returned again. Towards noon, taking out our sandwiches, we made our dinner as we rode along. I may here note another piece of knowledge which Fred displayed. Whilst resting for a while near the roadway he drew a cross in the dust as a crude idea of the sundial and placed a small stick upright as the meridian line. By observing where the shadow fell he gave the hour quite correctly in accordance with my watch.

After a ride of about ten miles our equestrian travel ended at a small village, the name of which I forget. There I had the last lunch with Fred. I shall not mark the last affectionate pressures of our hands, the mingling as it were of our mutual regret. I have never parted from a truer and more kind-hearted friend. "All on board!" shouted the merry stage-driver and as the coach pulled on, the last good-bye he cried, waved his hand, mounted his horse, and dashed wildly towards his lonely mountain-home high on the sunny hillside.

> "And he was gone! Gone like a breath,
> Gone like a white sail seen at night—
> A moment, and then lost to sight."

Last year I heard of his death. Let the weary be at rest—peace to his dust!

Towards evening I reached Coulterville, and next day continued by stage-coach to Stockton, where I exchanged the uneasy vehicle for the smooth-running railroad train on my way back to San Francisco.

CHAPTER IX.

A Visit to a Chinese Restaurant and Opium Saloon—My Initiation into the Mysteries of Opium Smoking—Its Consequences—Celebration of the Chinese New Year—Chinese Joss Houses and Funerals—Domestic Arrangements and Habits of the Chinese—A Stroll through the Chinese Quarter of San Francisco.

THERE is scarcely a tourist who does not as soon as he comes to San Francisco hasten to Chinatown to gape at its heathen wonders, and to gratify his pent-up hunger for Chinese delicacies or opium smoking in their restaurants and saloons. They are patronized by many gentlemen; and even ladies, it is rumoured, condescend to visit the opium-saloons in strict *incognito*. A friend directing me to a Chinese restaurant in Dupont Street said: "It is one of the best; there are others of the same sort where the food is as good, but less varied and served up less delicately, but in plenty for all that;" so I went there one evening with some of my friends. There were not many stairs, but we mounted them so slowly that I had ample opportunity ere we reached the mystic chamber of making myself acquainted with the smell of that which, if all went well, I should presently enjoy the felicity of tasting. I cannot say that the odour was very appetizing, and I began to have doubts lest after all we had come to a wrong place, but a searching question soon drew out clear evidence that we were all right. Having found the place we experienced no difficulty in making known our desire as one of the pig-tailed waiters proved to be the brother of a servant of one of my friends, whom he often visited.

He did not exhibit the least amazement that we should have a craving after the celestial luxuries. Once again was I doomed to disappointment—I had pictured to myself richly costumed mandarins of commanding aspect, but there were only shabby, shambling Chinamen there, whose apparel consisted only of the vulgar, common, blue calico, and who wore their pigtails wound round their heads in the ordinary fashion. The landlord on seeing us saluted with his cap, bowing with great cordiality and politeness as gracefully as his crooked legs would permit.

The quartette of us sat down to a little supper which was "little" only in the sense of there being only four of the party. It is a common and erroneous impression among those who have not investigated the subject that Chinamen eat little else than rice and a few other articles of plain food. This may be true among the lower classes, but the almost endless variety of edibles that may be seen served to better-class customers at some of their *bon-ton* restaurants fully attest the carnivorous appetite and the epicurean taste of the Celestials.

"Oysters for four" were ordered, and they were brought in, fat and tearful, on the half-shell. Fresh herring cut up into mouthfuls with sugar and chopped onions (a very toothsome combination), slices of smoked mackerel and eel, raw salmon, tinned anchovies, sardines, and other tit-bits by the dozen came next. When all these were tasted and disposed of, the pig-tailed waiter—enveloped in a steamy ether—stalked in with the soup. Shad followed. It came up from the kitchen a beautiful broil with all the pristine purity of its native waters escaping in a savoury vapour. Then a long array of cured and dried fish, dried oysters, shrimps and shell-fish of various kinds, roast fowl, dried duck, mouthfuls of tongue, beef in tiny round steaks, broiled and surrounded with hard-boiled eggs, and a great variety of cold meats assorted, hashed, roasted and cooked were served on small plates. The viands were all cut up into very small portions, of which, however, we could take as many as we pleased, for the waiter kept the dishes filled by relays from the kitchen. We fought very shy of some of the spiced and seasoned mixtures of a bilious, yellowish-brown colour, for tradition has connected the rodent and reptile species so much with the food of the Chinese that we had a natural distrust for many of the mysteriously compounded dishes. Roast pig, the *pièce de résistance*—the excellence of which, it is said, was originally discovered by the Chinese, and the peculiar toothsomeness of which is dexterously improved by them with various *compotes* of delicious fruits—just enough to flavour—with fresh vegetables, rice and peas, concluded the repast. It was high time that the four were appeased.

In conformance with an old saw that says "good eating deserveth good drinking," tea was served at last. Yes, tea came in proper order just now, and of this the gods themselves could not complain. It proved to be the best of the whole and went to the right spot. In the first-class Chinese restaurants tea is used costing from two to three dollars per pound, and it is a known fact that even the tea in common use among them is of a far better quality than that consumed by Americans and Europeans. Much of the food used by the Chinese in America is brought directly from their own country, and the superiority of the tea, rice, and all the condiments and conserves imported for their own consumption, is attested by everybody who has tried the experiment of dining in one of their *bon-ton* restaurants. After we had paid for our swell supper, the landlord looked at us inquiringly, smiled, made a deep salaam, rubbed his hands and bowed again. Perceiving that our attention was directed to lighting our cigars, he uttered with a grin the word "Smokee?" (the Chinese add an "e" to nearly every word they utter, and the ridiculous sound may be imagined produced by this adornment of the Queen's English), and added, politely pointing to a door, "Go this way and take a cheer."

At that moment I did not know what "taking a cheer"

means with the Chinese, but my friends hastened at once to declare that we were not in the least hurry, but would like to see the place and witness the proceedings. At his summons a queer-looking fellow, whose strangely-shaped head-cover looked as if its possessor was always falling and always managed to let the hat be underneath, took up a lamp and marshalled us up stairs to a room in which there was no table or chair or any moveables save a queer-fashioned bedstead that stood at the end of it. But the bed was even more remarkable than the bedstead, for it was made across the bedstead from side to side instead of being made lengthways in the usual way. On three sides of the "saloon" were arranged three tiers of bunks with the heads against the walls. Each bunk was large enough for two persons, who lie facing each other with a small oil taper-lamp between them. For a pillow a block of wood is used with two hollows for the heads. In this room, about twenty feet square, there was smoking accommodation for thirty persons. Economizing space seems to have been reduced to a science by the Chinese. Where two or three white men would feel crowded and cramped for elbow-room, a dozen Chinamen will live without a particle of inconvenience; and wherever a breath of air can be coaxed to fulfil its life-sustaining purpose, there one is sure to find lively and apparently healthy Mongolians. Over the bunks were stretched Chinese mattings and rugs and a few gaudy business notices greeted the eye on the walls in bright, red hieroglyphics. Their print and business signs read vertically instead of horizontally. Grotesque, diminutive figures, representing doubtless some idols, and various gilded ornaments, thrown together in confusion, were placed on the mantelshelf.

When we had surveyed the premises, the opium-master pointed to the bedstead, just as much as to say: "There, I think you'll be snug," and forthwith began to initiate me into the mysteries of opium-smoking, for the conjectures of how it was all done still puzzled my brains. He commenced the operation with much gravity, though the procedure did not look more interesting at the beginning than boiling porridge. Taking a smutty tin pot with some water in it and fixing a little sieve on the spout, he shredded some cake-opium as smokers shred cakes of tobacco, placed it in the sieve and put it on the fire to simmer. He explained more by gestures than by words that the essence filters through the sieve in the form of thinnish treacle, while what remains in the sieve is of no more value than common tea-leaves which remain in a tea-pot. He accompanied his observations and explanations with an expression on his pallid and wax-like face that betokened his fathomless pity for a person in my stupid and benighted condition, though I made but few inquiries, for fear lest too much exposure of my ignorance might turn his pity to downright contempt. The brew required some more care, for it was not—even after the stewing it had undergone—as yet ready for smoking. It had to be frizzled, and all ye who are guilty of the gross barbarism of smoking opium, be well assured that it should be cooked, stewed and frizzled before the process of smoking begins.

Then the opium-master, producing the tools of his art, beckoned me politely to the bedstead, which I mounted with a tremulous heart and not without some extremely dubious feelings as to the possible effects of the experiment. The presence of my friends, however, steadied me in my purpose, and I proceeded with a lighter heart to business, but was firm in my resolve to take my smoke sitting and not reclining. The opium-master then lit a little brass lamp, and stepping up he squatted upon the bed with the tools ready at hand. The pipe specially constructed for this kind of smoking is not at all like an ordinary tobacco-pipe. It is a hollow bamboo-stem with a wide open bore at one end, while at the closed end, about an inch from the extremity, is a screw-hole into which is screwed the tiny, egg-shaped bowl, fitted with a cover. And now the opium-master said that he was at my service. At this moment I would have gladly postponed my initiation in the art and effects of opium-smoking, but the sleepy barbarian took such pains to show and explain everything to me that I positively dared not say him nay. Out of a little box, which contained the prepared opium in the form of a paste with the consistency of something like thick tar, he took a slender wire bodkin, and twiddled it round till he had secured a piece as large as a pea. This he deftly manipulated over the flame of the lamp till it was done to his liking. The influence of the heat causes the opium to expand, and to break out into small blisters like soap bubbles when blown from a hollow reed. Then he spread the precious morsel upon the sides and edges of the pipe, after which he politely handed it to me, whilst with one of his friendly elbows he nudged my ribs to apprize my brains of the fact that the drug was ready for use. With a mixture of fear and disgust I took the pipe-stem between my jaws and tasted the dose, whilst the demon at my side steadied my faltering courage by shouting in my ears: "Pull-ee! Suck-ee! Melican likee smokee by-m-by!"

The fumes of the burning opium are of a whitish colour, not unlike those from ordinary tobacco, but the odour is strongly suggestive of carbolic hospital disinfectants. I pulled and sucked, and desperately endeavoured to swallow what I sucked, as the Mongolian heathen directed me to do, until I felt a strange sensation, like floating away in a sort of ethereal atmosphere, stealing upon me. It seemed to me as if I were in a dream, and was trying in vain to awake from it. I began to feel extremely drowsy, and a strong desire possessed me to spring to my feet and rush out of the den, but baneful and direful qualms beset me in rapidly rising tide; tinselled heathen idols and gaudy buntings were flaunting everywhere before me; fanciful shapes in indescribable confusion fluttered and flickered on all sides; a confused mass of gaudiness and glitter danced before my eyes; and under the feeling of tropical heat and suffocating fumes of smouldering incense, my senses slowly drifted off into vacuity. I became unconscious. Then came a marvellous sense of delight and ecstasy; I dreamt a wonderful and beautiful dream of the most delicious and entrancing character. I felt as if I were being borne gently through the air in the middle of a dense forest, and the enormous branches of the colossal trees, interlacing each other and stretching right across, formed a roof of foliage high overhead. The forest appeared to be full of birds, but I cannot pretend to describe the beauty of the brilliant rainbow hues of their plumage. Insects, too, quite different from any I had ever beheld, flitted to and fro amongst the gorgeous flowers. Their bodies glittered with scales of gold, and their little eyes sparkled like flashing diamonds.

There was apparently no end to these marvels. Beautiful fruits and flowers, delicious perfumes, and every element of physical happiness surrounded me. I felt exalted. For hours, it seemed, I sped through the air without effort and fatigue. My body was getting lighter and lighter; and, lost to every sense of a terrestrial existence, I soared amid visions of supernatural and transcendental beauty, such as only happy spirits are supposed to enjoy.

At last, with the slowly returning consciousness, a mysterious change came over everything. The fairy forms seemed to melt into the air, and the whole scene passed gradually away like a mist. The lovely flowers withered by degrees until they stood pale and perished, their bright hues faded gradually, and their sweet perfume gave place to nauseous odours. The branches of the trees no longer spread their leaves in graceful curves to the breeze, but hung flat and dank against the trunks. The foliage shrivelled and fell in showers to the earth. Great serpents swung from the trees across the paths lying in wait for their prey, and noisome beetles and huge squat toads scurried off into black stagnant pools. The beautiful birds also changed into all sorts of flying monstrosities, resembling nothing that I had ever conceived possible. In lieu of them the trees now swarmed with ugly and monstrous creatures, some taking the shapes of enormous bats which skimmed over the surface of the ground, others the shapes of owls that hooted as they flew and leaped from bough to bough. Slimy crocodiles and snakes surrounded me whilst I waded through mud and reeds, and stared at me, and opened their jaws. Other gaunt shapes, unutterably hideous, which had no likeness amongst all the human and brute creation, hovered about, and stretched out their long skeleton arms to lay hold of me and gnashed their teeth in a threatening manner. Suddenly above the buzz of the insects, the croaking of the toads, and the growling of many animals a terrific roar shook the air and I started shudderingly and opened my eyes. The spell was broken.

When I came to myself I was lying on the bed, my brain was confused, whilst the ceiling seemed to be swaying about over me, and the bed heaving as if rocked by an earthquake. For some moments I had scarcely power to move. A strong, pungent, though not altogether unpleasant odour filled the room. I felt as if I had been suffering from nightmare, and struggling to my feet I endeavoured to collect my thoughts. Then did the hollowness of this world with all its pleasures become fully and disgustingly apparent to me. I had a feeling of nervous prostration which however wore off for the moment when I took a few whiffs at a cigarette which the opium-master, observing the signs of my revival, hastened to roll up for me. My visit came to an end. "Two bit-ee, please," said the smiling opium-master, extending his hand, and I hastily pressed on his acceptance the asked for twenty-five cents, and was glad enough to find myself once more breathing the free air.

The result was precisely what might have been expected. I walked home like a man only half awake and very much subdued: making no familiarity with opium-smoking. I slept the following night like a log, and awoke very late in the morning with a splitting headache. The coffee at my breakfast was thick, the milk tasted sour, I was the unhappiest of men. If it causes so much misery to the uninitiated to make himself sick in a first class opium-saloon, what must be the consequences of smoking the drug in the gloomy cockpit berths of the low dens that abound at San Francisco? Th was my first and last experience of opium-smoking, and "*crede experto*" it was dearly bought, and I do not recommend it. I had had quite enough of it to last me my lifetime.

The Chinese New Year commences on the 12th of February, and Chinatown is then in a blaze of heathen glory for several days and nights. Its usual painful squalor departs as if by magic, and gaudy furbelows and bunting decorate the filthy domiciles. Their quiet, listless inhabitants change into jolly, rollicking beings, and the uninviting streets and lanes are made to ring with the music of drums, fifes, and cymbals, and are brightened with more than usual brilliancy by thousands of glittering lanterns and lights. The scene is one not to be witnessed often by a stranger in his lifetime. Their theatres, restaurants, music-halls, and Joss-houses are all fitted up in a most grotesque manner and at large expense; and celebrations and festivals are continually going on inside them as evidenced by the atrocious sounds produced throughout the day and night by their musical instruments. All these places are crowded by the pig-tailed gentry, and some of these fellows, on this festive occasion, spend their money with the prodigality and flourish of princes. They invest usually in opium first—every one can guess that by the dream-look in their eyes—and buy trinkets and articles of wear and food afterwards.

I met a Chinaman once who was wearing ladies' many-buttoned gloves, while the balance of his costume was made up of the usual blue calico. A patch on both knees, a blouse, and many-buttoned gloves! It is not possible to extract any "washee-washee" of a Chinaman during the New Year's week, because no work is the general feature of that week in Chinatown. Many of them at that time have their pictures taken at the little photograph galleries in the Chinese quarter. There they will prune themselves and fidget by the hour together, and if the picture does not look precisely as they want it to be, they express their dissatisfaction in unmeasured terms, and another picture has to be taken. The Chinaman scans every article purchased as closely as a connoisseur, even though he knows very little about it, and counts out his money with the precision of a bank-cashier. When the price of an article is told him he rarely asks a reduction, but when the purchase is concluded he wants something "thrown in." A dozen of them may be leaning against the counter, and when one starts to trade the others participate, and if an article is submitted that receives unfavourable notice from any of the party the remainder will chime in that it is not good, and compel the clerk to hand down something else which very likely is of inferior quality.

I went one day during the New Year's devotional exercises to a Joss-house on Jackson Street, where the almond-eyed celestials were engaged in their mysterious incantations, but I could not remain very long as the ever-present and stifling odour of the incense destroys anything like pleasant illusions. There were not less than eight images enthroned in this Joss-house, two of which were of female figures. Preaching or exhortations are not practised in these temples, only an array of edibles and condiments, such as it is thought the idols may have use for, is spread out from time to time immediately in front of them and a certain form of prayer is observed, but much contrition is not exhibited by the worshippers and very little adoration is paid to any of the Joss-figures. Here and there a little facetiousness appears in these erections, for I noticed that one or two of the idols had pipes sticking in their mouths, others had their noses ornamented with large spectacles.

The surroundings and accessories of this Joss-house however were not as aristocratic as those in another temple in Clay Street which I visited at another time. I had to pay a fee on entering, and doing this I looked about for some returns for the outlay, but not recognizing any, and coming to another door in a long, dark passage I parted with another trifling sum, and I must confess with very much the same result. I was beginning to lose all interest in everything that pertains to the Chinese nation when a Celestial came to me and asked if I would like to see the Joss-house. After having been trying for several minutes to attain that end, and paying twice for that privilege, I thought this rather a singular question, but I was even more struck when I had to pay again before I entered into the sanctum. There gaudiness and glitter surrounded me on every hand, and immense groups of wood-carvings, some of them of most elaborate design— were suspended from the ceiling and arranged around the walls. These carved groups were very conspicuous and even attractive, for some of them were really works of art and skilfully designed and executed—grotesque and exaggerated as they were.

There is one system of worship which seems to be common to all classes, and that is the worship of dead ancestors. They cherish the memory of those who have "gone before," and in this fact probably lies the secret of the universal practice of preserving the bones of the Chinamen who die abroad, and carefully conveying them home for their final burial.

I have on several occasions witnessed their quaint funerals. A whole roasted pig, adorned with flowers, wreaths, and gaudy ribbons is laid out on a kind of platform and driven on a waggon immediately behind the hearse to the Chinese cemetery. The pig in motion attracts as much attention in the streets as the hearse. A portion of the roast pork is laid into the temporary grave of the defunct, the larger part of it however, is consumed by the mourners in loving remembrance of the departed.

I have often since my return to Europe been endeavouring to decide to what other familiar smell, or mingling of smells, the odour in Chinatown might best be likened, but not yet successfully. The noisome stench and dank effluvia, perpetually arising from the filth which abounds, would be sure to breed a pestilence among a white population, and the wonder is that some malignant and fatal fevers have not again and again swept through these huddled nests of human beings ; but the Chinese seem to possess some physical qualities which serve as an antidote against infectious diseases. Offensive smells, fumes, and other impurities of the atmosphere are seemingly not injurious to the health of a Chinaman. I hated to pass through the Quarter, for the air there is never free from the disgusting smell. What would the inhabitants of any other town think and say of such a nuisance in the heart of their city?

The visitor on seeing the streets of Chinatown thronged and crowded with the pig-tailed inhabitants, is puzzled to know how and where all these people stow themselves in a division of the city which consists only of twelve blocks of houses. But let him make the round and thread the narrow alleys in some of the back slums, and peer into one of their filthy and unventilated dormitories, and he will find perhaps a dozen human beings, or more, packed like sardines in a box. Many of the houses in the Chinese Quarter are quite unfit for human habitation; and sleeping apartments are to be found there which any well-to-do farmer would feel ashamed to use as sheep-pens or dog-kennels, yet hundreds of Chinamen live and sleep in them. Their domestic arrangements and habits are disgusting to any decent human being. They cook, eat, sleep, and perform every function of the animal and domestic life in the same room, and in every attic, cellar, area or garret where a Chinaman can find shelf-room, there he will stow himself, and apparently enjoy good health and comfort. One building on Jackson street, formerly the Globe Hotel, which never claimed to have accommodation for more than two hundred people, is now occupied by over 1,500 Chinese. Another building very little larger than the hotel just mentioned, is packed with 1,800 human beings, yet there are many amongst them whose wages are good, and

K

whose savings accumulate to a handsome amount at the end of a few years. These are able to leave California, having saved enough by their industry and frugal habits to live comfortably in their native land.

A special Committee appointed to examine the condition of the Chinese quarter of San Francisco, issued a report of their inspection, a short extract from which will give the reader some idea of the opinion entertained of the Chinese in the said city: "The Chinese, alien to our laws, alien to our religion, alien to our civilization, neither citizens nor desiring to become so, are a social, moral, and political curse to the community. They live under conditions scarcely one degree above those under which the rats of the waterfront and other vermin live, breathe, and have their being. They huddle together in bunks; each bunk being occupied by two persons, and in many instances by 'relays' so that there is no hour of the day in which there are not thousands of them sleeping under the effects of opium."

Under the genial and intelligent guidance of a friend, an old resident of San Francisco who was thoroughly familiar with the locality, I sallied forth one day, during the evening hours, to take a tour through the Chinese quarter. My friend guided me through many narrow and almost interminable labyrinths which lead into the tenement houses and lodging dens of the pig-tailed race. The more I saw of the surroundings the more my feelings of surprise gave way to those of dumbfounded amazement. Our eyes, however, were not the only organs brought into play. The nose sometimes suggested the presence of odours not altogether those of "eau de Cologne" or "patchouli." The street peculiarities of the "quarter" are typical of its Mongolian character. The predominating colours which greet the eye are red and gilt, most of the signs and insignia of business consisting of bright red letters. The signs read vertically instead of horizontally, frequently extending from the top

IN THE CHINESE QUARTER OF SAN FRANCISCO.

to the threshold of the door. The side-walks on either side
are crowded with stalls for the sale of fruit, sweetmeats,
and a thousand articles familiar only to the Chinese appetite
and taste. In a space less than two feet wide and three
long, a cobbler finds room on the sidewalk to carry on his
trade. Every nook and irregularity between doors and flanking
entrances to basements, are occupied by cobblers, tinkers,
razor-grinders, fruit-sellers, and other "curb-stone merchants"
and artizans, busy at their various handicrafts, that seem
indispensable to the Chinese.

During the evening the principal streets of the "quarter"
are more thronged and crowded by pedestrians than any
other portion of the city, and yet they pass each other without
collision, and seemingly without any serious inconvenience.
At that time, too, the balconies and upper stories of the theatres,
restaurants, Joss-houses, and other buildings are fancifully
decorated and illuminated, and Chinese lanterns of all sizes
and shapes flutter and flicker in front of all public places.

The Chinese quarter of the city consists of twelve blocks
of houses, and the bulk of the Mongolian inhabitants—
estimated at more than thirty thousand—there herd together.
All over the city, however, and in almost every block, there
are numerous wash-houses bearing signs with the announce-
ment so comforting to the bachelor heart, that Sam-Sing, or
Chin-Kwong-Chong does washing and ironing at low rates,
with no extra charge for sewing on buttons. Chinese cigar
shops and small ware dealers are also scattered over the
city, and in the suburbs market-gardening is extensively
carried on by these people. But the "Glory of Cathay,"
the condensation and concentration of all that is quaint and
curious, the ingenuity and industry, the vices and abominations
of the Chinese character, are to be found only in the famous
"quarter," mixed up and literally sandwiched together in
indescribable confusion. All day long and far into the night
its streets are thronged with these peculiar people, and every
shop teems with busy industry and unflagging commercial

life. The variety and extent of the businesses carried on by these almond-eyed traders are simply wonderful, and some of them are incomprehensible to any one who has not been initiated into their mysteries. Outside the regular mercantile establishments, there are numerous mechanical industries carried on. The cigar manufacturers are more numerous than any other branch, and no American manufacturer can possibly compete with them. They have fairly monopolized that business all over California. Next to the cigar-manufacturing establishments, the Chinese barber-shops are most numerous in San Francisco—the basement apartments being chiefly devoted to the barber's art. These shops have a peculiar sign at the doorway, indicative of the business. It is a four-legged frame with the legs painted green, and on the top of the frame are red or gilded knobs. In all the streets in Chinatown these signs are seen every few steps. At first sight one cannot help wondering why so many of these establishments are needed, but a glance at the head of a passing Chinaman and the mystery is dispelled. Among them no toilet is considered complete which does not involve the shaving of a greater portion of the head and neck, a thorough cleansing of the ears and nostrils, and even a trimming and pencilling of the eyebrows and lashes. Razors, probes, and lances of peculiar construction are among the instruments used by these skilful artists. The process of shaving and cleansing is necessarily a long one, but when a Chinaman emerges from one of these shops he may be safely counted as thoroughly clean—above the shoulders. The combing and braiding of the queue consumes no little time, and the closely-shaven head must be scraped and rubbed again and again to give it the shiny appearance so much desired. Every Chinaman of adult years regards an occasional visit to the barber as a sacred duty, and in a place so populous as the Chinese quarter of San Francisco this requires the constant service of a numerous force.

Even their wealthy men (some of the *chefs* of the Chinese companies are said to be worth millions) don't make a great show of their wealth. Step into any of their stores and you are at once curiously impressed with the number of clerks and porters, apparently far in excess of the requirements of the establishment. But on closer examination you will find two, three, perhaps half-a-dozen kinds of business carried on in the same room. By dividing the rent they reduce the individual expenses, and thereby are enabled to undersell all competitors.

The practice of opium-smoking among the Chinese, while perhaps not universal, prevails to an alarming extent, and in nearly all the restaurants in the Chinese quarter accommodation and facilities are provided for opium-smoking, whilst the "saloons" and dens specially set apart for this indulgence probably number several hundred. Its effects are seen in the bleared and vacant expression of the eye, and a general air of listlessness and stupidity, not unlike that resulting from over-indulgence in strong drink. Of course not all the Chinese frequent restaurants and "saloons" when they wish to indulge in opium-smoking. Many of the better class smoke in their own houses, where plenty of room and good ventilation counteract in some measure the baneful effects of the burning drug. The habit of opium-smoking may be said to be confined almost entirely to the Chinese, and it is fair to presume that it is purely a Chinese invention. The use of opium in this form does not appear to produce such baneful results as arise from eating the drug, nor is there any danger of immediate death as from overdosing with morphine. Opium-smoking may be regarded as simply another—perhaps an improved—form of drunkenness, and it has this advantage —it develops no fighting nor destructive impulses. It is also, I believe, a slower system of poisoning than the use of alcoholic stimulants. The dens patronized by the lower classes almost defy description. They consist mostly of rooms about fifteen feet square, in which tiers of bunks are arranged with accommodation for about forty persons. Stupefied and drugged, scores of young people are in these places initiated into a life of shame, dissipation, and vice. In such a den I managed that evening to live through a brief period of suspended respiration. Passing a house which could only be entered through a heavy plank and iron door, we peeped in, and whilst my cicerone was explaining to me the cunningly devised trap-doors for escape in case of a raid by the police force, a pig-tailed fellow pushed open a side door, and invited us to come in. It was evident we did not look over-respectable in our night-slumming costumes, or we certainly should not have gained so easily the confidence of the opium-master—for this he proved to be. He guided us up a filthy, narrow staircase, and we followed him as he toiled slowly up like a person very ill. Large rats of surprising fatness scampered away in front of us as we passed along. Arrived at the top of the stairs he opened a second door, and the sickening odour which was lurking on the stairs instantly and most unmistakably increased. The atmosphere, impregnated with the fumes of burning opium, was tangible and stupefying. The room was an awfully dilapidated den, the much-begrimed ceiling spotted with rain-leakage, and broken here and there so that the laths were visible. The only method of ventilation was through the door, and this was closed and fastened as soon as we had entered. Ventilation seemed neither to be desired nor sought after. Taking a survey of the surroundings, I saw one expectant Chinaman on one of the bunks, who was greedily sucking, and to all appearance the ugly fellow was nearly translated from earth to heavenly spheres as we entered the room. His face was pale as the face of a corpse, but his eyes burned like fire. In about ten minutes the hideous figure evinced signs of revival. Observing this, the opium-master who was engaged meanwhile at the fireplace in preparing another dose of the drug, hastened to roll up a cigarette and lit it by taking a whiff at it himself, after which he handed it to the Chinaman, who was still squatting on the bunk. Then he rose from the couch yawning, and like a man only half-awake he staggered towards the fire, and sat re-

A CHINESE OPIUM DEN.

garding it in silence. He was not going yet; he had come for a "drunk" and would probably indulge in half-a-dozen more pipes before the night was over.

Footsteps were heard at this moment on the staircase, the door was opened and two dirty, savage-looking villains, evidently fresh from shipboard and sorely itching for an opium drunk, stalked in. Their very pigtails seemed to stiffen in anger as they scowled on us. The opium-master turned and in an apologetic tone whispered to the two new customers of his own nationality that we had been waiting some time, and it would be no more than just to let us have the pipes at once; but they were not thus to be put off. Observing this, we told the master that we would give up our turn quite cheerfully, and he in his quaint English thanked us, at the same time explaining that all could not be served at one and the same time. This little difficulty smoothed, the two dirty Chinamen, restored to good humour, flung off their caps and leapt upon the bunk with the agility and eagerness of cats bent on stealing some food. They curled down on the mat, and mumbled and grinned at each other as they wriggled into a perfectly comfortable position with their heads on the wooden bolster. Then the master squatted on the bunk, and the disgusting performance began. Nothing but what seemed to be the thinnest possible thread of purple vapour escaped from the pipe-bowl, and as one of the awful-looking beings rapturously sucked and sucked, the thread became thinner, his face lit up with a strange light, and his pig-like eyes closed till but two mere streaks parted the lids—two streaks that glowed as though his eyes had turned to opals. The smoke that was drawn up through the stem was not blown out from the mouth, but was swallowed or otherwise disposed of. While the one was thus tasting felicity the other villain was served, and presently they were a pretty pair. I never should have supposed the human countenance capable of wearing an expression so sensual, so bestial and revolting. Faintly and more faintly still they sucked till a gurgling sound in the pipes announced that the opium in the bowls was spent, then the pipes fell from their lips, and they lay still as dead men. After a while the eyes of the barbarians opened again— But enough. I could not bear to look at them any longer. I felt as though I were assisting at some sacrifice with a strong flavour of brimstone about it, and felt quite relieved as, after paying our fee, we regained the street and the open air. The Chinese quarter of San Francisco affords certainly a new and strange sight to anyone who has never seen the like before.

CHAPTER X.

An Excursion to the Sandwich Islands—Lovely Weather—Flying Fish—
First Sight of Maui and Molokai—Oahu—Harbour and Town of
Honolulu—Decrease of the Population and its Supposed Causes—
Costumes of the Natives—Freedom of Hawaiian Life—Excursion to
the "Pali."—An Amusing Incident.

BOOM! thundered the gun; the engines groaned; the steam-pipes wheezed. The great Pacific Mail Steamer rounded slowly from the wharf, wended deftly out of the forest of masts, and backed gently towards the centre of the Bay. Amidst a salute from the guns of Fort Alcatraz, and the screaming of the steam-whistle, we passed along the spacious docks and wharves of the wonderful city, steamed through the "Golden Gate," and we were gone.

To our left we caught sight of the "Cliff House," and the "Seal Rocks," bright with many a pleasant reminiscence of happy hours. With a strong breeze blowing, and gold-bordered clouds sailing swiftly through the blue, we were coasting merrily along, observing the flocks of seagulls and the graceful albatrosses on poised wings, following in the wake of our good ship without any perceptible effort; and watched the cormorants scooping with their shovel-bills the scraps thrown overboard. We kept on down the coast for some time until we turned westward, and before us stretched for thousands of miles the broad expanse of the Pacific Ocean; the coast-line sank into the sea behind us, and the hazy, blue mountains faded out against the clouds like a dissolving view. All was bright and pleasing without and within: the sea was smooth, the air was mild, the sky was lovely. Everybody was on deck. Hip-hip-hurrah! a few days will bring us to palms and brilliant sunshine. Good-bye to San Francisco; Good-bye to the beautiful Golden State! The weather was charming, and the sunset of our first evening at sea was exquisitely beautiful. During the night I watched the steering of our vessel straight on through the solemn silence of the sea. It was a perfectly calm night; such a night as lovers and poets like to talk about. There was nothing to be heard but the faint splash of the water against the hull of the vessel, and nothing to be seen but that phosphorescent light so often seen after dark in these western waters. Pale flashes of light chased each other incessantly through the gloom of the night, and the beauty of this strange spectacle was enhanced by the entire surface of the luminous water in the foamy wake of the ship being, as it seemed, covered by myriads of sparkling diamonds. There is a strange and wonderful charm in such phenomena, hard to explain. A sense of drowsiness stealing over me at last, I repaired to my cabin, and—fanned by the ocean-breeze—resigned myself to a comfortable nap.

As day came and light permitted us to look about, we could see several large schools of porpoises, and a big monster of a whale spouting his welcome to us, while treacherous sharks were skulking in our wake. These ever-summer seas are lovely. Out of the waves rise the flying fish, skimming in flocks through the air, and dropping down again just as we begin to believe that they are birds. The porpoises leap and dart by the vessel's side, and every now and then we pass a nautilus, cruising along in his shell, with his transparent sail wide-spread and sparkling in the sun.

Our steamer was speeding steadily on her course through this broad sea of deep-green blue, until early in the morning of the seventh day from San Francisco, we saw, to the southwest of us, the first land. It was the island of Maui, distinguishable by its volcano, Haleokla or Haleokala, rising to

THE ISLAND OF OAHU.

10,200 feet above the sea. Some of my fellow-passengers thought they saw a column of smoke rise from the crater; I squinted my eyes till they both turned yellow, trying to see it, but I could see nothing, which was—as I had later on the opportunity of finding out—quite natural, for the once active volcano is, and has been extinct for more than 2,000 years, according to a commonly accepted theory.

Another half day's steaming through the calmest water brought us in sight of the island of Molokai. Its shores look very sad and stern, and their bleakness is apparent to the least receptive mind. This island is converted into a leper settlement, and is entirely given up to these afflicted beings. The government provides them a liberal ration, and those who have the means erect comfortable houses for themselves, and are free tenants on the Government land. They cultivate patches of land for which they have no rent or taxes to pay, but there is no break in the monotony of their weary round of life. A visit to the shores of this island is strictly forbidden, even to the friends and relations of these poor victims of a terrible disease.

Westward still, through wonderful phosphorescence, we were slowly approaching Oahu, on whose southern side lies Honolulu. Viewed from the sea, the coast of this island presents a scene of great beauty. The richness of its tropical vegetation is unique and beautiful, and awakens a longing to go ashore in order to examine more closely a scene to which distance can lend such enchantment. The intense glare of the day was fading down the sky, when our attention was attracted by the huge bulk of "Cape Diamond"—the guardian of the harbour of Honolulu—on whose bare crest the sunlight was waning. We had a near view of the towering rock, which rises sheer out of the water, as we passed along its base. On entering the harbour through the narrow channel, which forms the passage to it, Honolulu became visible. A warm, roseate glow lingered still on its houses as we got the first glimpse of the town, which, surrounded as it is by cocoa-palms, large-leaved bananas and mangoes, has a truly tropical aspect. My cabin-companion compared it to "the dimple on beauty's cheek." Perhaps more cheek, thought I, than dimple. The town seemed to be a busy place, for there were many vessels, large and small (principally the latter) riding at anchor in the harbour, and storehouses and sheds to be seen along the water front. The sun was well down by the time the great steamer reached her moorage; and before all the passengers' luggage could be hauled out of the hold of the vessel to go through the ordinary inspection of the custom-house officers, it became quite late, so the majority of us remained on board until the next morning.

It was a cool, starry night, and I lingered on deck till late, watching the twinkling, lamp-studded heights and hollows of the town in the distance. The light was burning in the lighthouse; the wind had subsided to a zephyr. From the shore floated sweet, spicy odours, and perfect quiet rested upon land and water, broken only now and then by a faint bleat from some kine upon the meadows, or the far-off tinkle of the cow-bells. By and by all was absorbed in silence, and over all, like a benign influence, was the luminous face of the moon, whose bright reflection played upon the water below my feet. It was with reluctance that I withdrew at last from the deck and sought rest. O, these delicious, tropical nights with new vegetation on earth, and new constellations in heaven—the soft, vivid luxuriance of the shore, and the perfumed air make physical existence an absolute luxury. Doubtless the state of the weather had had much to do with this spiritual repose which I enjoyed at that time, for during the whole run of more than two thousand miles, the breeze blew gently and agreeably; the weather was clear, and the sea was almost without a ripple. Our voyage was as easy and as pleasant as a sail from one end of a placid lake to the other. That early navigator who bestowed upon that ocean the name of the "Pacific" must have traversed it under similarly favourable circumstances. It is doubtless its characteristic tranquillity which caused him to give it this appropriate and expressive name.

Early next morning I was awakened by the pattering of many feet overhead, and on coming on deck, the strange but pleasing and not unmusical sounds of the Hawaii language greeted my ears for the first time. A number of men and youngsters of all sorts and sizes, of whom some were clad in the scanty garb of their ancestors, hustled each other as they helped the crew to unload the hold of the steamer. The quaint and with some almost fantastic costume, the peculiarity of the faces and features, their complexion and their dialect, all combined to invest them with interest, and make of us gaping and wondering spectators. After a hasty leave-taking of my travelling companions, I left the steamer, preceded by a Kanaka boy, who, carrying my luggage on his head, guided me to the hotel where I put up for the nights.

My first impressions of Honolulu were most favourable, and I began to look forward to the choice hours which were to come with joyful anticipation. The town is snugly situated on the shore of a circular bay, and is a larger place than I had expected to see. It ought to be a good-sized place, for the majority of the inhabitants of the island of Oahu live there and in its vicinity. As the dry lava interior of this and the other islands presents few attractions, the settlements are chiefly found on the narrow girdle of land around the coasts, where the disintegrated lava is transformed into rich fields, gardens, and plantations of sugar-cane; for the lava when crumbled by the action of air, and abundantly irrigated, proves a very fertile soil.

Honolulu possesses a very important harbour, which is one of the stations of the American and British whaling grounds, and whither numerous ships resort for provisions and repairs, as the islands are in the direct route and in the path of the vessels from San Francisco to China and Japan. The town contains a good number of commodious houses and edifices, amongst which the neat villas of the American and English residents are conspicuous. The houses have generally piazzas around them, and nearly every house, cottage, and hut, seems to possess a garden—sometimes quite a large one—gay with every variety of bright-coloured flowers, which perfume the air. Many of the streets of Honolulu, as well as the roads outside the town, are in fact running between gardens (the business streets are of course exceptions) surrounded not by a fence or a wall, but hedged in with the prickly pear, so that when walking through the streets one sees only here and there the roofs appear above and between the waving mass of flowering shrubs and trees. Over the hedges are seen the broad leaves of the bananas, or the slender and scraggy stems, and feathery tops of the light-green cocoa-nut trees, rising above the other trees. The various shades of the foliage of the mangoes, bananas, lemons, oranges, grapes, and many other kinds of shrubs and trees of rich and unfamiliar foliage, mingled with the many-coloured and luscious fruits are a revelation even to one coming from California, and give the town more than anything else, its entirely tropical appearance. The Hawaiians are most enviably situated. All the fruits grow and thrive in the open air, and it is well-nigh impossible to realise their profusion. The residence of King Kalakaua and Queen Kapiolani, as well as that of the dowager Queen Kaleleonalani (commonly called Queen Emma [1]) the widow of King Liho-Liho Iolani (who was proclaimed King under the title of Kamehameha IV., and died November 30, 1863) are spacious and comfortable mansions, surrounded and shaded by many fine trees of different species. The gardens and all the spaces about the houses are crowded with beautiful flowers, among which the orange and lemon scatter their fragrance and exhibit their mellow fruit. Roses were in bloom everywhere; oleanders waved their pink blossoms, and magnolias spread their luxuriant shades over the street.

Honolulu harbours a good number of foreign inhabitants, representatives of most of the European and American and some of the Asiatic nations. All the pomp of a little court

[1] Died since this was written.

with foreign consuls in residence, and the busy idleness of a health and pleasure-resort for invalids and tourists, are focussed there. The English, American, German, and French merchants enter upon speculative ventures with their wonderful enterprise and boldness, and their stores, business-houses, and shops bestir themselves to supply the wants of native as well as foreign customers with all the luxuries and comforts of life with the bustling activity, that promptness and eagerness, which characterise these races. The Chinese are delving away at various employments in the town, and monopolize, as elsewhere, many industries. Thousands are scattered through all the islands on the sugar-cane plantations, and engage actively in various other occupations. After the death of King Lunalilo (who died only thirteen months after his predecessor King Kamehameha V.) the present King David Kalakaua I. (born 1836) was in the year 1874 called to the vacant throne, being related through his mother to the old regal family of the islands. This choice among three eligible candidates was strongly opposed by many, and party feeling ran even so high among the populace as to break out into open rebellion. The electoral assembly was attacked by the discontented partisans, the furniture was smashed into matchwood, and other damage was done by the insurrectionists during their temporary loss of self-restraint. Order and peace was only restored by the militia, assisted by sailors from American and English vessels lying in the harbour. Several years of a prosperous rule have, however, cancelled the grudge against the King, and the present government appears on the whole satisfactory to all parties concerned.

Queen Kapiolani is the grand-daughter of that heroic princess Kapiolani who at the time when the worship of the goddess Pélé, one of the most feared deities in the Hawaiian Pantheon, was universally observed, ascended boldly to the summit of Kilauea, and there, at the brink of "Hale-mau-mau," the ever-boiling and raging crater, declared publicly her belief in the true God of the Christians, and entreated His help for the propagation and spreading of Christianity among her race.

Hitherto whenever the natives had to pass near the crater, the supposed abode of the goddess, they hurried past it at the height of their speed, for it was in their belief the custom of the sorceress to prowl round about, and when she took a fancy to a handsome mortal to cast her spells over him, and to draw him under the boiling waves to dwell with her other victims for ever, or she killed him with her fiery darts. No bribe could be offered large enough to tempt the natives to descend into, or stop near the crater, whose sulphurous breath was considered blighting and fatal ; and not to give some offerings to the deified spirit was in their superstitious minds to induce certain death ; but this heroic deed of the princess had considerably helped to weaken the faith of the natives in the power of the goddess Pélé.

What a difference between the Sandwich Islanders of to-day and their ancestors who slew Captain Cook, and devoured his heart in order to acquire the mysterious power and art of the white sorcerer ! In lieu of the altars and haimaus for human sacrifices, many pretty churches, chapels and schools are now scattered over the islands, and the grass-huts and mud-hovels of the natives are being rapidly replaced by comfortable houses of all shapes, sorts, and sizes—the happy homes of thousands. Paganism in these islands was formally abolished in 1819 by King Liho-Liho Iolani (the son of the great King Kamehameha I.) who ruled over his people under the title of Kamehameha II., and by his sister Kamehamaru, who, after the Hawaiian custom of former times, was also his wife. In lieu of a tyrannical and bloodthirsty chief, these islands are ruled over at the present moment by a King who granted his subjects a liberal government, which consists of what could be called the upper and lower house. The members of the latter are chosen by all the inhabitants ; thus the people at large have a voice in the government through the representatives they send to the legislative council ; whereas the members of the former are mostly chiefs and nobles selected by the King. They form therefore a sort of elective peerage. The speeches and debates in the legislative assembly are delivered either in the Hawaiian or in the English language. The royal couple are childless, and the heir apparent to the throne is the young daughter[1] of Princess Miriam Like-Like, the King's sister, who is married to the senator the Honourable Archibald Scott Cleghorn. The young princess was born in 1875. One fact in the history of these isles is rather startling, and suggests the possibility—nay, the certainty, should the same state of things continue—that at some future and not very remote period the whole native population will become extinct. A census taken in 1832 reckoned the native population at 130,000; in 1836 at 109,000; in 1840 the number was 88,000, whereas at the present time it amounts only to 48,000. The disproportion between births and deaths, in a given period, is very great in favour of the latter, and thus nothing but destruction awaits the people. It is a sad scene in the history of human progress when the original inhabitants, instead of being added to the civilized nations, are gradually annihilated by a host of sinister influences. The aboriginal people learn our vices faster than our virtues, and drink has followed the white men everywhere as their shadow. There is something truly deplorable in the reflection that civilization—as is also the case with the aborigines of America and Australia—is sweeping the natives of the Sandwich Islands from the land of their fathers. This diminution of the population is ascribed to various causes; one being the emigration of the young men to other regions, as many of them take service as sailors in the whaling ships, and never return to their native isles. Some, however, bring in another agency, and attribute it to the excessive mortality amongst infants, due to insufficient nourishment and inadequate caretaking. But less than a hundred years ago the population of the islands numbered nearly half a million souls, although the women of the bygone generations were also accused of a heinous neglect of their children—to say nothing

[1] Her full name is: Victoria Kawekin Kauilani Lunalilo Kalani Nuiahi Lapa-Lapa.

of infanticide—which fearfully increased the mortality amongst them. Whether or not this last statement is true may be left undecided, but whatever it was at some past period, the account with respect to the present mode of child-nursing cannot be true, and these fearful accusations of the female population are evidently drawn from things as they were many years ago.

Amongst a number of smaller hotels, there is a grand American caravansary at Honolulu, whose guests are mostly people suffering from weakness of the lungs. The town has a pleasant climate—one that can be depended upon. It is warm and equable, and in every way suitable to the consumptive patients, who even during the winter months—if they can be called so—can bask in a blessed sunshine. The air is moderately dry, and one is able to live almost constantly out of doors under the blue skies. It is a spot where all care might be laid aside for some time and existence become one protracted hour of repose and soft delight. The above-named hotel looks large and cool. It is surrounded by a piazza, affording to those unable or unwilling to bear the fatigue of out-door exercise, perfect facilities for enjoying the fine view and refreshing breezes, for the temperature of Honolulu is at times undoubtedly so high that one finds it necessary to court shady places and avoid too much physical exertion. In the sun, and at mid-day especially, the heat is sometimes excessive, and almost unendurable to any but the copper-coloured skins of the aboriginal race, but it is not such in the shade as to occasion very great discomfort. In the mornings and towards evening I never found it too warm to go about sight-seeing in the town or along the harbour. The fine weather brings out the dusky belles, who are peculiarly ready to appreciate the compliment of being observed. The natives have a decided liking for gay attire, and the women especially dress very gaudily, bright-coloured dresses being very much coveted by them. Their original dresses and costumes have been mostly laid aside, but though seldom seen now are most picturesque.

A very large proportion of the people one sees in the streets wear suits of coloured linen, and only a few of the old people still keep to the garb of their ancestors, the "malo," the "paw," and the "kapa." The best time for obtaining a good view is on Sundays; then a crowd of peculiar bonnets, straw-hats, sunshades, and fans may be seen on their way to and from church. As a race, the natives seem to be hardy; the women are bright and pleasant, and both sexes are very fond of pleasure.

A few words about the freedom of Hawaiian life in towns and country will not be amiss. I do not exaggerate when I state that female society can be easily enjoyed by even a stranger, the natives—perhaps unintentionally—often sounding the praises of their pretty sisters or cousins. On several occasions during my rambles on these islands I noticed this freedom on the plantations and farms which I came across, and where I was hospitably entertained. In the vicinity of the plantations, or in their huts, they gather in the evenings, and often have a jolly time till late at night. They sing, chat, and laugh when they engage in their native amusements, and their voices disturb the stillness of the soft and balmy evening air. Fresh wreaths and garlands of a variety of beautiful colours and shapes are to be seen occasionally on the heads of the young girls, and they often coquettishly screen their faces and necks from the sun with broad fans made from a palm-leaf. They have plenty of small talk at command when amongst themselves, or when in society of white people who speak their language and are known to them. There is something of Arcadian simplicity in the way they enjoy their freedom, and their lives are perhaps more pleasurable than those of the girls of other nations who are cut off from nearly all society outside of their own families. The natives have also some vices of the civilized nations added to their own; thus drinking and gambling are carried on amongst them to some extent, though not so much at present as one sees in some of the larger towns of both hemispheres.

It is a genuine pleasure to take a ride or drive about

Honolulu. Many of the native women ride on horseback astride like the men, and both—male and female—gallop about from morning till dusk in the town and neighbourhood. What indeed could be more exhilarating than a ride in the glad, delicious air and sunlight of an early morning, with the big leaves of the bananas fringing the roads, and the feather-tufts of the tall cocoa-palms overhead, and the cool and thick acacia-foliage waving on each side across the streets, and the glittering gossamers spreading and hanging from bush to bush?—or when the sultry heat of a summer's day has been chased away by the soft evening breezes, sweeping gently over the bosom of the placid ocean?

One of my rambles, which I took into the country, is connected in my mind with a very odd and funny incident which still tickles my fancy, and I must write it down. I secured that day one of the one-horse vehicles which are to be seen in the streets, to take me to the "Pali," a hill in the neighbourhood of the town from where, as I was told, an extensive view of the interior of the island may be enjoyed. We started after breakfast; the driver cracked his whip, and away we went. It was a very hot day, and I made up my mind for a continuous vapour bath. In the streets, in the gardens, on the door-steps, lounged and lay the happy people, yielding to the soft, restful influence of the weather. Everything felt lazy, and it was not to be wondered at. The strong sunlight gave warmth to a scene of natural beauty, and induced to a lazy enjoyment. All went gaily on until we arrived at a spot from which the road led up the slope of the mountain. Here I left the driver with his carriole to await my return, and started on a toilsome walk up the steep mountain path. I lingered and paused wherever I chose, and when I reached a considerable altitude I saw before me the high walls of a defile. Approaching nearer, a blast of wind assailed me, the keenness of which was almost unendurable after the simmering heat of the mid-day sun, which I had to bear in coming up. The defile itself is like the area of a grand amphitheatre, walled in by beetling cliffs. A huge gap in the rocks affords a passage. From the summit the view is a remarkable and extensive one, for in this alluring climate the view is seldom obstructed by vapours; the land, however, beyond the abrupt hill did not appear very inviting. The hills and dales which sweep back from the rocky defile presented an aspect of almost desolate barrenness; the parched soil was in many places cracked, and only here and there was the country decked with green.

Whilst contemplating the scenery, whose jagged features bespeak the havoc of volcanic action of bygone days, I was interrupted by a regular uproar of yelling, shouting, and whip-cracking, mingled with the clinking sound of horse-hoofs. Turning round, I saw two young girls who evidently were enjoying a race, for they were switching terribly at their plunging and snorting ponies; the cracking of their whips, and their merry shouts disturbing the death-like stillness of the barren solitude. They galloped in wild career over rocks and stones which are there thrown together in a tumultuous confusion and roughness, and hallooed at their steeds, and made them jump over the loose boulders of black lava. Their long hair fell floating over their shoulders, and in their outbursts of childish wantonness they were romping, and laughing, and showing the pearls within their rosy lips. I listened to their shouts of mirth and joy, and watched their youthful gambols with delight. They looked so pretty. I do not travel with a mouth full of exclamations, although I have occasional bursts of enthusiasm; and I seldom saw a woman who would have justified the stereotyped, emotional descriptions which are so often used in the vain attempt to convey a faint idea of a beautiful creature; this time, however, I must confess that I looked at these two Kanaka belles in their bright-coloured dresses, and in their gay attire of fresh wreaths and garlands, with undisguised but respectful admiration. Their ponies were fine-looking animals; they looked all innocence, and guileless as doves, but they were so in no sense, for when one of the young damsels whacked her pony over the ears to make it clear a stone, it simply ducked its head; then a pair of hoofs flew out behind, and the pretty little butterfly whirled through space; then there was a scream and thud—and that was all. The next moment the pony stood alone, and the girl was lying gracefully on the ground, her face covered with dust and astonishment, and that of the pony with part of the bridle. After that the animal stood quite calmly as though nothing had happened. " O, what a fall was that! So lovely that one might not suffer the winds of heaven visit her face too roughly "—to speak with Shakespeare—and fallen so low! I hurried to the scene of the wreck to help her to abandon the reposing and to assume a perpendicular attitude; for a kind help is a little thing but it is recorded in the great ledger in heaven; and I strove to appease the ruffled equanimity of her mind with some consolatory reflections, for a kind word is a little thing, but it is strange what a soothing influence it sometimes possesses. And in doing so I could not help wondering how the same Divine hand could have made such a pretty face and such an ugly foot as she had, and I contemplated with astonishment the numerous rents and chasms which the envious tooth of time had wrought in her stockings and shoes.

Were I to tell and relate the various shifts and clever contrivances which she devised in order to conceal from my eyes her dilapidated underwear, some would smile; and some, to whom they would recall their own bitter experiences and the struggles between the wish to keep up appearances and the pinching gripe of necessity—would sigh. But beware! Let me not disturb that veil of oblivion which shrouds from profane eyes the hallowed mysteries of womanhood, beware! Your summer has ended fruitlessly and all your fields are turning brown; you found no love, oh, cruel fate! no tender heart; no faithful breast; your youthful years went wasted by —then why do you try to intrude into these mysteries, and conjure up the ghosts of oblivion? *Cui bono?*

Goodness gracious, the agility with which that girl jumped

into her saddle again and tore out from that place, and the velocity with which both vanished behind the rocks! And musing silently I soliloquized: "Now, that girl has a wealth of glossy, raven-black hair, is pretty, and her large, dark eyes have a look of tenderness and love; her pouting lips are roses gathered from the South; and her lover seeing this, no doubt worships her when her slight form rests in his arms; and her stockings—beware! I warned you once; I warn you twice!"

But how came this tiny, quizzical, little wreath here? It was a dainty affair, tied together with a long, straggling, bright-coloured ribbon. Deeply affected, I picked it up. Were I married I should have been almost tempted to present it to my wife. How the late wearer must have been startled when she found her head lighter than usual, and discovered that she had lost the ornament which she was perhaps so proud of! Who knows how many tears were shed over the loss of this fanciful wreath, for the colour of the ribbon was of that brilliant scarlet hue which is so universally admired in the Sandwich Islands. It evidently belonged to this child of distress with the sweet face—it was not mine, I was sure in my mind about that. I moved slowly down the hill, meditating on the truth of the Italian proverb: "*Chi va piano, va sano;*" and though conscious of the sad deficiency of my own crown, I nevertheless with Christian renunciation offered my spoil to the old driver who was impatiently awaiting my return, and moved his heart almost to tears.

CHAPTER XI.

A Visit to the Island of Maui—On the Way to Waikapu—Heat, Dust, and Blood-thirsty Insects—Riding to Makawao—Centipedes—Ascending the Crater of Haleokala—Disturbed Night—Return to Maalea Bay—Sugar Making—Planters and the Native Labourers—Work on the Sugar-Cane Plantations.

CRAVING pardon for the digression at the end of last chapter, I return to my description. In the whole group—which was named by Captain Cook "the Sandwich Islands," in honour of his protector and patron, Lord Sandwich, who was at that time First Lord of the Admiralty—there are eight inhabited islands, namely: Oahu, Hawaii, Molokai, Maui, Lanai, Kauai, Niihau and Kahoolaue (besides a collection of islets and rocks of different sizes) of which three claim attention either from the number of population or the convenient position of their harbours. Hawaii, the largest of the islands, measures about one hundred miles in length and eighty in breadth at the broadest part. Maui is about forty-eight miles long and twenty-eight miles wide, and Oahu—the smallest but most important island of the three—has a surface nearly equal to that of Maui. Hawaii is much larger, but Oahu has wealth—most of the other islands have merely size. I stayed for a fortnight at Honolulu, and after that time I resolved upon extending my visit to some of the other islands to see their fire-spouting mountains. The extinct crater of Haleokala was my first object of inspection. One morning, I stepped on board of one of the little coasting-steamers, and soon left the picturesque town behind me. As we cut through the clear water, and swept past the undulating shore, many a pleasant hamlet and beautiful prospect of rock-scenery and tropical

MAALEA BAY, ISLAND OF MAUI.

foliage came into view. In the afternoon we came again into sight of the island of Molokai, which lies nearly equally distant from Oahu and Maui. I was told that a young Belgian Jesuit missionary,[1] though unafflicted with leprosy himself, has voluntarily exiled himself to Molokai, and lives there to comfort and assist the lepers in their solitary confinement. A good man, indeed, is he who hazards his own manhood amongst suc'. unfortunates. I must leave to imagination the task of picturing to one's mind the yearnings for the associations of early life; but to pass voluntarily weary hours of simple endurance with a stubborn and unbending will without complaining, and to cherish loving and affectionate feelings towards such unfortunate beings, requires a high mood and a great exaltation of soul. It is easy enough to make sacrifices for those we love, but to overcome one's self for an afflicted fellow-being—such a deed is noble.

We arrived at Maalea Bay on the western part of Maui. The island is divided into two halves—East and West Maui—which are connected by a narrow isthmus. The shore looked very uninteresting from a distance. The steamer stopped; skiffs were seen approaching from the shore, in which Kanaka boatmen were seated; they pulled up near the steamer, and carried some parcels, bundles, bags and chattels (I suppose some of them contained the mail) to land. Then we—that is, a native woman and myself—were being rowed ashore through the surf in one of the boats that had come off for that purpose. The shore looked as if hundreds of factories and foundries had deposited their cinders, ashes and refuse on it—at least, the dreary surroundings bore not altogether an imperfect resemblance to it. A skinny old woman greeted me with much effusion as soon as my feet touched land, and wanted to guide me somewhere—where I did not understand, for she talked the vernacular idiom. Having been previously informed that I could find accommodation at Waikapu, I asked of the old

[1] Father Damien de Veuster contracted the disease and died in the autumn of 1889.

woman how far that place was. I received a reply, but not an intelligible one. There we stood and talked, and what I said she seemed to guess, but what she said I could not understand. This fact dawned at last on her mind, and after some deliberation she said something with great emphasis which sounded like: "A very long hour." To tramp through a lifeless desert, devoid of vegetation, in an oppressive heat for more than an hour, was anything but a pleasant prospect. I declined firmly, but politely, her offer of assistance, as I had no faith in her bodily strength to carry my valise that distance, and hired a man who, after pulling his battered straw-hat tighter on his head, shouldered my valise, and we started on the weary tramp to Waikapu. On getting clear of the coast, our walk, or rather crawl over the rough stones of disintegrated ancient lava-flows, which jutted out of the deep dust and cinder heaps through which we had to wade, was not enjoyable. The heat and the fine black dust, which rose under our feet, made things very unpleasant indeed. How my guide managed to carry his load I do not know, for the strain must certainly have been very fatiguing. Arrived at the place of our destination, we presented the appearance of chimney-sweepers. If my clothes had been drawn out of an ash-barrel they could not have been more dirty, and my face—the perspiration pouring off it profusely— was still dirtier. As I looked in a looking-glass in the cottage where I took my abode for the night, I grasped the arm of a chair to save myself from falling—I never saw my face so dirty before. And here I might mention, for it was strongly impressed on my mind during this tramp, that one of the most prolific crops which the lava-dust develops is the playful flea. He is a merry, though troublesome little nomad, and wanders around on warm days in a reckless sort of a way. One no sooner begins his gymnastics on your legs than a whole regiment marches up, and begins skirmishing over your body in a manner that is very perplexing. You clap your hand down violently and with great precision on some tender part of your body where the little rascal is pleasantly grazing; down comes your hand like a sledge-hammer, and—away skips merrily the flea. It seems hardly respectable to complain of these tormentors, but they are really a greater plague than the other inquisitive insects thereabouts. Minute and sharp as needle-points, they seem to abound in the dust, and as the dust is everywhere, so are they. The people on the Sandwich Islands stuff their mattresses and bolsters with "pulu," a vegetable growing there, as being obnoxious to fleas; but I have no faith in their antipathy to pulu. Some persons will perhaps say that women have more tact, and skill, and perseverance than men in overcoming such little difficulties of life, but I have on several occasions myself seen the native women despairingly—well, I would not for worlds say what I did see; however, I saw enough to convince me that they suffered just as much as I did from these bloodthirsty insects.

The next morning I found it blowing very hard, and proceeding on horseback to Makawao, in company of another native, whom I had hired the previous evening, we had a difficult ride against the wind; to which was soon added another treat in the shape of a smart scud of rain which, however, soon passed over. I applied to my guide for some information, but the fellow—whose origin a Darwin might have traced perhaps back to the calf species, judging from some external manifestations—had not the remotest idea of anything. His mind was peculiarly foggy, and he seemed as ignorant of the history and nature of the country as the animal he was riding. His conversation was almost wholly confined to an occasional grunt. On his way he yawped at the horses now and then, and the time between he succeeded in filling out by singing one and the same tune over and over again in a lurching sing-song, which I could not choose but hear. Frequent expostulations were of no avail, and my patience was fairly worn out. I smothered him with questions, but it would have required a surgical operation to get a common-sense answer out of him. The reason why, and for what purpose I had come, was beyond his depth of penetration, and appeared to be a matter of profound indifference to him. It is not always safe to judge by appearances, but nature certainly did not give that man the countenance of a hedge-hog without a purpose.

No doubt on a fine day the ride would have been enjoyable, for there were here and there indications of picturesque scenery appearing; but riding as we were for about twenty miles in tempestuous weather against the wind, which blew the dust in our faces, we were not in a mood to admire the beautiful.

We must have presented a very sorry appearance when we rode into Makawao, covered as we were with a good coating of dust and dirt. On hearing of my intention to ascend Haleokala the next morning, the people at Makawao told me that it would be a long while before I should be able to do it, as the weather would probably continue to be boisterous for some time. That was too bad; I could almost have sat down and cried. Oh, it was too terrible—this walking, or rather jolting, and riding for two days over the dusty and dirty country, and then when I had arrived near the place of destination to be told that it would be a long time before I could ascend and see the crater. This suspense was becoming hard to bear, but I comforted myself with the reflection that the unpleasant prognostications might prove false; and hoped against hope, in the teeth of adverse auguries, for favourable weather. During the night and the following morning—alas! gray-coloured clouds drifted low across the country, and with a heavy rain falling, my prospect looked anything but bright. To endure the dull monotony of waiting, I went to inspect a mill for crushing the sugar-cane on one of the plantations, which was something entirely new to me. The whole place—houses and fields—was curious to look at, and I shall return to it later on, and give a short description of the process of sugar-making on the sugar-cane plantations. For the present moment I must continue with my narrative. I was right after all—as the sequel proved—to persist in my determination to wait; for in the afternoon the weather cleared up a little, and for the rest of the day we had no more rain. I had had quite enough of it, for on my way to and through the plantation, the water found its way to my skin through my clothes, which I had to take off and dry before a fire after my return to Makawao. The sun peeped in fitful glances through the clouds which chased each other across the mountain-slopes, and Haleokala loomed in the distance like one vast massive rock of several miles in length; his brow being veiled by a wreath of floating mist. I could not rest for the very delight at the brightening up of my prospect, so I prevailed upon my guide to start with me at once for the crater, for I had been informed that there is a lava-cave near the summit where people often remain over night. A promised extra dollar awakened some slight symptoms of vitality in my guide, and packing some provisions into the saddle-bags, we prepared for our start. Whilst thus engaged, a blithe and bonny young woman with eyes dim with tears brought a dead centipede into the house, where I was filling the pockets of my mackintosh with eatables, and with a plaintive voice related that she had been bitten by it whilst cane-stripping; whereupon my hostess squirted and rubbed some very pungent liquid into the wound. I took the many-legged and venomous insect into my hands, but noticing a sad though sardonic smile still playing around its tail, I decided to lay it down again. It gave a few faint parting kicks and convulsive motions, and with a look of calm resignation and a touching expression of melancholy on its face it passed away. It is one of the unpleasant features of these islands that, besides the numerous inquisitive and impertinent insects, centipedes abound everywhere. These pests often lie coiled up in the stalks of the sugar-canes, and the stripper is not aware of their presence till he feels their fangs in his hand. Their bite is poisonous and painful, and causes very often a great deal of swelling, but by speedily applying ammonia, or some other antidote to the wound, the result is seldom dangerous or fatal.

It was now about five in the afternoon, and we had a three hours' ride to the cave before us. The ascent is not steep, but the path is all covered with stones. First we rode amongst hills covered with scraggy shrubs and guava bushes and trees, which quite stopped our seeing anything; then we emerged upon a vast lava-field where only a few withered and weather worn plants were growing and waving in the wind between the rocks, but soon even these ceased. Dimly seen through the veil of the curling and wreathing mist, the deep recesses of the huge mountain-dome looked weird and solemn. My mind was filled with peculiar emotions in the midst of that barren, desolate, uninhabited, and otherwise God-forsaken region. Some parts of our ride were rather fatiguing on account of the stones being very slippery from the recent rain, but the guide, who rode ahead, was ever on the alert that no accident might happen. The path which was now and then nothing else but a narrow and scarcely perceptible trail, was so rough in some places that we had to dismount and lead our horses. Gradually but constantly ascending we at last reached the cave, and were now close on the end of our jolt; only having another mile, or two, to go to the brink of the crater. On arriving at this altitude we found it blowing in gusts, and clouds of scudding mist were being driven before the sweeping wind, and floated over the valley beneath. Much rain had evidently fallen on the summit the previous night and during the forenoon, for the air was still very moist and chilly, and the crevices and holes among the rocks were filled with water, with which the poor horses quenched their thirst. I was very tired and hungry, and as it was growing rather late, and the ground is unsafe after dark, we thought it better not to proceed farther; so stepping inside the cool, dark cavern we sat down and ate our supper, and prepared our berths. There were no traces of grass or any other vegetation to be seen, so the horses had a very meagre feed, having only a small bag of grain between the two of them. We wrapped ourselves up, and lay down at the farther end of the cave, but the howling and moaning of the wind was so awful that I could not sleep. What excited my fancy most was the sound of the wind.

Now and then it was heard sombre and complaining like the soughing and murmuring of the autumn breeze which steals gently up through a forest, loiters a moment, and rustling, passes away. Now it was swept far away, now came back again more powerfully. Anon its echoes were monotonous and nearly akin to those from some unseen spirit choir, or to distant organ music in a church; then again it roared forth its harmonious anthems like the forcible rush of a hurricane—solemn and grand.

The wind increased during the night to a regular gale, and soon the rain fell again in torrents. This seemed at the time likely to prove another "tight fit," for had the gale continued we should not have been able to descend the track down the mountain. To increase my discomfort, my guide added to his many other objectionable qualities and disagreeable habits the almost unparalleled atrocity of snoring. Despite the whole artillery of the raging blast, this contributed much to "murder my sleep." His snoring was in fact the only thing that pretended to compete with the wind in mightiness and vastness. "Not poppy, nor mandragora, nor all the drowsy syrups of the world could have medicined me to that sweet sleep which I own'd yesterday." At one time during the night I heard a rumbling noise, which made the very ground shake under us. This awoke the guide from his slumber. He said that sometimes tremendous masses of rocks, disintegrated and loosened by wind and rain, fall thundering down into the vast pit. The cannonade was absolutely terrific, and the reverberation was so deafening that I was rather alarmed.

The wind, which had its lulls and relapses, gradually subsided, and towards morning I enjoyed some sleep until I was aroused by the moving and shifting about of the guide, who was already munching an early breakfast. Having no very pleasant recollections of the kind of food I got the evening before, I partook but sparingly of our provisions, and soon stepped out of the dismal chamber into the open air. What a welcome sight! The clouds were dispersed as if by magic, and the sky was almost clear. The horses having been saddled by this time, we hastened on, and about halfway to the summit we had a fine view of the distant islands of Molokai, Lanai, Tachoorowa, (I write down the names as my guide pronounced them) and—well, the words are too long for my nervous system. The last name is long enough, and life is too short to use so many compound words. White vapours of the early morning-mist were still creeping up the sides of the hills in fleecy clouds, which lingered for awhile, but soon disappeared before the cheering rays of the sun.

At last we reached the edge of the great crater, having passed previously one or two small ones. A region of chaotic grandeur from which all the blooming flush of life had fled—a desolate surrounding of lava and cinders! Hills tossed and torn by the action of fire into every imaginable form, and tremendous masses of rock, hurled from the heights above, are tumbled together at the bottom of the yawning abyss. These fragments from the wreck of ages tell us yet, after the flight of many centuries, in their own silent language of the fearful catastrophe which shattered the whole summit of the mountain. It is impossible to give an adequate description of the overpowering grandeur, and without seeing it one cannot form an idea of the size of the immense cauldron. Its walls are scarred by the storms of ages, and their crumbling ribs, strangely coloured, present a never-to-be-forgotten sight. I stood spell-bound and in silence at the brink of the lightning-splintered rocks, filled with thoughts on the sublimity of this vast scene of Titanic convulsions, and as I gazed my thoughts wandered back to sunny Italy where years ago I stood on Mount Vesuvius. Poor Vesuvius is but a hillock when compared to this, and could easily find room inside the stupendous crater of Haleokala. The sun shining brightly allowed me to gaze into the chasm, at the farther end of which I could plainly discern several smaller or secondary craters. But these were mere pigmies, and sank into insignificance by the unapproachable immensity and magnitude of the great crater, which they seemed to be trying to

PART OF THE CRATER OF HALEOKALA.

imitate. What an expansive outlook on mountains and rugged hills we had! The mountains honey-combed and scarred by lava-courses that belched out in some past age and mark the headlong rush of the once molten torrents—bare, rugged, and bleak. Here and there beyond the black shadows of the mountain the slanting rays of the sun threw over the country a flood of golden light; and stretching far away below us lay the blue expanse of the Pacific, and long lines of smoke in the distance showed where a steamer was ploughing towards far-off shores. The heavenly vault was arrayed in pure blue, until next to the horizon it became lost in the hue of infinite space. The cane-fields, lying deep beneath us, were clad in pale velvet green, and looked doubly bright in contrast with the deep blue water of the sea, and the melancholy desolation around. To the southward, dimly seen through the veil of distance, we could see the island of Owyhee or Hawaii; and above masses of floating clouds its highest mountain Mauna Loa. A column of smoke hovered above the volcano, which still utters now and then most terrible hints of power. Silence reigned around in this desolate seclusion—silence so profound that it oppressed my heart. The world, how far it seemed, and God, how near! How deep the chasm from which rose pearly vapours—how calm the deep blue sea enshrouded in solemn mysteries! Man has erected many a magnificent church through which the sounds of sweet and solemn music ring; but Nature, carrying out her handiwork by unvarying laws, has built here a grander temple, where sermons without words are preached—a shrine at which to worship God and be impressed with His vast omnipotence and power.

The great crater of Haleokala (the meaning of the word is "House of the Sun") is on the top of the mountain, at an elevation of 10,200 feet above the sea, and is said to be twenty miles in circumference. The huge pit is above two thousand feet deep, and several cones rise from its depth; one or two being specially prominent. Its sides are precipitous, and twisted about in all sorts of jagged and fantastic shapes in a manner peculiar to the volcanic agencies which were working in its womb. I could see no signs of the avalanche which disturbed us the previous night, but amongst such a vast heap of shattered rocks it was difficult to distinguish between the fresh and old *débris*. They had probably fallen at a distant part of the precipice.

Whilst I had been engaged in examining the grisly wonders of the place, evening drew on; and the glowing ball, casting long lines of crimson over the wide sea, sank slowly down. We had to start on our return ride. I watched the sun go down as we jolted downward along the zig-zag path, and admired the play of the exquisite colouring upon the few clouds that were visible, as they moved slowly along. The sea reflected vividly the hues of the celestial arch, but the scene so ravishing to my eyes gradually passed away. The light faded down the sky, the tints grew fainter and fainter, and by and by a thin, filmy haze gathered over the scene, and absorbed it in tranquil and pathetic silence. The glory had departed, and after the sunset came the exquisite twilight peculiar to these islands, until all was hushed and wrapt in the sable robes of night. But soon the darkness changed to a scene of silvery radiance. The immense stars came forth suddenly and seemed to float in mid-air. I almost fancied I heard them twinkle; they were so big and so brilliant. I was deeply impressed with the surpassing loveliness of the night; a soft breeze cooling the atmosphere, and turning the ghastly desolation around into a fairyland of mysterious beauty.

On our way down the mountain we met a party of tourists, coming up with two guides, and several horses carrying great heavy baskets on their backs. At one place we had a pretty lively time of it, as we lost the track, and it took us a while to find it. Spurring our horses to a brisk trot, whenever the condition of the track allowed us to do it, we rode quickly, and at last got safely back to Makawao. I put forth every effort to ride in style to the house where I was hospitably installed, and cleaned as much as I could my muddy garments, which were so demoralised that they would have made a show, and caused surprise anywhere, before I entered. Clambering down from my horse, I hastened to join my hostess and the bonny young lassies of her family, who were anxiously awaiting my return. They told me with laughing faces what a woebegone appearance I presented. What mattered dirt and muddy clothes; the excursion was none the less inspiring, and was thoroughly enjoyed by me. I was greatly favoured by the weather after all, having had such a beautiful view of the crater; though I had not as much time to examine it as thoroughly as I should have liked to do.

A long day's ride the following day, brought me back once more to the lava-bound shore of Maalea Bay. The ride was absolutely exhausting; the mid-day sun shining on my head made me feel most unpleasantly hot. I stopped my horse at one time, for my sight grew dim, my throat was parched, and thirst became intolerable. I was afraid of sunstroke, and tried to turn my horse to the margin of the sea, so as to be able to cool my throbbing temples in its sparkling waters; but the beast would not deviate from the road, which was worn down by the feet of the passing animals. It was useless to whip and pound him; he could stand more beating than a sitting-room carpet. I did not give it up, though, but secured a firm seat in the saddle, and after a good deal of kicking and twisting the animal clambered down over the rough blocks of lava which jut out into the sea, and then I jumped from the saddle, and was very soon enjoying a delicious bath. This caused the guide, who evidently—judging from his general appearance—rarely, if ever descended to such common-place matters as washing or bathing, to watch my movements with grave suspicion. The aphorism of cleanliness being next to godliness did not appear to be understood and appreciated by him, for he seemed to be surprised that water can also be utilised for cleansing purposes; the idea apparently never struck him before. Then donning my clothes again, and shading my face—of which the skin was nearly burned off— with my slouch-hat, I proceeded on our journey with a cooler head and lighter heart.

When nearing the Bay, the guide, drawing rein and turning towards me, said "See, there she lies, and gets up steam." That was the only coherent, and the longest sentence he spoke during the three days he was in my company.

"What gets up steam?" I asked of him.

"Why, the steamer—there she is," he answered, pointing with his sunburnt hand across the sea. I hastily turned my dimmed eyes in the direction of his hand, and there she was before us, lying peacefully at anchor on the calm water beyond the surf, with the warm sunlight glittering on her sails and masts. We were almost at the beach, against which the heavy swell dashed the curling waves. There was no time to lose. After paying my taciturn companion his due, I hurriedly stepped into one of the skiffs which were close in shore, and soon the heavy thumping of the oars of two Kanaka boatmen brought me in safety to the little steamer beyond the heavy surf.

To return to the theme of sugar-making on the Sandwich Islands. The cane is, when eighteen months or two years old (though some kinds will mature in one year) cut and carted to the mills to be crushed. There, the cane, which is from five to eight feet in length, and almost as thick as one's wrist, and hard and stiff as young saplings, is stripped bare of blades, cut, and thrown in heaps into a large cane-yard. A dozen men and women stand ready to throw it in arm-loads into the mouth of the grinder, which crushes every drop of juice out of it, and tosses forth the broken and withered stalks, to become fuel for the engine. When the cane is thrown into the grinder amid the shoutings of the men, and the din of the mill, it passes between two large, round, smooth, revolving stones, which crush every particle of it, and the juice flows out into a trough, which conveys it to the large tanks within the mill building; the grinder being outside. Near the hopper, close to the mill wall, where the juice passes in through a sieve into the trough, sits a woman with a hand-brush to draw away the foam and the loose pieces of cane which might interfere with the free flowing of the juice. Inside the building the sugar-making is done. The juice goes into numerous large tanks, where lime is thrown into it, and it is then boiled. The skimmers, with long-handled shovels, keep on skimming off the sediment, which boils up to the surface of the tanks till the liquid is pure. Then it passes into a vacuum-pan, a large air-tight tank, where it is again boiled till properly toned and grained, and then it goes down into the drying pans, called centrifugals. Half a dozen of these pans are going at a time, and fly around with such rapidity that the thick, massy juice has the liquid element entirely eliminated, and after a few moments comes out the dry, brown sugar; and what was sugar-cane in the morning may be nice sugar at night. From the centrifugals the sugar goes into a large bin, where the poor and good qualities are mixed; the poor being improved, and the quality of the good reduced by the mixture, so that all can be sent to the United States of America for refining, without having to pay the duties that would be demanded on the best quality of sugar. From the bins the sugar is sacked and weighed, and conveyed per vessel to Honolulu, and thence to California. Most of the profits go to the agents of the large American sugar-merchants in Honolulu. These agents often lend money to the planters to put in the crops, one of the conditions being that the planters must agree to sell all their sugar through them, for which they charge a commission. Besides, the planters must buy all their sacks, boxes, and farming implements through them, on which they make also a large profit. Yet a great deal of money can be made at the business by those who have money enough to be independent of agents and all other monopolies.

Perhaps a few lines about the fields, the planters, and the native workers may not prove altogether uninteresting. The first thing which a man starting in the business does, is to look out for the best kind of ground. Land covered with guava bushes is generally considered the richest, because sugar-cane grows best where the guava tree grows, and the ground is not very difficult to plough up. The land, once secured, must be fenced in, which is sometimes partly saved by a deep gulch running on one or more sides of the plantation. Hedges of cactus, prickly pear or lantana are also sometimes made to serve in the place of fences, for there is much land owned on the Islands upon which the owners pay but a trifling tax, and leave all improvements to be made by those who lease from them. When a lease is obtained, or a purchase of land is made, the intending cultivator erects a house or a shanty according to his means. The planters' homes are not as a general thing highly finished, nor are the surroundings such as denote great wealth, but the freedom from care and anxiety make them desirable and frequently homelike. The huts for the accommodation of the labourers are put up around or near the principal building, or on such parts of the plantation as it may be most convenient to have them. Ordinarily there are several men living near the main building, who have wives and children to look after and support. When they are frugal people this is not a difficult task. They live pretty well, and of the pomps and vanities of the world they know little and care less. The labourers are engaged for one, two or three years on a plantation, both men and women, for outdoor manual service, during which period they are voluntary slaves, though the laws of the kingdom are all in favour of the labourer as against the employer. This gives the natives an independence which they would not otherwise possess, as they can bring a master who beats or misuses them into court, and have him heavily fined, if not imprisoned. The male hands are paid from ten to twelve dollars per month; the women work for less, receiving from twelve to fifteen cents per day. They are almost all fed by the planters with poi and rice, and a certain amount of meat is doled out to them in weekly quantities at the beginning of the week. When everything else is in order, the planter purchases or sometimes hires yokes of oxen to break up the ground. From six to ten yokes, that is from twelve to twenty oxen, are put to a big heavy plough, turning but one furrow at a time. Two or three Kanakas walk beside the oxen to drive and goad them to the work; whilst one man holds the plough. The master comes occasionally to the field to oversee the work, though this is usually intrusted to the "lunars" or foremen; one being with every gang of men and women in the fields. When the ground has been ploughed, harrowed, and furrowed four or five feet apart, the two-wheeled cane carts, with from two to three yokes of oxen attached, begin to bring the cane-tops from neighbouring plantations into the field for planting purposes. The cane is thrown in heaps between the furrows all over the field, and is there cut by some men into pieces of from one foot to eighteen inches in length. These the women carry along and drop into the furrows, treading them in place with their feet. The cane thus deposited is covered with a sufficient depth of loose earth. When the cane grows up, the cultivation with the hoe begins, and the weeding and thinning continues for a year or more, till the cane is clean and not too thick in the rows. The cane looks very pretty while it is green and growing, and the blades and stalks wave and bend gracefully to the nursing lap of the passing breezes. At length, when the cane is twelve or fifteen months old, the stripping time arrives. Then, sometimes eighty or a hundred men, women, boys, and girls will be turned into a field of a morning before the sun is up. Stripping the dry blades from the stalks is very hard and hot work. The stalks are often twice as high as a man, and with a bleaching tropical sun over the heads of the toilers, and the breeze shut out from between the rows of cane, the work is very exhausting. None but the natives can endure it, and they are often obliged to desist at mid-day for a few hours. The dry, sharp-edged blades are almost like sword-blades, and very hard on the hands. All the strippers are obliged to wear mittens of some kind, or they would cut their hands. The dry blades, torn from the cane, are spread thickly over the ground, and serve the purpose of fertilizing the ground when they decay. At last the cane is ready to be cut and carted to the mills, to be converted there into sugar, as I have described above.

Sugar-cane may be planted at any time during the year, but March and September are considered the best months on the Islands. The planters generally try to locate where the summer-showers sweep around from the sea; otherwise they must irrigate. The only disgusting thing in the business is that the Kanakas and Chinamen stand in the bins with their feet bare when mixing the sugar with their big shovels: and as they stand in the sugar the perspiration flows freely from their naked bodies down to their feet and mixes with the sugar—a fact which sugar eaters will do well to forget. It may comfort them however to know that the sugar afterwards all passes through the refineries, where we will hope that everything objectionable remains behind. The sugar-house is a hot place in a tropical clime, with the addition of steam and heat. Such a sugar-cane plantation is well worth visiting; and truly there must be a charm in living on it, as many people from America take kindly to plantation life, and will not change it for any other.

CHAPTER XII.

A Garden under Water—A Beautiful Sight—Kawaihai—Landing at Hilo—
A Ride to the Kilauea Crater—Painful Intensity of the Heat—On the
Wrong Track—Descent into the Crater—A Boiling Inferno—Eruption
of Mauna Loa in 1880—Attractiveness of Hilo—Return to Honolulu—
Farewell to Hawaii—Return Voyage to San Francisco.

REVERTING to my voyage, it may be mentioned that there are two or three little steamers which make a weekly circuit of the islands, calling at several ports and settlements on the way. It so happened that the steamer was almost ready to start on her southward trip when I boarded her at Maalea Bay. Standing on deck I caught glimpses of places through which I had just passed. Before us dashed the surf into creamy foam, which contrasted finely with the sombre, wildly grotesque lava-flows, curving roughly in and out of the shore. Looking over the rail my attention was attracted by the marvellous clearness of the water around the vessel. The steamer with all her cargo and human freight seemed to be floating in very shallow water, yet its depth, as I was told, was fully thirty and more feet. I could see the banks of sand and masses of sea-weed with wonderful distinctness, and every stone at the bottom could be seen as one sees stones at the bottom of a little brook. The hues and tints of colour were lovely; the white, sandy bottom, the stones, shells, and pebbles lying on it, here and there a large rock covered with sea-weed, and the fish swimming slowly around. I could distinguish every detail with accuracy—the star-fish and other sea creatures lying perfectly still, with the yellow and white sand below to set them off. Sea-fans, purple and green, spread themselves out from spurs of coral, and large bunches of the brightest green waved under the pellucid water as trees wave in the wind. Sea-feathers, whose beautiful purple plumes rose three or four feet high, and curious coral formations, branched like trees or made up into many fantastic forms and shapes, grew high and low on the coral rocks. Many-hued plants, lichens, and vines that looked like long strips of ribbon—purple, pale-pink, deep-yellow, and green, interlined with lemon or streaked with orange and vermilion, or straying into crimson, could be seen at the bottom quite plain with the naked eye, and all glistening wet beneath the clear crystal water. Colours, in fact, ran riot, and through all this chaos of curious sea-plants, among their nodding branches swam the fish large and small. Some were brilliantly coloured, some were striped, some were yellow, others red, or had bands of black and purple across their backs. This was one of the many curious things I saw at the Sandwich Islands, and description fails in the attempt to convey the impression received from such a glimpse of the ocean-world.

Late in the evening the steamer got into motion. The night was mild and balmy, and a blue sky studded with stars made the stopping on deck very pleasant. The vessel sped on her course through the calm sea, and the only sound that struck our ears was the gentle lap of the water against the ship, and the dull, monotonous thumping of her engines. On the following morning we touched at a place on the northern shore of Hawaii, called Kawaihai, where we took several new passengers on board, one of whom, as I soon had every reason to believe, singled me out as his victim. He was a man of shining pate and bushy beard—indeed, he was so heavily bearded that the hair seemed to have left the top of his head to grow on his cheeks. He introduced himself as a missionary (by the by the Islands seem to swarm with missionaries), and poured into my ears the story of Captain Cook's murder by the aborigines of this lovely island. In vain did I tell him that I had read and heard everything connected with this mournful occurrence; but all to no purpose, he madly persisted in his narrative; so I let him wander on and talk, till there was every prospect of his telling the same tale ten times over. For the benefit of the reader, however, I may mention it here, that Captain Cook landed in Kealakeakua Bay on the west side of the island of Hawaii on January 17, 1779, and was murdered there on Sunday the 14th of February following. An old decayed tree-trunk indicated the spot where the gallant Captain fell, but I was told that a few years ago the English residents of Honolulu have erected a plain stone obelisk at the place, to commemorate the exploits of their famous countryman. The island, seen from this place, sends up several high peaks into the air, which are seen far off at sea—Mauna-Kea, Mauna-Hualalai, and Mauna-Loa; all these volcanoes, can be seen simultaneously. The last-named—an active crater of the grandest description—gives forth a stream of smoke. Its last eruptions in 1868 and again in 1880–81, (which latter lasted for nine months) were most destructive. Rounding the northeastern shore of the island, on continuing our voyage, we had at one time a beautiful view of several waterfalls. Here the shore is high and rocky, rising in some places hundreds of feet above the sea-level, and enchanting cascades fall cheerily over the jagged rocks. Some leap down from rock to rock, foaming as they dash on their way—others plunge in unbroken columns of water into the sea. There are a series of glens rising one above, or one next to the other, and many narrow and romantic gorges receding from the shore through which the sparkling streams come leaping and flashing in rapids and cascades, and find their exit to the sea.

"This is Hilo, sir," said the loquacious missionary to me as we obtained the first distant glimpse of the town which stretched before us along the water-front. I was soon lost in the contemplation of this wonderful little Eden. Quaint houses, interspersed among tropical fruit-trees of almost every variety, peep through the thick foliage; and, scattered all round in the midst of the waving mass of vegetation, are the thatched roofs of the natives' huts. I was told before I arrived at Hilo that I should find it a charming place, and the description fitted quite. The town stands immediately on the shore, and behind it the abrupt hills seem to frown on the pleasant place and the sparkling waters. On landing there was a crowd of darkhaired and dark-eyed people assembled on shore (the natives have almost all black or dark-brown hair and eyes, and as a rule excellent teeth) who chatted amongst themselves in their own lingo, and laughed and showed plenty of the white ivory of their teeth. The scene was lively and promising. Some children offered us for a trifle bouquets of flowers and feathery grass, shells, handsome corals, and graceful sea-fans. When parting from my friend the missionary—the merry and entertaining soul—my sense of delight was similar to the feeling one has at being relieved from an oppressive cold mutton (ugh!) and cabbage nightmare.

I spent very pleasant days at Hilo, during which I was shown many beautiful sights of the place. It is a place of warm and fostering sunshine—a very home of peace and poetry. As one saunters through the streets, under skies that are blue with the blueness of the corn-flower, the view is often lovely. The tall cocoa-trees with their tufts of long feathery leaves wave on either side, until in the distance they seem to touch across the streets that run through the mass of foliage, broken only here and there by the roofs that rise out of the green. I was shown through several gardens. They have almost every kind of fruit growing there, and very often I had a feast of fruits such as one does not get every day. Among the trees may be seen the orange and mango, the luxuriant guava, the graceful papaw, the broad-leaved plantain and banana, the beautiful cocoa-nut, and many other useful and fragrant as well as ornamental products of that land of perpetual spring.

Hilo Bay is sometimes also called Byron's Bay, in remembrance of the commander of the English ship *Blonde*, which anchored here for a protracted period, after having conveyed and delivered to the sorrow-stricken people the dead bodies of their King Kamehameha II. and his Queen, who both died within a short time of each other whilst on a visit to England. The Queen died on the 8th and the King on the 14th of July, 1824, in London, both being attacked by measles.

Having spent a few halcyon days of lounging and dreaming, I thought it was about time to start for my intended trip up to the Kilauea crater, for which purpose I had come to Hilo. After some inquiries I heard of a suitable guide and forthwith I went to look after that man. I found his abode, opened the door, and peeped in. A dog came bounding with menacing growl and yelp towards me, and the noise brought out an old man from some shadowy nook of the hut, and also his granddaughter, a child with a great scarcity of clothes on. Good-nature sat in the old man's eyes, a thin stumpy beard was sprouting on his chin, and his lips were ridged with tobacco-juice. "Good day!" said he, grinning from ear to ear, "and what may it be that has brought you here?"

"My legs," replied I. "I was walking."

"Good luck to you then, sir; you are welcome."

He chewed and snuffed, but declared that he never took liquors; which was a consolation to me. On asking him why he did not abstain also from chewing and snuffing, he answered that the people thought as much of him with these objectionable habits and imperfections as they would without them. We had a long palaver, during which the child gave vent to various expressions of discontent. I tried to pacify it, but the baby only poked her finger in my eye, and answered me with a weak imitation of "how the rooster crows," which wasn't at all satisfactory, nor in the slightest degree applicable to the case under consideration. I engaged the old man for the following day—weather permitting; although that may almost always be counted on bright and glorious—to ride with me to the Crater-House; but with that exactitude which distinguishes the character of guides in general and Kanaka guides in particular, he failed to put in an appearance at the appointed time. At last he came with the horses, and nothing could have exceeded the cordiality of the greeting he gave me, save the amount of snuff he thrust up his nose. Gentle reader, excuse this unsavoury joke.

We started. The morning promised well for a hot day, for the sun was powerful enough, early as it was. No clouds floated in the limpid blue, not even a breath of air bent the ripening cane, which under the scorching rays of the sun twisted its stalks. The way, when out of town, led us at first past plantations, where we could observe between the rows of cane a great number of rats, scampering off on our approach amongst the blades. They are, so my companion told me, great pests and cane destroyers, climbing and eating the stalks, and otherwise injuring the crops. Over the fields and along the roads, amid clouds of dust, a motley crew of rough-looking men moved behind yokes of oxen, plying their whips, which crack like pistols, and exercising their voices to the fullest capacity of their lungs. Quails seem to be very abundant thereabouts. We saw a whole bevy of them flocking about. They are most beautiful birds; in a flock together upon the ground they look like little troopers. Their uniform is between a blue and a brown in colour, and a plume nods on their heads as they march soldierly along. Wild pigeons are also plentiful, they are larger than common pigeons, darker in plumage, with a white ring about their necks.

Later on during the forenoon we rode through a belt of forest-land amongst beautiful bushes and trees, many of which were unfamiliar to me. The ground on both sides of the road was thickly overgrown with lantana and guava bushes and cactus plants, and many other species the names of which I do not know—botany being a weak point of mine. The cool shade amongst the trees was delicious, and the glimpses of over-arching foliage and of many slumbrous nooks of densest shrubbery were marvellous. Coming out of the woodland on the open lava-fields we felt at once a very perceptible change in the temperature; the bleaching tropical sun sending his fiery, scorching, penetrating rays straight down on our heads. In some places where the lava was disintegrated by the action of air, grey lichens, those forerunners of vegetation, were germinating, and here and there even some thorny shrubs were already struggling for existence in the corroded substance. Higher and higher ran the path along edges of lava-flows and rocks, and the heat became more and more oppressive. On the high plateau the sun beat down with extreme fierceness, and the heat was reflected back from the sun-dried and exposed shelves of the intricate old lava-flows with painful intensity. The air became stifling. In several places hung high embankments of lava rocks over our heads, which if broken off might have crushed a caravan. It was now two o'clock, and the heat was simply intense, and what I expected with grave apprehension and dread every moment, happened. We took a wrong track, and had to ride back for a considerable distance. After a weary and vexatious buffeting among the jagged blocks and lava-flows, which were twisted by the action of fire into all sorts of curious and intricate forms and grotesque shapes, we found the right trail, and rode on silently under the blazing sky, through the heated, simmering air. Should the reader ever desire to have a thorough acquaintance with, or only a peep at the magnificent scenery on the Sandwich Islands —then let me pour forth into his listening and I trust sympathetic ears, the advice to bring with him a guide from his native heath, for he may rest assured that he will know just as much about the islands as the native guides know.

Soon we reached the last steep portion of our climb, over rough and loose stones, which by the agency of convulsions and earthquakes were scattered about. This we accomplished after much groaning on my part as well as on that of the guide. We had both come to the conclusion that we did not like clambering over glittering lava-flows in such an oppressive heat. At last we gained a tolerably even plateau and rode along it for about half a mile to the house, which is perched 4,000 feet above the sea. I was too tired and hungry to wait long watching the boiling gulf beneath. Under the hospitable roof we no more blamed our fortune for treating us cruelly, but fell tooth and nail on our supper, after which peace and oblivion of the exhausting thirty-mile ride and the broiling heat, was soon obtained in bed.

Mauna Loa rises to a height of nearly 14,000 feet above sea-level; and its principal crater, Mokua-wéo-wéo, is quite on its summit, and is almost inaccessible. Its second crater, Kilauea, with the Crater-House, is situated on the eastern slope of the mountain, at an elevation of 4,000 feet. The Crater-House is occupied by a German, who is ever ready to explain and show all the various sights of the place, and to accommodate visitors. Under his sheltering roof the traveller soon feels quite at home. The immense pit of the crater, which is about 600 feet deep, can be descended, and at one extremity of it is situated that remarkable freak of nature, "Halemau-mau," the inner crater. There the traveller may climb and stand directly on the edge of the seething lake of burning lava—if he has firm nerves and a quick step, for the ground is in many places treacherous and unsafe.

I was soon astir the next morning, and in company of the host walked along the rim of the crater. The pit was still partly filled with vapours, but the clouds drifting away now and again, gave me a glimpse of a faint gleam of fire in the background, and here and there the glimmer of the molten lava through the thin haze. Later on, a kindly breeze and the powerful sun dispelled the smoke altogether which was hovering over the cauldron, and revealed the glittering background, but it was not until we were inside the huge crater that I could fully appreciate its—what shall I say—grandeur or indescribable hideousness? The descent was not difficult, and a part of the way we had fairly good climbing, but lower down, and nearer the burning lake, it was like a huge cinder-heap. The contorted walls, over which subsequent lava-flows seem to have been hurled and twisted about in a manner peculiar to themselves,

THE BURNING LAVA LAKE IN THE CRATER OF KILAUEA.

are furrowed and scarred, and here and there of a reddish-brown colour, whilst in some places they are whitened and lined with a thick crust of sulphur and pumice. Plodding cautiously along in the midst of this desolation, we saw some very curious and intricate formations of the hardened lava. In some places large pieces were lying about, almost transparent, resembling in a remarkable degree the slag or vitreous sediments of scoria which one sees near glass-factories.

The stench from the sulphureous fumes became more and more unbearable the farther we advanced and the nearer we came to the burning lake. We had to walk very carefully, for the faithless ground gave way easily under our feet and crumbled into dust. Here and there were holes, down which we could look into the subterranean vats, and could hear the hissing and gurgling, whilst occasionally the muddy mass bubbled over the rim, or was forced sputtering into the air through one of these nasty holes. The ground all around these cisterns of brimstone-stew was covered with fine pumice mixed with sulphur, and the nauseating stench which arose from them was something awful. I followed on after my uncanny guide, who unfortunately seemed to be quite indifferent to nasty smells, and only anxious to get over the treacherous ground in safety. However, on we went till we saw before us a stretch of lava hideously streaked with a nasty-looking sulphur scum and pumice-froth and mud. That was all that intervened between us and the seething lake. We approached as near as it was advisable to proceed, and then I remained spellbound for the moment. The impression created by this scene was most powerful, and the appalling sight of the boiling cauldron filled my mind with a sense of amazement and bewilderment, of which it is easier to speak than of the causes which produced it. The crater had been for several weeks before my arrival at the scene in one of its periodical ebullitions, and it was my rare good fortune to see the cauldron whilst it was still in a very effervescent mood. This boiling inferno upon earth, this veritable abode of the evil one himself, with its tanks of inky black, and vats of brimstone and sulphur, with its awful stench and nauseating vomitings of seething lava, presented an indescribably hideous appearance. My senses were quite dazed and dulled from the fearful sight and the awful smell. I stood lost in awe, oblivious of everything save the scene that was being enacted before my eyes. Pale, dismal flashes chased each other incessantly through the smoke, lighting up for moments the surrounding rocks, and giving glimpses of ghost-like and startlingly weird and unnatural effects.

Such a sight I never saw before nor since. A gleam of fire here, and a sudden flash there, like forked lightning of great intensity, followed one another in rapid succession. And even as I gazed I could see and hear the process going on, for presently a projecting rock gave way, tottered, reeled, and with a splash went down to boil again—there another cone burst, and the steaming mass was tossed against the scorched banks, until the burning flood mingled with the flaming, smoky sky. It was the phantasmagoria of a wild dream, a continuous transformation scene such as no pen nor tongue can describe. One might as well try to discuss the colours and forms in a kaleidoscope. At Kilauea[1] it did hold that "distance lends enchantment to the ear as well as the sight," for the boiling gulf looked better and much more solemn and mysterious from afar. The hours above all others to realize its awful and impressive grandeur were towards night, when twilight had succeeded sunset. As we loitered about in the gloaming, and looked at it from the heights above, a purple-grey cloud of steam canopied the eerie scene, and no sounds broke the silence except those of the bright glittering blaze, which crackled audibly through the still air. Sometimes only a faint glimmer broke through the smoke, anon lurid flames flashed out, and in the creeping gloom of twilight the terrific belt of light in the background became more intensely brilliant, against which the

---

[1] At the beginning of last year a great eruption destroyed Halemau-mau.

surrounding jagged rocks loomed out near, huge and dark. Sheer inability to give a fair idea of this soul-affrighting place as it then existed, and to transfer to paper any reflex of the impressions which its sight had deeply engraven on my mind, leads me to abandon a task in which few writers could succeed.

To add a description of our journey from Kilauea back to Hilo would only be a repetition of much what I said when describing our ride to the crater.

One of the most terrible eruptions of Mauna Loa occurred in the night of November 5th, 1880, and the lava-stream travelled fully forty miles from the summit of the mountain. It ceased to flow on August 25th, 1881, after nine months of continuous outbursts, and stopped within fifteen minutes' walk from Hilo. People who have seen it describe it as inconceivably grand—if the idea of grandeur could be conceived amidst such fearful scenes of destruction. For miles there was one unbroken line of slowly marching fire, which pursued its onward march with a continuous, dry, shrieking, terrible sound. For months it raged with unabated fury, bearing banners of flame, and everywhere on its dreadful path it finished its awful work of destruction. The horizon was brilliant with a long, quivering band of vivid crimson, and the seething lava, flowing in several columns, leapt up towards the sky and poured down in some places over stupendous precipices. The deafening roar of the flames was like a prolonged boom of a tremendous cannonade. It seemed impossible that Hilo should be saved : it was apparently doomed to annihilation. The terrible crisis lasted for months—nearer and nearer came the dreaded flood, until, when it approached within a few miles of the town, the flow ceased. Hilo was saved.

Now, in contrast to the preceding description of ghastly scenes, let my busy pen fill up another page of this record which shall hereafter wring my heart with too fond memories of these lovely islands. But how shall I describe their gleaming shores? how shall I turn all their wealth of bloom and fragrance into plain, prosaic language? The groves, where luscious fruit ripens all the year beneath a sweet and balmy sky, the gardens in a glory of roses, heliotropes, geraniums, and orchids; the free sea; the burning mountains;—powers to delineate all this fail me.

How beautiful is this snug, neat town of Hilo, nestled amongst trees, when the sun is shining brightly upon it! Its beauty sank deep into my memory, and rises ever and anon in the guise of cherished remembrances and pleasant recollections even more delightful than the reality itself. I think that it would be worth while to attempt a sympathetic description of the emotions which this little Eden awakens.

The house where I resided during my stay at Hilo, any artist might have delighted in. It stood on high ground and was surrounded by a pretty garden. Heaven opened on all sides its golden gates, and from my windows which fronted the bay I had a clear view of the green promontory stretching far away into the sea, and of the huts and hamlets scattered amongst and peeping through the embowering foliage, with here and there small patches of cultivated land hedged in with bristling, long-armed cactus and prickly pear. It was the most tranquil place I ever was in. It seemed quite out of the world, and I felt as if I could have bidden a farewell to all, and taken up my abode under the shelter of this cosy little house for the rest of my life. Looking at such a scene as I surveyed from my windows, it seemed that anyone with a soul in his body could not but calmly drift down the vale of blissful happiness and contentment. In the dusk of twilight, when nestled on the bank in front of the house and enjoying dreamily the glorious evening air, a pleasing sense crept over me. The ineffable tenderness of the scene was beautiful almost to sadness. I burned my weed with the spirit of one who offers a sacrifice to some adorable but invisible object; I scented the perfume of the golden-hued oranges, heard the water bubbling in the shells of the cocoa-nuts, and saw the luscious fruits through the canopy hanging amongst the glossy green leaves above me. Sight and hearing faded away in a delicious oblivion—the world was forgotten, I never thought of it; all the past seemed to me only as a dream.

The sky was glowing in colours when the sun was sinking behind the horizon; the deep shade of the trees reflected beautifully on the smooth surface of the water, and the sea without a ripple and the air without a sound—such was the glorious scene repeated almost daily. Sometimes the sun went down in a yellow mist that hung over the sea like a veil. It seemed as if some mysteries were concealed behind it, and that all the glow was the flame and the lurid smoke of sacrificial fires.

At sunset the landscape was characteristic in colour—peculiar to these islands. The eye fell first upon a strip of green meadow-land, and beyond it, a mile or two back, rose a low range of bare hills. There was a steep, rose-coloured cliff to the left and some melancholy palms beside it; the palms as brown as chocolate, tinted so by the slanting rays of the setting sun. The sky was usually of the brightest hues, with a golden lustre over it all. Upon the soft background of pure sky, trees and foliage lay pencilled with wonderful distinctness, and the silent sea was sometimes broken up into restless little waves that at night tossed hither and thither the gleams of moonlight or of the stars. Those were sights that evoked a vision of paradise, and which for many years it will be a pleasure to recall.

The calendar told me that it was autumn, but the beautiful scene that greeted my vision told me that it was spring. Overhead the sky was serene and cloudless, the air felt so pure, the sunshine so balmy, the hazy mountains smiled so sleepily upon the glassy sea, and the voices of the birds were distinctly heard and their forms distinctly seen.

The meadows were covered with sweet-scented grasses, the trees were laden with blossoms, and all around the flowers were in bloom, and flung their perfume to the balmy air.

Gardens, meadows, and fields were gaily strewn with fragrant gems. Roses, blue-bells, buttercups, golden-crowned dandelions and daisies nodded on their stems, clusters of wild violets blushed sweetly from among the herbage, and white azaleas and honeysuckles sent forth their faint aromatic scent in at the windows. I was awakened in the mornings by the musical wings of the humming-birds sipping nectar from the roses and fuchsias beneath my bedroom windows; bees and butterflies vied with each other for the sweets of the buds, and green-robed and red-breasted birds skipped amongst the boughs in the garden, chirping a low, plaintive song. What halcyon days I have spent amidst this lovely surrounding! They were like a dream of peace, and every evening reminded me, as it closed in, that another beautiful morrow will come with fresh pleasures and enjoyments. Happy days when I could weave in my dreams to my heart's content! My thoughts stream very often to the fair place which it has been my endeavour to describe, and memory, after many days, will find me lingering amongst its flowery and shady walks. My short visit there had been a real idyl, and I never left a place with such a pleasurable regret.

I got under way again on my return to Honolulu. I curled up in a corner of the foredeck, with my cigar alight, waiting for the late moonrise. There is nothing better in these western latitudes than the sunsets with their after-glow, and the divine nights that follow. Not a sound broke the settled stillness save that of the night-breeze sobbing and wailing around the ship. The big stars sparkled with unusual brilliancy, and threw long, glittering wakes on the water, which seemed decked with myriads of sparkling crystals, and the dark outlines of the trees and rocks along the shore passed by like spectres. Several boats were seen in the distance engaged in spearing fish by the aid of gleaming firelights, and suddenly the swish of oars was heard, and sweeping round a bluff promontory several skiffs and boats, well filled with men, drifted by us, but out of speaking distance. Their paddles sent the white foam flying into the air, and as they passed along, their voices joined in one of their Kanaka boat-songs, which had a charming effect. Then they gave us a few parting cheers; the wild shouts, being borne by the breeze, rolled and rang over the silent water for a minute or two, and all was quiet again— only the slender palms along the shore rustled their plumes in the delicious air. Just above these palms rose later on the moon in unclouded grandeur, and almost on a sudden every leaf was lustrous and sparkled faintly, and the whole scene became flooded with a deluge of mellow light in which we were all crowned with glory and transfigured. Soft breezes bore us slowly and noiselessly onward, our ship looked like a fairy-ship with sails of softest silk, and bright flames played upon the water under us like a fretwork of silver. Not even a cloudlet passed across the face of the moon, who, throwing a weird sheen on the vast expanse of water, climbed up the heaven in all her chastened glory, and did what she could to smother the light of the stars, but they are not easily outshone in those crystal skies. I sat on the deck in the clear night as in a dream. The scene was most impressive, and it was with a sad thought of the unlikelihood of seeing them again that I saw the rocky shores of Hawaii recede into the distance. I felt as if they were one of the gates of Paradise, and this gate was to be closed on me for ever.

Six weeks and more on the Sandwich Islands, and they have gone by like six days and less. My days at Honolulu were also ended. The steamer was lying at her moorings in the harbour ready to start, her crew were dozing on the deck waiting for the tide, and the cabin-passengers went downstairs to supper in a body. The stillness of sleep lay over the landscape. Leaning over the rails, I looked down upon the glassy waves, and recalled to my memory all the strange emotions which my stray soul had treasured during my brief stay on these dreamy islands. I could not master my feelings and prevent them from sinking. The budding flowers from the shore shed their fragrance on the air; in the windows of the houses and huts in the distance sparkled a hundred lights, and Cape Diamond, the high cliff watching the sea, stood like a solitary tomb in bold relief against the pure, starlit sky. A few short, jerky shrieks, and finally a long-drawn scream from the brazen throat of the engine-whistle, and we got under way. Soon after night closed in, and the beautiful panorama faded from my eyes. I shall see it no more. Hawaii, farewell! I shall climb thy lava-rocks no more.

After a few days' I found with regret that the voyage was almost at an end. After living for weeks on the water, with a constant change of scene, the prospect of being shut up in a house was like going into prison. Alas! I had to go back again to that tedious world I had turned my back upon. The rugged rocks of the Californian coast presented themselves to our view. In the far distance "Tamalpais" and "Mount Diablo," reared their massive heads in dark and mystic grandeur, illumined now and then by the slanting rays of the brilliant sunshine, and the "Golden Gate" and its surrounding rocky ridges received the magic influence of the sunbeams which revealed their ever-varying outlines. Now we were brought in sight of "Fort Point," and that dear little place Saucélito; it appeared like a sweet, familiar face—unchanged. The steamer was making her way to her moorage in the docks on Brannan Street wharf—the voyage was ended.

Oh, hills and waves and glowing skies, too feebly and faintly drawn—after waiting and striving and longing all my life's brief spring for you, I saw you at last—so late! so late!

CHAPTER XIII.

The Town of San José—The "Lick Observatory"—On the Santa Cruz Mountains—Salubrity of their Climate—Los Angeles—San Diego—With a Mule-Train through Arizona—The Start—Difficulties of the Journey—Camp Life—Fort Yuma—Gila City—Arrival in a Mining Camp—Placer Mining—The Hydraulic Method of Mining—Arrival at Tucson.

THE day came at length—all too soon—for my final departure from San Francisco. I can hardly give any other reason for leaving this, to me always dear and interesting city, than that I wanted a change. My thoughts turned again with an intense yearning towards the Bohemian freedom and fresh excitements of travel, and I discovered that my ramblings and wanderings during the past few years had only served to upset all ideas of returning directly to Europe. Recollections of the surpassing beauty of the scenes which I had seen in the Yo-Semité valley, and on the Sandwich Islands, were continually intruding themselves upon my thoughts, until my mind became so completely absorbed by the idea of pushing my way to the South, that finally I could not resist the temptation, and one early summer day I found myself again in a train of the Southern Pacific Railroad, whirling towards the town of San José, fifty miles south of San Francisco. This little place lies in one of the finest and loveliest valleys I know of, being hemmed in by mountains whose summits are picturesque and beautiful beyond description in their varied outlines. Mount Hamilton lifts his old head majestically above the rest. On his highest eminence is located the " Lick-

Observatory," which contains the largest telescope in the world. This institution was founded by one of San Francisco's most wealthy citizens, the deceased James H. Lick, who bequeathed 750,000 dollars to build and furnish an observatory. San José has a population of about 8,000, and is connected by the far-famed "Alameda" with the little town of Santa Clara, three miles distant, the inhabitants of which number about 3,000. This fine Alameda (or avenue) was laid out by the old Jesuit missionaries. They planted willow-trees the whole length of the road, and these trees now look grand and venerable with years. They are fully a century old, and are gnarled and twisted with storms and age, and the hands that planted them long since have turned into dust. Along this fine avenue the street-cars are constantly rumbling, and it forms one of the finest drives in California. In San José and Santa Clara are located some of the best schools on the Pacific coast. The old mission of Santa Clara is now a large college kept by the Jesuit fathers. I was kindly shown over the college, and the beautiful gardens and playgrounds which surround it, by the Rev. P. Varsi, principal of the institution. The fathers have very fine apparatus for studying natural science, indeed the most modern appliances have been furnished to assist the teachers as well as the pupils in their studies. The ranches and farms in the valley are surrounded by beautiful live-oaks, which the residents have wisely spared from the axe. These trees abound everywhere in the State, and stretch away through the valleys like a boundless orchard. They are splendid old trees, and being always green, their wide-spreading boughs invite to repose beneath their refreshing shade.

After various discussions and plannings I resolved to spend a few days on the Santa Cruz mountains, some twenty-five miles distant. I determined upon riding there, since I could easily hire horses and a guide, and I should thus have an opportunity of seeing the country more thoroughly. After passing Los Gatos, at the foot of the hills, we commenced the ascent of the mountains, and for ten miles onward our steeds continued to climb. When near the backbone, or divide, of the range the scenery was very grand. We looked down upon the tall trees, and below in the valley a dancing mountain stream sparkled in the sunshine. From the mountaintop we had the finest view imaginable : east, west, and north the mountains lifted their heads in sublime grandeur ; peak towered above peak, but old Loma Practa looked down in majesty upon the rest. In a south-west direction we looked out upon the Pacific, and for miles and miles its broad bosom was shimmering in the sun, till it seemed to melt into the blue of the sky. South, we gazed upon the Bay of Monterey, which resembled a great placid lake ; and beyond the bay we saw the mountain-range that borders it. Below us, seemingly almost at our feet, we looked upon the town of Santa Cruz, a pretty place of about 5,000 inhabitants. A few miles to the left of Santa Cruz the town of Soquel was plainly visible. We could espy steamers, sailing vessels, lighthouses, and the railway locomotives with their trains puffing along the coast, as well as farms, dwelling houses, stock-yards and sheds, fields of grain besides vineyards and orchards bearing many kinds of choice fruits, semi-tropical and otherwise.

The remainder of the road along the crest of the mountain, until the Redwood hotel is reached, is a very pleasant ride. I established myself at the hotel for a few days, where very snug and comfortable quarters can be obtained, and it was a grand sight in the mornings to look down from this lonely spot, so high up among the mountains, upon the clouds that hung below us in the valley. As the sun rose they looked like great sunlit billows, or a mighty ocean lashed into foam by some furious storm. The mountain-peaks that towered above these clouds looked like islands, but as the sun rose higher the clouds gradually faded and floated away, leaving us the grand old ocean instead to gaze upon. Such was the scene at sunrise, but the picture of the rough glens and wild woods at the vesper hour was one of perfect beauty and repose. Above was a canopy of stainless blue with peaceful rocks and trees around, while before us lay the bright waters of the sea, the depth of whose blue could hardly be excelled, and on whose surface the occasional sail of a distant vessel seemed resting like a sea-bird's wing. The lesser hills were clad with evergreens, while lower down in the valleys the fields, purple with clustering vines or yellow with ripening grain, were suffused by the waning light of the sunset. Then the soft and witching twilight came and its weird-like presence was felt. I admired the grey old rocks around, rugged and overgrown with moss, which glittered in the sun and showed the most brilliant colours; and the high mountains, standing in bold outlines against the blue sky, furnished beauteous and ever-changing images. Oh, what a grand view of surpassing magnificence!—a combination of the beauty and sublimity of mountain and ocean scenery was there. Nothing was more healthful or exhilarating than scrambling up some of the neighbouring crags and peaks. Discontented and debilitated people should go there, and they would return with a fresh bloom upon their cheeks and new fire in their eyes, new hopes, new aspirations, new—I was going to say new boots, but that would be a slight deviation from truth, for my dilapidated boots might have been deemed, after a few days of climbing these mountains, a pair just loaned from a tramp and constructed on the most improved principle of ventilation, for they had not been made for the rough wear and tear of the mountains.

The climate near the summits of these mountains in winter is said to be warmer and the air more balmy than in the valleys, which are subject to fogs which roll in from San Francisco Bay; whereas on these mountains the fog very seldom appears, and their reputation as health-resorts increases every year. Not only is their climate in winter warm and equable, but the air is very dry. Why the climate should be milder at so high an elevation has puzzled many scientists, but it is generally believed that this range lies in the course of a warm current of air from the ocean, and that this causes the mildness of the climate. The farms and ranches upon these mountains also surpass those in the valleys for fruit—the mountain fruit always commanding a better price in the market than that of the valleys. Any one who, for profit or for health, is seeking a new home might well consider the advantages and charms of residence in a land where roses, geraniums, and many other flowers bloom the whole year round, and where the climate is one eternal spring, whose enlivening and exhilarating sunshine and air send the blood coursing more briskly through the veins, and lighten one's spirits. These peculiar attractions draw to the Santa Cruz mountains a great many invalids and persons of delicate constitutions. Many of the people that live there have fled from death in other climes and countries, and are now buoyant with health. Breathing such a life-giving air the wasted or diseased lungs are strengthened, and the health of the patient improves from day to day. Invalids, I was told, who have been brought up on a stretcher have been seen walking a short time afterwards without aid.

Having quitted my pleasant abode on the Santa Cruz mountains, I proceeded on my journey and a ride of several hours on the Southern Pacific Railroad brought me to Los Angeles—a town, the very name of which recalls the beauty of its surroundings. The eye runs along miles of undulating hills whose gentle slopes are clothed with vines and fruit-trees, and all along the line orange-groves, vineyards, farm-houses, and cheerful-looking cottages, snugly nestled in a profusion of greenery, arrest the attention of the traveller. Indeed, it is hardly possible to realize the fact that vines and fruit-trees are able to thrive in these seemingly dry sandhills.

Los Angeles was now left behind, and San Diego was finally reached. This was the last and southernmost town in California which at the time of my visit was connected by the railroad track. Beyond it stretch miles upon miles of sand-flats, intersected by greenish-brown bluffs, and smooth grass-covered slopes, rising up in gentle waves from the level of the plateau and ending often in steep, rocky declivities where a few scrub-oaks and bushes find shelter. One of the first indications of my approach to a frontier town was the sight of a mule-train, which was preparing to start over the plains to some settlements in Arizona. These mule-trains travelled backwards and forwards from one mining camp or settlement to another, forwarding the necessary provisions, utensils or luxuries to the settlers and miners. Prompted by curiosity I made inquiries about these "prairie schooners" which led me to desire a closer acquaintance with this then to me really novel way of journeying. After a few distant approaches and cautious questions, I soon managed to arrange for a berth in one of these caravans which was to start eastward in a couple of days.

By five A.M. of the appointed day sixteen huge canvas-covered waggons, laden with merchandise and provisions worth thousands of dollars, were drawn up side by side on the plaza. Teamsters were bustling about to see that all was right as the long lines of kicking and rearing mules were being harnessed, and the traces fastened to the waggons. After laying in a small stock of extra provisions and luxuries for my journey across the plains, I arrived at the place just as the teamsters were cracking their raw-hide whips, and had got the mules and the first waggon off with a bound. The start of some of the other waggons was not so successful; the mules began backing and turning, but catching the foremost by their bridle-bits and flogging them, the teamsters started them at last in good style.

Our train consisted of about two hundred mules, and more than thirty men. There were sixteen waggons in all, the freight of which contained diverse articles and commodities, such as barrels of flour and sugar, sacks of potatoes, blankets, grindstones, tin-kettles, axes, iron-pots, barrels of nails, files, bags and chests of coffee and tea, cotton-webs, various fire-arms, boots, knives, tobacco, gun-powder—everything in short, that a miner or Indian trader can think of or desire, and each waggon, with ten to twelve mules attached, was

"PRAIRIE SCHOONERS."

guided by two men. There was also a number of mules driven along with the waggons, to be used in time of need. After winding for a few miles along the edge of the dried-up course of a little stream, which found its way down from the distant mountains in the rainy season, we got upon a sandy plain of uneven surface, alternating with stretches of undulating grass-land, dotted over with patches of scrub-willows and covered with coarse, spare, and withered-looking grass. As we advanced the country for miles maintained this dry and monotonous character; stretch upon stretch we traversed, and rough work it often was. Crossing the plains with such heavy and clumsy waggons means a great deal of roughing and of bodily fatigue; yet the teamsters bore the hardships of the journey without a murmur and often with much hilarity. The dust lay foot-deep in some places, and over some parts of our trail were scattered rough stones, which rendered the driving dreadfully bad. Our heavy waggons gave many a doleful groan, jolting and knocking against the obstructions in the road—if the track formed by hoofs of horses and mules, and the wheels of passing waggons could be so called—yet in spite of the continual exposure to wind and heat, and of a life of isolation—for our party was doomed to solitude during a large part of the journey—our mode of life was very enjoyable and amusing. When we arrived towards sundown at a suitable spot for encampment, the teamsters unyoked the mules by the roadside, the heavy, canvas-topped waggons were drawn up together so as, in case of need, to form a sort of fortification and defence; the feeding mules were tethered about, and the thin, blue columns of smoke soon rolled lazily up from the flickering camp-fire. Provisions were then unloaded and unpacked, and above the crackling blaze were soon to be seen the requisite number of pots, frying-pans, and kettles, containing the viands for our supper. Our party was divided into four messes of eight men each, and at each meal the captain gave out the rations of flour, dried meat, and other provisions to his people, and one or other of the men cooked for all the others belonging to the same mess. These teamsters, like hunters, and miners, lived well—at any rate when there was a good supply of provisions, or game about; for each one knew how to roast or broil meat and make good coffee and tea. If any one has ever eaten a piece of venison cooked in the open air, he need not look for any greater delicacy on this earth, for he will never find it.

After our supper had been disposed of, which was the principal meal during the day, the hour of story-telling set in. Sitting around the fire—not from want of warmth, but to shield off the troublesome mosquitoes—most of the fellows became talkative, and stories and jokes were sure to be told for the general amusement. One or other of the company related his individual adventures and stirring incidents whilst hunting; another told of narrow escapes and terrible fights with Indians; and each in his turn was prepared to out-do his neighbour in a lively and exciting yarn. Whilst conversing in this strain, time crept on, and the night was generally half spent before we retired to sleep. There was especially one fellow, an experienced "old hand" formerly a scout, and as rough as a grizzly bear, who, not a little proud of his feats, of which he was fond of boasting, often lifted up his horn on high and vaunted loudly of the marvellous prowess which he had displayed in his desperate encounters with the Indians. I opened their eyes and ears sometimes wild-wide when I told them of the large and beautiful cities in Europe; so much so, that one evening a dark-skinned, wild fellow formed the resolution of visiting Europe, if—as he added with a grin—it was his fortune to live till then. In discourses of similar nature time was materially shortened. Sometimes the song went round until our brains and noses gave hints of a strong disposition to doze, when the whole party (with the exception of two who guarded the camp) crept into the waggons, where by an artful arrangement of the bales, bundles and boxes, and with the help of our blankets, we managed to make ourselves tolerably comfortable.

At. night the camp formed a hollow square into which the mules were driven and staked. The men who kept awake as guards were relieved once or twice each night. Although little danger hovers nowadays over travellers in that lonely stretch of country, still it gives one a little shiver around the roots of the hair to think of the possibilities which attended such a party not many years ago, for marauding Indians often raided from the innumerable gulches and water-courses where they were hidden, and after giving a flying lick, were back to their hiding places where the white men dared not follow. One would think that the teamsters could have scarcely slept under their canvas-covers for dreaming of some of their murdered predecessors, whose bones are buried in this sandy waste; but they seemed to be as easy and unconcerned about it as if they had been taking a drive of a few miles into a populous and hospitable district.

In the morning the patient mules were drowsily switching their flanks and nibbling at the tops of the spare, thin grass, and judging by the furtive glances they threw around, seemed to know that their hour of toil was approaching. Then the teamsters, aroused from their sound sleep, bestirred themselves whilst breakfast was being prepared with arranging the equipage and harnessing the teams; and after a hurried breakfast the camp would be raised and everything re-packed, and refreshed by our first pipes we again set forth. Gay and lively songs echoed along the line of the caravan when the light morning breeze sighed along the prairie, which were, however, effectually stopped later in the day by the fatigue as well as by the dust raised by the hoofs of the toiling animals. About noon we usually halted for lunch, but as this meal needed no fire, it was not allowed to occupy more than an hour. The men, many of whom had gone over the same track more than once before, were dressed in linen jackets, and high boots over buckskin pantaloons, and all were well armed with revolvers and knives in their belts. A good supply of ammunition and some rifles were also stowed in the waggons, handy in case of need. So we were not defenceless, but for many days we did not encounter even an Indian on our solitary way. Thus we drove on and in due course reached Fort Yuma, where we lingered a few days and then set forth again. Arizona City on the confluence of the rivers Gila and Colorado; Gila City forty miles farther on and several villages and settlements we passed in succession, and now the monotony of our journey was enlivened by an occasional freighter's train which hove now and then in sight. But the general aspect of the country remained unchanged; miles of loose, sandy soil, and wave after wave of rolling prairie sparsely covered with bushes and with here and there a few cotton-wood trees and scrub willows, which dotted the banks of a dried-up stream and made a scattered fringe along its edge. Occasionally however, when passing through a swampy tract, we came upon a green spot— an oasis grown over with fine grass, which seemed to me like the wildest luxuriance of vegetation in the midst of a barren waste. There the jaded mules were generally allowed to halt, and eagerly they grazed on the verdant sward, and stamped about in the muddy water to escape the flies. The heat was often oppressive, yet I thought it sometimes better to brave the unclouded sun, than to seek the shade of the sparse clusters of scrub-trees, which fringed these marshy hollows, as the profusion of insect-life that hummed and buzzed amid the rank grass put anything like rest out of the question. Unfortunately we had sometimes to camp near marshy bogs of this kind, and in the absence of any other, had to strain and skim the lukewarm, nauseating liquid, before we could use it in the tea-kettle. However, the tea which we concocted from it in large, queer-looking earthen pipkins was nevertheless refreshing and reviving after our day's toil. We had, as I said, a small herd of extra mules, besides those which were drawing the waggons. These were driven by a muchacho, mounted on a bony mule, and followed in the rear of the train, ready to be used in case of an emergency; for it happened occasionally that one or other of the mule-trains turned adrift any mule unable to keep up. This fact seemed to account for the heaps of bones which we saw lying by the wayside, whitened by exposure to the air. The track in some places was literally lined with them, and the poor animals to which they once belonged, having died from exhaustion or starvation, had offered, no doubt, a banquet to buzzards and other beasts of prey. Toiling and resting and toiling again, we wore away the days, until late one evening, after jolting the whole day long over the plains, we arrived at a mining camp and jogged up to the few cabins which were scattered by the side of a sluggish creek. They were very primitive structures, with crevices filled with mud and turf, but wearied out as I was, I was truly thankful as I crossed the threshold of one of them. On a frame of planks which was fashioned into the shape of a huge bedstead and filled nearly half of the inside of the cabin, four of us enjoyed a sleep that night. This improvised bed was big enough of a certainty, for man, wife, and a whole family, and had always been used—as I was told—by three to four men sleeping together. However, I was agreeably surprised the next morning at breakfast when a dish of stewed wild turkey and dried beef in a sauce of pepper and tomatoes was put before us. It caused my breast to heave with emotion, although there were heaps of pepper in it which made me cough against my will after I had swallowed the first mouthful.

After breakfast I took a walk by the side of the creek with one of the miners to see the washings. A few men were engaged in scooping out the sand and loam from the bottom of the creek, whilst their mates, standing in the water, filled their pans, and by rocking them washed off the earth. Gold-washing in the creeks and rivulets abounding with running water at one time or other, is the simplest and easiest of the various methods employed for gathering the precious grains, which had been carried orginally by floods and freshets from the mountains and rocky bluffs to the valleys and plains. This mode of gold-washing is called "placer mining" and pickaxes, hoes, shovels, mattocks, and a few tin-pans or cradles for washing and rocking the gold-bearing sand, are all the implements which are necessary for that purpose. The cradles are rocked with a rotary motion, so that with every circular turn some water with part of the sand and liquefied loam splashes over the edge, while the heavier grains of gold remain at the bottom of the pan. The gold is coarse, and is generally found in grains from the size of a small pin's head to that of a pea scattered amongst the fine, reddish sand, which is often mixed with sand of a blackish colour. But some layers of a brown-coloured clay also contain gold in considerable quantities—in fact, it seems to be distributed throughout the mass, from the surface to the bed-rock, but it is most abundant at the bottom of the drift.

The first deposits of gold which were discovered in Arizona more than thirty years ago, yield now but a meagre return for the fatiguing labour, yet there are still men to be found digging and toiling in the same places where gold-washing has been carried on for many years, and consequently only small quantities of the larger gold-grains can remain. But even here the persistence and dogged pertinacity of some of the miners is occasionally rewarded with a handsome find. Some of the men engaged in this precarious pursuit become, after much experience, such excellent experts in their art that they find "pelf" where others find nothing. As only the smaller particles of this heavy metal can be carried by the currents into the lowlands, the gold-diggers track the creeks and streams up to their sources in the mountains, between the rocky seams of which the richer deposits are hidden. There the mining is carried on in subterranean pits and shafts, where the gold-veins ramify between the seams of the silicious rock, and where nuggets of the size of pebbles are found.

But there is still another mode by which gold-washing can be conducted in places of an abundant water-supply, by what is called the "hydraulic method." This is an improvement in the art of "placer mining," and originated among the gold-diggers along the Stanislaus and the San Joaquin rivers and their tributaries in California. An elevated flume or water-conduit is erected, through which the water flows sometimes from a long distance towards the bluff which is being worked. At the end of this sluice a reservoir, built on the top of the bluff, receives the water which, descending again over the slope to the level of the workings below by means of long hose-pipes of leather attached to the bottom of the reservoir, is thrown in powerful jets against the base of the bank. The overhanging mass of drift and loose stones falls to the ground as soon as the supporting earth is washed away, without having been even touched by pickaxe or shovel. The only labour necessary is to remove the loose stones and boulders out of the way as they fall down, but the earth is not touched except by the water which carries the loose, diluted mud together with the gold-bearing sand into a long drain, at the bottom of which the grains and nuggets of gold—being the heaviest fragments of the drift—collect. The largest lump of pure gold which has been taken out from one of the washings on the San Joaquin river in California weighed four pounds.

After two days of rest during which the waggons, being much in need of repair, were overhauled and "fixed up," we hitched up again, and prepared to resume our journey. As we had delivered some bales and packages of miscellaneous wares at Fort Yuma as well as at the camp, the weight of our cargo was considerably reduced. With the usual torrent of oaths and a terrific cracking of the whips we started again, and the mules resumed their gait. For a few days more much the same landscape as I have described before spread around, till I came to feel as if this might go on for ever. However, some bluffs streaked with brown and tawny yellow appeared finally in view, and reaching at last the Rio Santa Cruz, we turned into a dusty and well trampled road, and clattered along between adobe houses with flat roofs, into the streets of the town of Tucson.

CHAPTER XIV.

My Interpreter—An Unexpected Meeting—The Chief of the Indians—
Distributing Presents—Dissatisfied "Bucks"—An Extemporaneous
Interlude—A Sketching *Séance*—Parting—A Wild Ride—We come up
again with the Redskins—On the Trail—Our First Halt—Water
Discovered—A Restless Night.

ONLY a few days before our arrival at Tucson, one of the most prominent and characteristic of Indian festivals,— the "Sun-dance"—was held about forty miles eastward from that place on the banks of the Rio San Pedro, a tributary of the Rio Gila. A great many lodges and tepees, I was told, arrived from far distances at the rendezvous, to participate in the ceremony, which appeared to have been a great event. Having heard that many of the lodges had not yet broken up their camp, and feeling some curiosity to see something of their doings, I resolved, if possible, to proceed there. I lost no time, and through the intervention and kind assistance of a U.S. officer stationed at Fort Yuma, but at that time on a visit at Tucson, I engaged the services of a young Indian boy as interpreter, to accompany me on my intended visit to the camp. Pikavu was a smart and intelligent boy who had acquired a fair knowledge of the English and Spanish languages at Fort Yuma, Gila City, and Tucson, at which places he made himself useful in the capacity of officers' servant, interpreter, teamster, and in various other occupations. There he undoubtedly picked up the choice expressions of cheeky slang, with which he fairly astonished me from time to time.

Having taken in addition to the necessary provisions, several bags of tobacco and various packages of powder and shot, beads, brass-bells, small round looking-glasses, paint, and such like trumpery, which I had bought the previous day as intended presents for the Indians, we set out early one morning on our Quixotic expedition, and directed our course along the bank of a dry river-bed, over a fearfully rough and broken-up country. The ponies we rode were but sorry beasts, yet though shaggy and ugly they were very steady, and jogged patiently along if allowed to choose their own way. When we had covered about fifteen miles we were suddenly greeted by the sight of several men on horseback, hovering at some distance on the brink of a rugged bluff in front of us; and on our nearer approach to them, we discovered that they were a number of Indians riding at the head of a long convoy of lodges. I felt a little nervous at their sudden appearance, but riding close to them, my guide crossed his hands upon his breast and stood for a while quite still. The whole convoy stopped at once, and many braves, and even their squaws came galloping from the rear and from the neighbouring rocky declivities; and fairly swarmed around us. There were amongst them oldish men as well as tall and young "bucks," who had their broad faces painted out of their natural resemblance to humanity, and whose half-naked bodies also displayed a great variety and combination of yellow and red ochre. I felt something like a man feels who is carrying eggs in his pockets through a crowded street when the painted savages gathered around us. They began parleying with my guide, and amongst themselves, until several of the braves dismounted from their ponies, and squatted in true Indian fashion before us. Pikavu conducted his harangue in a manly voice with great fluency and animation, and the braves soon became very friendly. One of them, a tall and powerful man, whom I afterwards learned to know as their chief, after a while filling his pipe, lit it by means of a flint stone, drew a few whiffs and handed it to me. Being acquainted with the custom, I handed it in turn to my neighbour, and the pipe was passed on until it had gone once or twice

round the circle, every one drawing a few puffs from its bowl.
The chief of the band of Navajos Indians—for such my new
acquaintances proved to be—was the very type of his race.
He was very tall, broad-shouldered and lithe-looking; his body
seemed all muscle and strength. He had a fine head with
an expressive countenance, his nose was slightly aquiline,
and his black eyes, glittering and scintillating as he spoke,
were certainly the most wonderful I ever looked into. As
he puffed the smoke in huge volumes from his mouth, and
it wreathed and curled around his head, he looked the very
beau-idéal of an Indian. His dress consisted only of a few
articles; buckskin trousers, moccasins and a blanket. That
was all his clothing, and his companions were dressed very
much like him, except that he wore large earrings in his ears
and rings on his fingers.

In return for his friendliness and with the intention of
gaining his confidence, I opened some of the packages containing the presents, and gave him a small, round looking-glass
in a brass frame (by the by these small looking-glasses, brass-bells, &c., are expressly manufactured for the Indian trade),
some smoking tobacco, and a bright-coloured scarf, which he
immediately tied round his throat and smoked his pipe with a
self-satisfied mien. The braves squatting in groups around,
were remarkably quiet, and no one would have thought,
seeing them sitting upon the ground with staid countenances
like statues that they were the very pick and choice of the
most reckless and daring among the numerous Mexican tribes.
I began to enjoy the whole scene, which might possibly have
become still more interesting if it had not been suddenly
interrupted by an episode of a somewhat alarming kind. It
happened that, whilst I was distributing some of the trinkets
and tobacco amongst the men squatted nearest to me, some bucks
(that is the young men who have not yet passed through the
ordeal necessary to obtain the distinction of braves or warriors)
who were farther away from me, having received none of the
showy trifles, and feeling, no doubt, provoked at the preference

that seemed to be given to some of their comrades, started to their feet, and whooping and howling in horrible discord began crowding around me. I could scarcely control the alarm which their diabolical yellings and howlings occasioned me, until the chief started up and hastily struck some fearful blows on the heads of some of the noisy crew. He looked the embodiment of the spirit of retaliation as he distributed cuffs and blows right and left This mode of infusing tameness into his subordinates, and the racket that accompanied it, struck the yelling fiends with a temporary panic, and they ran away with the utmost precipitation, leaving me alone for some time with the chief and a few squaws, who laughed heartily and seemed to enjoy the fun. When the hubbub of this extemporaneous interlude had subsided most of the bucks looked moodily upon me from a distance, but did not approach nearer, so I seized the opportunity of inquiring through my interpreter where the cavalcade had come from, and where they were bound to. The chief answered all the different questions put to him in a free and open manner, and the pompous air with which he waved his hands as he spoke, was a thing worth—seeing at all events, for though I could not understand a single word of the palaver, it possessed the charm of novelty. I was made to understand that they were returning from the Sun-dance festival, and were moving back across the border into Mexico. Being also told that the other lodges had already left the camping-ground of the late ceremony and dispersed in different directions, I felt very sorry and disappointed that my intended visit had thus been frustrated.

It was now about noon, and the scene with the chief sitting opposite me, and the groups of Indians around, some squatting, some lying drowsily on the ground and smoking their pipes, made a very pretty subject for the pencil. As I was desirous of having at least some remembrance of our meeting, Pikavu communicated my wish to the chief, telling him that I should like to make a quick sketch of one or two of the braves or squaws, and asked his permission to do so. Receiving an

affirmative answer, Pikavu tried to obtain the consent of the
taciturn and sullen bucks whom I selected and pointed out to
him for my models, but they flatly refused unless—as I was
given to understand—I presented them first with some tobacco.
I gave Pikavu a few handfuls of the not very fragrant weed
for distribution, and fondly imagined that all the preliminaries
were now settled, but whilst he was handing it out pretty
freely, I was again startled by a perfect bedlam-like noise,
which could not by any means be taken for expressions of joy
or satisfaction. Wrangling and contending angrily amongst
themselves, the majority of them walked away with their
booty, which in their opinion was undoubtedly so much lawful
plunder from one who—as they probably thought—had no
other intention but to cheat and defraud them. My anger
boiled up within me, but for reasons easily understood I
thought it but common prudence to say nothing. Angry words
would certainly have been very inopportune, though I felt
very much annoyed at their faithlessness; but after a while
the chief consented to have his picture taken, and as soon as I
was ready to commence my work, some of the braves, dressed
in their best finery, came with noiseless steps and squatted
down before me with an air of perfect complacency and com-
posure, and I sketched the whole group. By the side of the
chief stood the medicine-man, and as many of the bucks and
braves as could find room were squatted around. It was an
extremely amusing sketching *séance*, and after its conclusion
the calumet went once more round the circle, passing from hand
to hand. Then the chief rose from his squatting position and
his example was followed by all. With a peculiarly dignified
air he nodded his head, gave a few friendly grunts at parting,
and soon after this the whole convoy moved rapidly forward,
the young bucks dashing around on their wiry, little horses
and giving vent to many echoing whoops.

Immediately after their departure I started with Pikavu on
our return ride, and while drowsily jogging along, the shades
of evening began silently to wrap everything in darkness.

ON THE TRAIL.

Whilst I was thinking of my disappointment in not having been able to see the late festival, and while ruminating over the scenes which I had just witnessed and which my imagination could not have fancied more weird, the strange and rather fantastic idea of continuing my journey in their company intruded itself upon my thoughts. When I communicated this to Pikavu with the view of sounding him and hearing his opinion, he did not evince any very great desire for renewing his acquaintance with the braves from whom we had only just separated; but the prospect of having his engagement prolonged induced him, no doubt, to acquiesce in my proposal to return and overtake the convoy. Having come to this resolution, we lost no time about it, and after a short canter over the desolate plain we quickened our pace to a sharp gallop and gave them chase. It was a wild ride; lustily sprang our ponies, and did not slacken pace till after about forty minutes we saw them dimly in the far distance moving steadily forward. Pikavu used his whip with the most frantic diligence until we got within earshot, and then he gave vent to a few sharp yells in quick succession which reached the ears of the men in the rear of the convoy, and about a dozen of them turned round and advanced to meet us. Having reached them, we communicated our resolution to them, and they conducted us before the chief, to whom Pikavu imparted our wish in a somewhat prolonged address. The chief expressed his approval and satisfaction by some loud, deep grunts, and some of the more sedate of the braves joined him in his expressions of joy and unmingled delight with a series of whoops and yells, which the entire band echoed in even louder refrain.

Resuming the trail, we rode a few miles farther along the open plain until we reached a long ridge of rugged bluffs stretching away into the far distance which were dotted over with low scrub and a few dwarfed cedars, but the vegetation chiefly consisted of a multitude of low, prickly bushes in an endless variety of shapes. Some signs of water were however discovered by some of the bucks among stones in a hollow, and descending to the cavity we found a little spring. This treasure-trove was hailed by all with joyous acclamations. It was soon exhausted however; and then the bucks began to dig it out and enlarge it with their axes and machetes, until they had excavated a large hole which was soon brimful again with water, of which, after the squaws had filled their tin-pails and pots for the camp's use, the horses and dogs eagerly drank. We encamped here for the night. The lodges were soon collected, the tents erected, and a few fires were lit, whilst the horses were trying to pick up a meal amongst the surrounding stones and scrub. Wrapped in my blanket, I sat with the chief in front of the smouldering fire, and I must confess that I felt a nervous sensation stealing over me. I lapsed into a reflective mood, casting now and again a furtive glance towards him as he sat in perfect silence, blowing white clouds of smoke into the cool evening air and gazing with a sombre countenance into the grateful glow of the fire. Meanwhile some dried meat had been broiled, and the braves were helping themselves to their shares of the common repast. After the dry scrub-twigs and small faggots of brushwood were entirely consumed by the fire, the squaws made a little mound of the glowing ashes, and producing a prairie-cock from their larder, removed its entrails, salted and peppered it thoroughly inside, and buried the bird as it was, feathers and all, in the hot ashes. As soon as the stifling smoke which was emitted during the process of baking had ceased to rise, they took the bird out, and drew off the burned skin whole, with all the ashes and dirt adhering to it, as one would draw a glove off one's hand, and offered the white meat to us in all its purity and whiteness. To my palate, not being as yet accustomed to their cookery, it tasted somewhat smoky and hot from the quantity of pepper in it; but after I had added some of my own provisions to the meal, the chief and I fared very heartily.

When I had at last retired with Pikavu into the ragged skin-tent which had been assigned to my use, and all was dark, and no sound save that of the night wind broke the silence around, the wild solitude of this mighty waste became appalling to my mind, and I felt awed and almost frightened at what I had undertaken. The Southern Indians had often been represented to me as being revengeful, and as I thought of what I had been reading of their bitter hatred and contempt for the whites, I felt too restless to sleep during the long hours of that night, as much as I was in need of rest. I had a vision of scalpless spectres wandering about for ever, and the melancholy gusts of the night wind which soughed along the rugged bluffs, sounded like their sighs and groans as they were driven hither and thither about this howling wilderness. As far as my own scalp was concerned I ought to have been quite easy in my mind about it. My crown being already bare, it would have been no easy matter to take it, but still it made me "grue," and I felt like the Scotchman about his head, that while "nae much of a scalp, it would have been a sair loss to me." However the braves were buried in deep slumber during the whole night, and with returning daylight I plucked up courage, and my fears were dispelled. I made up my mind I had gone too far to retreat, and from this time I dwelt for nearly two months with these hardy sons of the wilderness, sharing their joys and woes, and though I had to endure many hardships, I met with nothing but good-fellowship among them. I found kindness where I should have least expected it.

CHAPTER XV.

Life, Character, and Customs of the Navajos—Indian Trading Stations—
Language of the Parushapats—Their Clothing and Ornaments—Confirmed Smokers—Their Weapons—Indian Dogs—In Camp—Wigwams
—Evening Amusements—War Dance—Courtship—The Medicine Men
—Vigils by the Dead—Funeral Ceremonies—Methods of Burial—
The Sun Dance—Self-inflicted Tortures—Their Religious Belief and
Superstitions—A Doomed Race.

MY new companions were, and probably are to the present time, of a nomadic disposition, and had no fixed habitation. The tribe to which they belonged, and which consisted of several bands speaking the same language, has dwindled down to a few thousands, and is dispersed over a wide tract of land. Some live in New Mexico, others roam over the arid plains of Arizona and Sonora, and through the cañons and barrancas of the Sierra Madre. Their common name by which they are known is "Navajos," but the band with which I fell in, called themselves "Parushapats." The chief possessed an absolute control over his camp, and all the braves were at his command to execute his orders. This position was not hereditary amongst them, but was assumed by the man who had the most influence and power in the tribe. The climate of the immense district over which these nomads range being dry and warm most of the year, they were quite indifferent whether they had any shelter or not. It seems to be their inborn nature to cling to the tribal customs of their forefathers, for they are content to live in the same fashion and to jog on very much as their ancestors did many years ago. Their general character is a strange mixture of barbarity and chivalry, but I am inclined to believe that what there is bad in their character is chiefly due to the failing so common with their race—drink. They have coarse habits when heated by the detestable fire-water, and offend one's sense by a plethora of profanity and blackguardism, and a fluency of oaths so vehement and yet so unnecessary that one expects to see the utterers crushed where they stand. They drink to excess, and often indulge in beastly debauches. At the same time most of them, I found, were good-natured and kind at heart. I had evidence of this in the fact that they never had recourse to any contemptible attempt of extorting blackmail from me, though I was entirely at their mercy, and the slightest interference with my comfort (relatively speaking) was resented by the chief, of which I had various proofs on several occasions. Nor did anything that I possessed test their cupidity but my colour-box. This seemed to be the only thing in my possession after which they hankered whenever they caught sight of it. They did pilfer my colours, but besides this I scarcely ever detected them in any act of dishonesty. They were fond of their native pulque and mascal, but when they were across the boundary line, the liquor they obtained at the trading-stations and gin-mills was not whisky but alcohol and molasses diluted with water, or still worse, a stuff like molasses with vitriol in it, to give it life.

The tobacco which they got in exchange from the white tradespeople was also of very inferior quality, and thus they often became dissatisfied and disheartened, and abandoned themselves to vice and dissipation. "If you deceive an Indian once, he never believes and trusts you again" is a well-founded saying, and they naturally perceive very soon that the ruling passion of the white traders is self-interest. They make them first drunk with fire-water and then cheat them. All the good traits of the Indian, in whose heart some virtues have never germinated, are swept away like chaff before the wind as soon as he comes in contact with the vices of the whites, and from that time forward he looks upon vice, rapacity, drunkenness and dissipation as inseparable companions to civilization. The boys especially when they have been amongst the whites for some time, are apt to develop into very imps of mischief, and are very coarse and disgusting in their manners and conversation. By degrees they get accustomed to profanity and ribaldry, and abash one with their glibness in the use of it, for they are left to grow up as they can; their fathers—being too careless to take any trouble in controlling them—disclaim all responsibilities on that score.

At the beginning of my stay amongst them we carried on our conversation after the deaf-and-dumb method, shifting hands and fingers freely. They joined signs to their words which were so expressive that I could generally apprehend their meaning; if not, Pikavu gave me a literal translation word after word, just as they came from the lips of my interrogators. I adopted the same method to help them to understand my mixture of English and Spanish words. Mentally they are a fairly intelligent race, quick of apprehension; the boys especially taking up ideas very smartly. Pikavu took great pains to instruct me in their language, which is not unmelodious. It is abundant in words and names replete with vowels, and seldom terminating in a consonant. They pronounce it with a clear accent and inflection, and their power of expression is wonderful. For almost every object they have a separate name, though I observed that the living representatives of some of the species of indigenous animal life, especially those of small birds, have but one. I soon learnt a few words, but my companions found it exceedingly difficult to pronounce English words, probably because they abound in consonants, for Spanish they pronounced with great facility, and some of them spoke it even pretty fluently. Nevertheless, after a short time we found no great difficulty in making ourselves mutually understood even without the aid of my interpreter, who followed me everywhere like my own shadow.

All the braves had leather or cast off trousers of some sort or other, which they bargained for at the trading-posts, but the rest of their bodies was usually exposed, except when they were near a settlement. Sometimes during the heat of the day many of the bucks did not even wear their inexpressibles, and other parts of their dress were equally conspicuous by their absence. Thus they were *in puris naturalibus*, unencumbered save by their long names and a narrow strip of cloth or skin wound round their loins, the ends of which were brought between their legs and fastened at the back of their bodies. On their feet men and women wore moccasins which they made themselves of skins. The ordinary clothing of the women was also of the simplest form; a thick fringed blanket tied with a belt about the hips in the shape of a tunic not unlike a skirt falling to below the knees, and another blanket thrown over their shoulders. That was all the girls and women were dressed in, with the added decorations of some strings of beads around their necks and feathers and flitter in their hair, but still some of them were quite fair to look upon. The old crones, who were generally the very embodiment of ugliness, and some of the squaws also, threw off like the men all they wore on the upper part of the body as low as their waists when they were on the move, and it was only the young girls as a rule who exhibited a modest reserve and decorum in presence of the men. There were, however, also exceptions amongst them, but the exceptions were mostly those who appeared to have never been remarkable for their personal beauty. The braves fastened feathers of birds of prey upon the tops of their heads, and to many this ornament was very becoming. Their hair is usually black, and very abundant upon their heads, but never on their faces. Of its colour and liberal growth they are very vain. The chief and the sachems of the band painted their faces on festive occasions and distinguished themselves from the other braves by buckskin leggings, one or two blankets of better quality, and a tuft of hair on their crowns, to which were attached some wild birds' tail-feathers. Their rather showy costume was completed by rattling strings of antelope-hoofs fastened around each ankle and by the "wampums" suspended about their waists. This made up their full

P

war-toggery. The wam-pum is a girdle ornamented with bright-coloured beads, which they wear in front. These girdles, which are much admired and highly prized by the Indians, are manufactured by the squaws by fastening glass-beads or sea-shells of light and dark colours on a skin-belt. Some of them look very pretty, showing occasionally very nice patterns. Their squaws were skilled in various other manual occupations; thus for example the wicker-baskets in which they carried on their backs their little papooses, were very neatly made by them. The men took it comparatively easy when in camp, but the squaws were busy from morn till eve in preparing food, looking after the tents, horses, pigs, and dogs, and in performing the usual labour of beasts of burden. Besides this they had the care upon them of their babies, but for all their toil and hard work these poor, willing drudges received but a scant and trifling compensation from the braves.

All the men, and even the squaws as a rule, were confirmed smokers. It was quite a sight to see them smoke. Squatting around their camp fires in high glee and good humour, they blew clouds of smoke, thick enough to have shamed a railroad locomotive. They puffed the smoke through their nostrils as well as out of their mouths, so that it kept curling and rolling round their noses, and up their cheeks, and into their eyes, and through their hair, while their swarthy faces beamed with happy contentment.

When the camp was collected, it consisted of about thirty lodges or wigwams, formed of poles stuck in the ground, tied together in the shape of a cone, and covered with skins. These lodges had a rather dirty appearance; the very skins which covered them were black, tattered and stiff with rancid grease and dirt exhaling a very offensive odour. Cleanliness, which is popularly supposed to promote longevity, was conspicuous by its absence, yet despite this and a certain populousness of the tents, concerning which the less is said the better, a heterogeneous crowd of men, women, children and dogs huddled under them together. I became acquainted with strange

bedfellows, and vainly endeavoured to expel the dark rovers that nightly came crawling from the seams and folds of my tent. The young bucks did not care for shelter generally, and slept mostly in the open air amongst rocks or under bushes, with their spears and machetes lying near them. As for their weapons, the bow and arrow I presume were their natural weapons, but nearly all of them had muskets and shot-guns of some sort or other. The younger men and boys were very fond of shooting and bodily exercise and were very expert in the use of firearms, Occasionally there was plenty of quails and jackass-rabbits around whilst we were under way over the vegas, and the bucks with their old-fashioned shot-guns and pistols did great execution amongst them. Repeatedly they brought numbers of rabbits to camp which they had ridden down and pistolled or killed with their bows. Indeed, the frequent cracking of their guns rendered our camp very often anything but a peaceful resting-place. The shot-guns and rifles which the Indians obtain at the trading-stations, are very cheap ones. They shoot pretty well, but are apt to burst very soon. Sometimes our boys were compelled by scarcity of ammunition to practise with the bow and arrow, which is an adroit weapon in their hands. Besides the guns and bows they had spears, axes, hatchets, tomahawks, and Mexican machetes (strong, short, sword-shaped cutlasses), and I have also seen the boomerang amongst them, with which they killed smaller animals, and even flying birds at a considerable distance. This instrument was, I believe, originally used by the natives of Australia. It is a slender crescent-shaped piece of hard wood, about two feet long and two inches thick. When jerked up into the air it circles and whirls around with great velocity, whizzing with a humming sound, and returns in a curved line back to the thrower.

I walked about the lodges with great freedom, and the easy conduct of some of the squaws left no room to doubt that that freedom could have been carried still farther. Sometimes after sunset I sat outside the tent, and my friends gathered around me and seemed to be scrutinising me in all directions. The capillary deficiencies especially, which the "envious tooth of time" has wrought on my scull seemed to attract the special attention of the braves, who looked critically at it, whilst the squaws chattered amongst themselves, fed their squalling and kicking babies, or scolded the bigger papooses who were sprawling on the ground round my feet, examining my hard shoes and playing with the shoe-laces. There was one young girl with a soft mellow voice, whom I often enticed to sing by small presents of glass-beads or coin. Her tunes were generally rather gloomy, yet her singing had a pleasing and tender effect. Commencing in a low tone, her voice was joined by others, until it sometimes swelled to a full, round and modulated chorus. Singing and dancing in fact were sources of frequent delight and pleasure. Very often in the gloaming of a fine, cool evening, when camping in a favourable locality, the bucks would have a song or dance. Sometimes on these occasions songs were sung also by the women, but oftenest by the bucks alone. Occasionally one or other of the older men recited in a low voice one of their legends about the good or evil spirits, which had been handed down from generation to generation. The Indians are generally morose and taciturn people, yet they also descend sometimes to such commonplace matters as laughing and merry-making. One evening I witnessed the performance of an improvised war-dance, which will not soon be forgotten by me. Some of the young braves, with painted faces and huge bunches of feathers on their heads, danced hither and thither, bowing down now and then to leap up again with a fearful yell. They held each other with one hand, whilst with the other they brandished a spear or club above their heads, and with a rush like that made by some wild animals when they are released from their lair, they jumped high into the air, yelling at every leap. They played their part faultlessly and neglected nothing which could have rendered their bodies and faces hideous and deformed. Their wild cries and some of the frightful contortions of their limbs

EVENING AMUSEMENTS IN CAMP.
THE "JUGWEWAGUNT" (MEDICINE MAN) RECITING A LEGEND TO THE "BUCKS."

provoked great merriment, and occasionally the whole audience was seized with a fit of laughter, and displayed a peculiar tendency to mirth and frivolity. They shook and rocked their bodies in their frantic delight when one or other of the buffoons thrust out his tongue to an incredible length or gave vent to a yell, grunt or whoop of more than usual strength. The exciting performance was accompanied by loud beatings of their tom-toms, which were struck continuously during the progress of the dance. Their monotonous sound was interrupted every minute or two by a loud bang on their big drums, which even more than the tom-toms increased the already deafening din of yells and shouts of applause of the lookers-on. The whole scene looked so weird and wild that I thought I must be dreaming of the Walpurgis night on the Blocksberg. Thus the midnight hours passed by until the bucks, no doubt thoroughly tired out, retired to rest from their exertions. I was heartily glad when the last of their unearthly yells had died away, and the noise and revelry had given place to silence in the "'sma' hours o' the morning."

Their dogs were snappish curs of a rather small mongrel breed, the puppies of which they fattened, and their flesh roasted and prepared after their manner was as tender as that of a sucking pig. Boiled with cebollas (onions) and other ingredients of which they were fond, it made a soup not at all inferior to those of our cookery. They ate lizards, snakes, and other choice tit-bits, nothing in fact which land and rivers afford came amiss to them. Upon tamales, limes, zapotes, chillis, frijoles, and various other Mexican luxuries they also fed heartily when they could procure them.

They have a somewhat peculiar and curious mode of conducting their courtships. When a young buck falls in love, he haunts the places to which the girl is accustomed to resort, and keeps his face covered with his blanket—the custom of the Indians when smitten with the tender passion, as they consider it to be unmanly and unbecoming of a valiant brave. When in her presence, the love-stricken swain utters a kind of low, swelling groan, which he repeats on every occasion of their meeting. There is something very touching in this expression of despondency and sadness, although one unaccustomed to it would scarcely suspect the cause. When he has attracted her favourable attention, his nearest relatives go to her father, uncle or guardian with his proposals, the number and value of the presents which he is willing to give as compensation are enumerated, and if a bargain is effected, all is well. After a feast on hog or dog-flesh, which delicacy falls somewhat less frequently to the share of the common people, the red maiden is transferred without any other ceremony to the lodge of her new master, where she begins to age almost before she is grown up.

The only knowledge amongst them of which I could detect any trace, consisted in an acquaintance with the names and healing properties of various plants and roots; yet the "Tugwe-wa-gunts" (medicine men) of the various tribes make use of this little knowledge with more accuracy and success than will be generally believed. The Indians have a tendency to be very long-lived, and all their destitution and want of comfort seem to have only a pickling effect upon them. There were three or four old men and women in our camp who, though far beyond the ordinary length of life, were strong and healthy and likely to live for years yet. One of them, an old crone, with hair as white as snow, although as I was told close upon ninety years of age, was still a splendid physical specimen of an American aborigin. She seemed hale and hearty and appeared to enjoy life well. The medicine men also pretend to cure ailments by expelling the disease with certain charms and ceremonies. There is for example a bag of stones, amongst which they place a few tufts of hair of the sick person, hung up over the fire, and as the smoke penetrates this it is supposed to influence and dispel the disease.

When one of their number dies, the relatives and friends keep vigils or wakes by the corpse, and give vent to bitter lamentations and moans. These expressions of sorrow continue night

INDIAN CEMETERY.

and day; the relatives being relieved by relays of mourners. Sometimes the assembled people chant wild dirges to which the relatives respond with shrill cries and dismal screeches; and the women, as if writhing in a frenzy which their grief is supposed to have inspired, strike and beat or scratch themselves, as was the case with a young squaw whose child died whilst I was among them. The hideous wailings, which gradually subside until they entirely cease, sound extremely mournful and melancholy.

This brings me to speak of their nocturnal funerals, and the rites and ceremonies belonging to them. Their methods of burial are like those of other Southern tribes. They bury their dead at night, but instead of under ground, they deposit them above it, either by placing the corpse on a kind of scaffold which they erect for that purpose, or among the branches of trees under a covering of bark. The scaffold or kind of platform is prepared by setting upright stakes, eight or nine feet in height in the ground, and on these layers of sticks or saplings split in halves are fastened horizontally, on which the corpse is placed, closely wrapped in skins and blankets. On or near this catafalque on which the body is deposited, the relatives of the deceased place a pipe, tobacco, and some food. This latter observance is never omitted at funerals. In order to secure the bodies from being interfered with, they always choose a secluded and out-of-the-way place, or a spot between the converging branches of a tree in the midst of thick foliage. I had an opportunity of seeing some of these scaffolds—there were several in a group together—which presented a singular sight. They formed a veritable cemetery rising into the air above the ground, and my sensitive organ of smell, with a little imagination, almost made me shudder as I looked up and saw some of the skin-coverings loosened, out of which portions of mortality were protruding. In some cases when a chief or sachem of the tribe dies, a horse is sacrificed at his burial, and occasionally when a death occurs among them whilst they are near a trading-station, they procure a box and transform it into a coffin. The lid of this improvised coffin, after the corpse has been placed inside, is never nailed but only tied down, for they believe that the spirits of the departed pay terrestrial visits to the bodies which once held them. Sometimes even a small opening is made in the lid, to make the fancied egress and ingress still less fatiguing to the spirit.

The principal ceremony and the greatest event amongst the Indians of America has always been the " Sun-dance." This remarkable festival, which was formerly of almost universal observance among them, is still, with slight modifications, practised by some of the tribes. It generally occupies several days, most of which are given to feasting and to various martial performances and superstitious rites which impart to the festival both a religious and a warlike character; but one day is entirely devoted by the young braves to the barbarous work of inflicting cruel tortures on their own bodies. This ordeal of undergoing self-inflicted pain, necessary to obtain the distinction of warrior is—to the Indians at all events—the most interesting feature of the ceremony. Ingenious artifices are resorted to in order to attract notice by their novel and sanguinary character. Here might be seen a young Indian buck with a knife cutting long gashes down his sides or legs, or in his breast; and here another having two apertures made through the skin and muscles on his shoulder-blades, through which a leather thong or string is passed, both ends of which are tied to a rope which again is fastened to a pole standing erect in the ground. Thus the victim, suspended clear of the ground and supported only by the leather thong which passes through his back, continues to swing until it cuts or wears through the flesh and skin, and he drops to the ground. On the occasion to which I referred at the beginning of the preceding chapter, only one buck was able to sustain the racking pain of the last-named horrible torture without fainting; he proved to be the bravest. Among some tribes of the Mexican Indians the young braves have yet another, but not less painful way of putting themselves to torture. On the appointed day during the festival, long before daybreak, the votary takes his position on an elevated place and awaits the appearance of the sun. As soon as it comes in sight, he fixes his gaze and continues to look steadfastly upon it. Through morning, noon and evening the Indian with uplifted face maintains his position; his unfaltering gaze is fixed upon the scorching sun until it disappears in the West; or overcome by its fierce rays he sinks exhausted to the earth.

The Indians who occupy the plains and mountains of the Far West, and live still in their primitive and original fashion, are nearly all of them heathen. They are opposed to adopting either the customs or religion of the white men, and cannot be induced to change their mode of life. Among the Southwestern tribes there are a few partially christianized and civilized, but even these seldom care to relinquish entirely their former habits, and notwithstanding the efforts and exertions of Jesuit missionaries, they have as a rule imbibed very little of the spirit of Christianity. In reference to the religion of the Navajos—if there be any at all—one cannot use the term paganism nor idolatry, for they have no actual idols. Their religion is of a very vague nature and consists mainly of superstitious practices which have very little influence upon their morals. I was not able to obtain from them a clear statement of their religious belief, as there was little external evidence of what their belief really was; and all their statements were so perplexed and veiled in contradictions that I found it impossible to acquire a clear and consistent idea of their faith. They have not any priesthood, nothing more than what they call "Tu-gwe-wa-gunts" (medicine-men) and the few legends existing among them are also of little value towards throwing light upon their creed. I will, however, relate what I learned of it whilst listening to their wild superstitions. They believe, as their ancestors did, that a great and good spirit exists who rules the universe; and a faith in various good and bad deities, as well as in magic and witchcraft prevails amongst them. Expressions of reverence for the good, and fear of the evil ones, whether by words or gesture, are constantly recurring features in their daily life. They entertain with many other tribes the fanciful belief that their deeds and actions in life do not influence their future state of happiness but that, as soon as they shake the dust of earth from off their feet, they soar at once unimpeded from the land of shadows to the happy hunting-grounds in the regions of celestial bliss. Yet in spite of the crudeness of their moral conceptions and principles, they are possessed of traits which challenge one's admiration, and which seem to link them in a kind of brotherhood, so that as a rule they live together in harmony and good fellowship. Were it not for the bright hope in the future which they cherish, the monotony of their daily hardships would soon break their spirit of fearless daring and reduce them to mere savagery. Truly, the aborigines of America are a doomed race. For what purpose was the red man created—was it to make room for another race from the old world, and to vanish before the march of civilization? The tribes along the coast of the Atlantic ocean have nearly all dwindled away, and from the shores of the Pacific the whites will eventually crowd all the Indians into the defiles of the Rocky Mountains, where they will meet the remnants of the Indian tribes from the east side; there seems to be their last place of refuge. And even this "great back-bone of the West," as the Indians call the Rocky Mountains, has been cut through by the white men for their iron track across the continent, and the Indians now hear the thunders of the locomotive as it sends its startling, whistling sound through their habitations in the defiles of the mountains. Territories after territories have been successively taken from them, treaties after treaties have been made in good faith only to be violated by the white pioneer settlers. Tales of rapine, murder and robbery committed by Indians have been written in profusion by writers who see

in the Indians only hordes of demons standing in the way of
progress and civilization, and who must and ought to be
destroyed; but a man who has a more intimate knowledge
of Indian character and life, sometimes forgets their baser
traits, and sees only their virtues, their truth, their fidelity
to a trust—for even in the humble abodes of the Indians
which the shadow of poverty darkens, virtues and vices grow
strangely together—and any one who is impartial and unbiassed
must wonder why, or with what right we destroy that primitive
life. They are said to be revengeful and to distrust every
"pale-face"; but who would not acknowledge that the Indians
were sometimes compelled to fight the white intruders, who
despoiled them of their property, and encroached upon their
rightful domain—their native forests, plains and hills, to which
they were attached with the same affection as any other people
are to theirs? What people are there on earth that would
not defend their rights to the land which gave them a living
by waging war against the usurpers? Is it a thing to be
wondered at that the red man is discontented and looks
upon the white people with contempt, or that scenes of
bloody reprisal were often enacted? One's blood tingles
with shame and boils with indignation to hear of the cruel
acts formerly wreaked even upon harmless tribes, which
were applauded by men who ought to have been pleading the
cause of these poor, untutored people so long as an ear was
found to listen or a heart to feel for their sufferings and their
wrongs. Thus for example, there is not perhaps in the history
of the Indian race a more striking instance of wanton cruelty
than the removal of the Cherokees, the survivors of a once
powerful tribe, from the soil of their fathers in Georgia. To
emigrate was very disadvantageous to all of them, but the
avarice of the white settlers put such a pressure on Congress
that it decreed their removal beyond the Mississippi river,
though the Government of the United States had previously
made a treaty with these tribes by which they were allowed
to dwell unmolested on their fertile reservations. Thus in

spite of solemn treaty and in violation of their rights, the whole tribe—the aged and infirm, and mothers with infants in their arms, were conducted by force from their peaceful homes, where they had seen their first days and where the hunting grounds and the graves of their parents were, to the wilderness of the Indian territory—a distance of nearly two thousand miles. Several other instances of heartless cruelty might be quoted against the Canadians as well as the Americans; but I must forbear. Abler and more eloquent pens have taken up the story of their wrongs which I have but touched upon, and pleaded earnestly and tenderly on their behalf though unfortunately with but little result.

CHAPTER XVI.

A Ride in Northern Mexico—With Indian Caravan through Sonora—Scouting—The Head-waters of the Rio San Ignacio—Aggressive Insects—Bathing and Toilet-Mending—Indian Trails Discovered—Unwelcome Visitors—Encamped on the Banks of the Rio Sonora—A Sad Incident—Mourning—Burial—Arrival at Ures—A Trying Journey—Scarcity of Water—Mexican Pedrigals and Vegas—A Dreary Region—Rio Yaqui—A Narrow Escape—A Timely Help—Leave-Taking.

IT is now time that I should continue the description of our journey, though space does not permit me to give a detailed account of our progress. Riding steadily for two or three days, we got clear of the boundary line and proceeded in a south-easterly direction. The ground over which we now travelled was becoming more and more rugged from day to day. There are few countries about which so little is known as Sonora. The plains which stretch away for many a long mile to the South and East, are almost void of trees, and covered only with a scanty herbage, mostly of stunted nopal and mesketis bushes and low cacti, which nestle among the sand and stones. Open, bare, and uninviting as the country appeared at that stage of our journey, the sense of desolate dreariness was enhanced by the apparently boundless expanse of plain which met the eye. Except at a few points where a few sickly trees were struggling for their existence, not even a knoll broke the monotony of the landscape. Our rate of travelling was about fifteen miles per day, which in the warm weather and often limited supply of water was sufficient both for man and beast. While creeks were pretty numerous, most of them were apparently quite dry, and in none did we find running water, yet my companions managed, nevertheless, to extract from them some decidedly stagnant water, which was collected in "pockets" under the stones and water-worn boulders that were freely strewn over the bottoms of the creeks. We required to keep a good look-out for marauding Indians, and great precautions were taken for fear of a surprise. The convoy also carefully avoided passing through or even near a mining camp or village, taking often a long detour to evade even a cattle-ranch. The scouts riding in front often returned with the intelligence that they had found a trail, whereupon the whole cavalcade immediately stopped, and all was commotion. The smallest object in the distance, the faintest sound startled them, and it was not until the scouts, who were sent out to reconnoitre, had come back, and they were sure nothing was amiss, that their confidence was renewed. Then the whole troup moved on again; the scouts in front, and behind them followed the main body of the band with children and squaws in the middle. The squaws rode generally straddle-legged like the men, with one or two papooses before them in the saddle, and sometimes a squaw had a child carelessly thrown over her back. The bigger children too rode on horseback—often three on one pony, with the baby in the middle—and each horse dragged a load of commodities besides. The horses were yoked to the tent-poles, one end of which being fastened to their saddles whilst the other trailed on the ground, and the loads were heaped and strapped on top of them. The whole arrangement was altogether so unique and absurd that I never got tired looking at it. A large proportion of the lighter transport work was also done by the dogs. These poor canine drudges had occasionally a bad time of it whilst the camp was on the move, panting and tugging at loads which were sometimes heavy and cumbrous enough for a pony. Behind them came the vanguard driving the packhorses and the pigs.

My saddle, until I became somewhat accustomed to its primitive character, was a source of great discomfort to me.

The articles Pikavu procured before starting from Tucson could hardly have been called saddles at all, as they consisted of nothing but a wooden skeleton of the commodity with the girth and stirrups attached. The object of their simplicity was, no doubt, to render them light and cool to the horses; but to mitigate their hardness to some extent at least, I had blankets strapped above as well as beneath them. For about a fortnight we thus proceeded, dodging from one place to another, and passing successively within sight of Babasequi, Arispe, and several other small towns and villages without any incident worth remark occurring, till we struck the headwaters of the Rio San Ignacio, where we came to a halt. The margin of its banks was worn out by water, but at this time the river was below its general level. In some places, however, the river-bed was widened by swampy holes and bogs, in which myriads of the inevitable mosquitoes and flies were hatched. These marshes were, through the influence of moisture and heat, covered with a fresh growth of grass, which was delicious to look at after the recent miles of scrub and sand unrelieved and simple, but alas! this multitude of the aggressive insects soon made me long to be again on the march, for rest seemed but a fiction to me. My companions slept soundly, but I could not close an eye owing to the venomous swarms which surrounded us at night, though Pikavu, in the hope of keeping these active blood-suckers at a distance, had kindled a fire of dry grass and rushes in front of our tent which emitted dense clouds of smoke. But all was in vain. The next morning my hands, face and neck, which had been exposed to their fury, were covered with innumerable poisonous bites. Mosquitoes are troublesome chiefly at night, but flies are increasingly so to man and beast as the day advances and the air gets hotter. One and the same fly will continue to alight on one's face or hand, although it had been many times shaken off. Yet in spite of, and defying all these nuisances, during the following day we performed our ablutions in the river, after which nearly the whole camp sat along its banks, bestowing the greatest care in arranging and mending their scanty toilet.

Whilst the boys splashed and romped about, the squaws bent over the water, dashed it over their faces and heads, and then old and young, comely and ugly ones of both sexes held the little, round looking-glasses, which every Indian carries suspended from his or her neck, before their faces with great complacency and satisfaction, and combed their long raven hair—the women more particularly—with the most primitive of wooden combs I ever beheld.

We had thus far travelled for a good many days without having seen any human beings, though we often found indications of their presence at one time or other in various spots which we had passed; but one day towards evening we were suddenly greeted by a sight which put every one in our camp on the *qui vive*. Some of the bucks fell in with a small band of Indians, and brought them into our camp. They fortunately were a friendly tribe. They dismounted and sat on the ground, and an hour or two were spent in eating, smoking, and a little talking. The most liberal hospitality prevailed during the evening. While their lords were eating or idly smoking, the squaws looked complacently upon them, or smiled at the little potbellied papooses who crawled on the ground quite naked, and played with the dirty dogs which sneaked around.

The new comers encamped near us for the night, but I did not much like their appearance, nor was their neighbourhood very agreeable either to me or to Pikavu, who had to watch the whole night for fear that our belongings would disappear. Some of these fellows were skulking and gliding with noiseless steps round the camp till late at night, but the whole band moved off early in the morning and left us in sole possession of the ground.

After a few days of rest we started off once more. I do not propose to narrate at full length all the incidents of our journey, and without entering into more minute details, suffice it to say that the next place where we enjoyed a long rest was on the banks of the Rio Sonora. A very sad incident occurred in our camp before we left this locality. The first-born and only child of a young squaw died suddenly one evening. The illness to which it succumbed was croup, and the grief of the mother—almost a child herself—knew no bounds. The sight of the rigid corpse forced her at intervals to tears and to convulsive sighs of tenderness and sorrow. She frantically scratched and wounded herself with her nails, wailing ceaselessly. Her female relatives, squatting on the ground, rocked themselves as if in dire grief, and bursts of passionate crying resounded on all sides. · The father of the child, a handsome fellow of about twenty, with the figure of an athlete—a very bundle of vigour and nerve—seemed also to be really afflicted at his loss. He sat silently by, lost in meditation and staring fixedly on the ground, and now and again he took the dead body in his arms and passed his hand gently over its tawny little face. During the whole night the air was filled with the sound of sobs and groans and shrieks of women and children, which gradually became less frequent and at last ceased. When the squaws got through their mourning performance they were fairly exhausted. It is generally said that the Indians possess very little or no sentiment, and that grief and sorrow never fills their breasts. The scene just described may help to refute this erroneous opinion. The father of the dead child improvised a coffin by using a wooden box which I possessed, and which contained tins of preserved meats and biscuits when we started from Tucson. Into this the little corpse was laid, and the box with its contents deposited upon the branches of a stunted acacia tree, and covered with bark and moss.

Our horses were much recruited by the long rest and good pasture for renewing our route. We passed now through a tract with plenty of grass in the glades, until eventually we reached Ures. Upon approaching the place the whole convoy halted, dismounted, and carefully combed their hair, and arranged their garments, and yet it is the common belief that Indians care little for their personal appearance. They are, in fact, very vain, and trim themselves up, and adorn their

Q

coal-black, glossy hair at every opportunity when they think that they are going to be observed. We encamped near the town, and soon a crowd of lookers-on were standing and gaping around the tents. I went to see the place to escape the heterogeneous assemblage of visitors, and wandered about the streets among the closely packed native huts forming the town, where family groups were lounging on the door-steps of the dilapidated houses.

Our sojourn at Ures extended over two days of vivid sunshine and sweltering heat, after which our party again toiled on, and travelled for a considerable distance along the course of the river Sonora to avoid the fatigues and hardships of the dry vega. The region into which we then entered was indeed a region of bad lands, a solitude absolutely appalling. Over the whole vast expanse no human habitation was to be seen, and for miles spread an interminable wavy stretch of land which for desolation had no parallel even in the poor country which we had thus far traversed. Thick mist rose every morning, and when it had been dispersed by the rays of the sun, the country lying before our eyes was a waste, barren, empty, and pathless as the Sahara. A wearier-looking desert could scarcely be imagined. Not a tree was visible, nothing but low scrub away on all sides to the horizon. The ground, partly rocky and broken-up, was in some places covered with a heavy sand into which the horses sank up to their knees. Frequently we had great difficulty in obtaining a supply of water for the camp, and the painfulness of the journey therefore was now extreme. One could easily understand the privations which the prospectors and mining men had to endure in former years when they struck across the dreary country in search of silver and gold, so alluringly shadowed forth to them in the distance. In some instances water was obtained by digging deep under the stones in the bed of a creek, but often we found them dried up to the bottom. It was, indeed, a wearisome and often repeated disappointment to enter a hollow that might have held a cold and bubbling spring, and to find everything dried up, or but a bog alive with insects, yielding nothing but some stagnant and tepid water which, under the pinch of strong necessity, we often had to drink,

I wish I could graphically describe the peculiar character of those wild, desolate pedrigals and vegas, broken-up and sown with sand, ashes, and alkali, which form so large a proportion of Sonora. Drearier prospect we had not seen since we were on the move. The great circle of the horizon receded as we advanced, and the extent of the view, dimmed by the haze of the golden light, was limited only by the powers of one's vision. One could wander from day to day across this untracked waste where desolation's dwelling is; over this land of silence, dreams, and shoreless deserts; lose all reckoning of time, seasons might pass, yet one could journey on and on through space, marvelling at the distances. It however seldom occurs that any one save the Indians break upon the appalling solitude of these melancholy regions. They are as drear and solemn as the ocean and seem as boundless—all is vague, monotonous, and infinite. No work is going on; one hears no sound of industry; sees no population. One looks off into immensity, and is only conscious of one's insignificance and feebleness; the soul is lost in their simplicity and vastness, and forgets its individuality, its pride, its restlessness. It is a pathless, monotonous waste, only diversified now by sunrise or sunset, now by scudding mists and winds, contending for the right to herd and drive the clouds each its own way. This is the Great Lone Land; the land of unknown distances where, as the Indians say, the sun and moon lie down together and bring forth the stars. I could not help being strongly impressed with the change after the lapse of only a few weeks, from the crowded streets and noisy bustle of San Francisco to this desert far beyond the limits of civilization, where all sounds of population and almost of life were gone.

Though the days which saw us on the track over this bleak expanse were ordinarily very warm and serene, there were also times when the wind got its back up, and forced the gritty dust into our eyes and lungs. However, after a weary ride of many a mile, the first real signs of a change were afforded us as the sparse herbage became tinted with green. The dull monotony of the landscape gradually changed, and greatly to its advantage, until one evening a dim, distant speck, then a long reaching line of low hills and swelling ridges, beautifully tinted by the slanting rays of the setting sun, hove in sight on the horizon and brought their variety of colours to the scenery. We were travelling for two or three days with these hills constantly before our eyes and seemingly close at hand. The rare, clear atmosphere on the plains annihilates distance entirely, and wraps one in endless deceptions. Having gained and scaled them at last, we finally descended from their steep brow to the level of the Rio Yaqui, and encamped on the bank of this river.

A little way from the spot where our tents were pitched—lower down the stream—there was a strong rapid, and a furious gush of water over the broken bed of the river, where many large boulders rose up and caught the current, hurling the water back in white foam. The water was crooning a soft low tune above the rapid, while at its base a fierce whirlpool was seething and hissing in fury. One day I met with a mishap on this spot, and got a thorough sousing in the water. Having sallied forth with my sketch-book, I clambered down the steep bank and over the stones lying in the water, clinging sometimes to roots, sometimes to frail and yielding bunches of grass until I found myself on a large boulder in the midst of the stream. Near it was a shelving rocky platform, between the base of which and the boulder on which I stood, ran the seething current. Thinking that this would be a safe perch from which to take a sketch, I caught hold of the extending boughs of a mesketis-bush, by the help of which I thought to reach the top of the rocky shelf. The "dexterous" jump, however, was a dire failure; for taking a good swing, with my shoes and my sketch-book in one hand, I was just reaching the top, when the treacherous bush gave way, roots and all, and I slid into the

ON THE RIO YAQUI. (THE WHIRLPOOL.)

A NARROW ESCAPE.

foaming water. The current swept me down with lightning speed, but passing a large boulder I made a desperate grip at it and stopped myself for a moment; but I could not hold on, for the current was too strong. Again the irresistible power of the rapid carried me several hundred yards onward, and thoughts of being hurled against the rough rocks were seething through my brain as I was dashing headlong down, straight towards the whirlpool. A few yards lower down there was another cluster of rocks, from the base of which a calm eddy tailed off—for every rock in a rapid has a long tail of still water below it. As I flew past these rocks I hugged and clung to one of them with a desperate effort, and seeing my chance I struck out with might and main for the eddy. Darting from rock to rock, and gaining a few yards at each dart, I reached it at last, and suddenly came to a halt in shallow water in the very middle of the stream. Standing to my loins in the water, I was congratulating myself on my escape from drowning, when I saw a young buck from our camp dash boldly, with a yell, from the opposite bank into the stream. He witnessed my mishap whilst fishing near by, and without losing time to undress, he hastened to my assistance, much to my delight, as I could not see my way back. His swim against the impetuous motion of the water was hard and fatiguing work, taxing both arms and lungs to the utmost extent; yet the daring fellow's eyes sparkled with reckless spirit as he reached me. Then by wading, clambering, and jumping, we finally gained the high bank in safety, though in doing so I bruised and scratched my bare feet and hands dreadfully against the rough stones.

My sketch-book and shoes, of course, disappeared under the shadow of the fall. The loss of the shoes, after the hard service they had seen, was not of much consequence in itself, but as they were my only pair I was placed in rather a queer predicament. However, I would have gladly left them in their watery grave if I could but have recovered my book, which contained many drawings and notes of essential value to me. After a short rest from our exertions, we laughingly shook the wet from our limbs, although I was almost stupefied with the sensation of terror; and went back to the camp, where I had to seek the solitude of my tent whilst my drenched garments were drying outside before a crackling fire. Pikavu was in great alarm when he heard of my little adventure. In these eddies of calm water between the rocks, our boys caught many a fine fish. They had nets and hooks of bone to catch them, but they generally speared them. From morning till evening one or more of the bucks were enjoying this sport; and good luck it was, for had this accident happened to me when nobody was near, its consequences might have been more serious.

The moccasins which I procured in camp to do service for my lost shoes, were but a poor makeshift, for I felt every stone through them on which I trod, and the sand came continually shifting into them when I was walking. However, they had to pass in the emergency.

Nearly two months had now elapsed since I met with my Indian friends, and for various reasons I began to feel that the time for leaving them was near at hand. I had been now for a considerable time a stranger to the abodes of civilization, and had grown somewhat accustomed to what was at least a partial assimilation to a state of nature, yet in knocking about the country with my Indian friends, I learned that a gipsy life of that kind has considerably more of hardships than pleasure or romance in it. We were fifty-four days reaching the Rio Yaqui, during the whole of which time we were never under a roof save that of our tents; nor did I enjoy the comfort of bed, table, or chair. Seeing an opportunity of reaching Guaymas, on the shore of the Gulf of California from which, I was made to understand, we were about eight days' journey distant, I set about making preparations for this lonely ride. The last evening before my departure, we sat around the fires in real good humour. The tobacco which I distributed enlivened the bucks, and brought out snatches of song, whilst the happiness of some of the squaws, who received beads and other trinkets, seemed for the moment complete. Of the things which I offered the chief, nothing appeared as acceptable as tobacco, powder, and beads ; however, when I handed him a few bright Mexican silver dollars in addition to these, a look of satisfaction lighted up his countenance.

In wandering about the world as I have done, one gets somewhat used to leave-taking ; yet I unhesitatingly aver that when the moment arrived and I had to take leave of these people, I found it rather a hard job to come to an end of it. We were pump-handling away at each other with great energy —the chief being specially exuberant in his handshaking. Time had passed quickly, and—with the exception of a few rough night-bivouacs and weary rides—I can even say agreeably, among these free children of nature. I met with no worse a misfortune than indifferent food, bad nightquarters, and a ducking in the river. But taking into consideration their condition as well as that of the country we traversed, whose wildness is not yet tamed, it would be impossible not to experience some hardships. I took with me their hearty good wishes, and many were the friendly grunts and whoops we heard as we parted from our interesting companions.

CHAPTER XVII.

Mirage on the Plains—A Welcome Sight—A Hospitable Hacienda—Our Next Halt—A Disreputable Company—Attack by Robbers—Fortunate in Misfortune—A Lassoing Scene—Arrival at Guaymas.

HAVING quitted the camp, we began to make our toilsome and devious travel towards Guaymas. I am speaking in the plural, so I scarcely need to say that I was again accompanied by Pikavu. We pursued the track, and rode on in the blazing sun hour after hour along an open, sandy plain, which was intersected by many a rocky gully, and here and there grown over with prickly bushes of yuccas and acacias. The following morning at sunrise we witnessed a beautiful mirage. There appeared in the pure sky one of those phenomena which are so often exhibited on plains; and on this occasion just as the first rays of sunshine were striking aslant the glittering sand, we saw rising perpendicularly from the verge of the horizon a colossal rock with a rounded crest. Along this and an adjoining, overhanging promontory, tall columns and towers seemed to stand, and spires in distorted and changing outlines came into view. At first scarcely visible they became gradually very distinct and well defined. Indeed we could plainly distinguish domes of churches, and the roofs of houses. The image was repeated several times in short successions, and for several minutes the strangely grand phenomenon lasted, until its outlines gradually faded and changed, and as the sun rose higher they were entirely obliterated and lost in the ethereal space. The deception was so perfect that it might well have been mistaken for reality.

The country became gradually more and more hilly—quite the reverse to the boundless, flat stretches which we had recently traversed. We took many short cuts across the slopes and bare hillsides, for we were obliged to get on as fast as possible so as to reach one of the villages or plantations through which, we were told, we should pass, before our small stock of provisions gave out. Thus our little horses carried us across many a rugged bluff, and many a ridge we zigzagged up and down, which involved toil and fatigue. We varied the routine of our travel by taking a *siesta* during the heat of the day—for the midday sun and the dust are two terrible things during the warm months—but we trotted along till late at night, and when the first faint—very faint streak of dawn was breaking through the eastern sky we were on the trail again. Though at daytime there was no suspicion of damp or chill, the nights—to say the least of them—were sometimes very disagreeable on account of the heavy dew which often fell then, and made the ground damp, soaked our blankets, and rendered such nights anything but pleasant. However, these hardships of rough travel amid strange scenes, and of sleeping in the open air, no doubt, benefited my mind, though scarcely my body. And onward through paling sunset glories and freshening evening airs we sped ; weary rides over monotonous, scrub-covered wastes were taken, until the fourth day of our journey—it was a magnificent evening, and near the time of sunset—after surmounting a considerable eminence which by its steepness had greatly fatigued us, a welcome sight met our gaze. I rubbed my eyes open and stared in apprehension that another mirage was deceiving our senses— why, there was a sheet of water rippling in the sunlight, and farther on fields, and houses and huts scattered over them, the reflections of which we could see in the bright water, shining like a mirror smitten by the sun. Wearied out with climbing up and down, the view of this first human habitation after a ride of several weeks impressed me as if I had come upon the dazzling glitter of a precious stone in this barren land. We stood for a while with feelings of joy, absorbed in the contemplation of the scene. Hastening on, we at last reached the outskirts of a plantation, and turning into a road between fields of maize, we met several ox-carts, the drivers of which, saluting with a friendly "*Buenas nochas, Señor*," directed us to the hacienda.

The lime-washed house, in front of which we jumped off, and into which we dragged our stiffened limbs, was superior to most of the posadas that I saw afterwards in this part of Mexico, and was inhabited by the manager of the plantation and his wife, a German couple who vied in showing kindness to their visitors. Some of the furniture standing round the room, and even the pictures on the walls showed the origin of their owners. However, my huge and healthy appetite did not allow me to indulge long in examining the pictures, whilst the perfumes that floated from the next room, hinted at supper. I did not wait for a repeated invitation, but fell to and fared heartily on jerked beef with sweet batter pudding, coffee, bacon, rice, chilies, tortillas, and other Mexican dishes. After the excellent meal, which would have suited the fastidious palate of an epicure, I asked myself: Am I so dear, am I so respected beyond the ocean, or is there anything so imposing in my individual appearance that I should be thus regaled? That night, for the first time after a long interval, I enjoyed again the luxury of a night's sleep in a bed, till the shrill clarion of a chanticleer the silence broke who loudly began his early matin-song. I was robbed of several articles before we reached Guaymas, amongst them was a valise containing several notebooks in which the route of my travel through Western Mexico was jotted down, and it is thus impossible for me to give the name of this hospitable hacienda, and to connect my description. This mischance happened to us two days later—however, I must not anticipate. The following day we passed through several villages, with their unvarying flat-roofed mud-hovels and tumble-down adobe huts. The situation of some of them was about as remarkable as can be seen anywhere, and I wondered on seeing them, how people ever came to live there. The huts and the few patches of fields that were visible seemed literally hung upon the precipitous hillsides. Some of the huts presented an aspect which indicated that at one time or other they must have slipped down the hill, or been shaken by an earthquake, for they were almost in ruins, their walls being cracked all over.

The sun had sunk behind the distant hills and dusk had fallen, as we pulled up in front of a miserable *paradero;* a wretched, low, dirty, and ruinous structure—one of the ordinary rough-and-ready wayside inns on which the few passing travellers must depend for refreshment and accommodation as much as they may dislike it. On entering we found it to be closely packed—indeed, jammed to overflowing—with a crowd of peons and teamsters sitting around a long table, which was covered with bottles, flasks and glasses. Some talked together and smoked and drank, lolling on the seats; others slept stretched at full length on the rude benches round the walls, probably intoxicated. The first man my eyes fell on, struck me as the dirtiest and most disreputable creature I had ever seen, but the next seemed worse, and so on until I was utterly bewildered and gave up trying to decide this point; but one thing I am certain of—that a more dirty and dissipated-looking lot never got together in one room. The heat in this den was simply terrible, and its squalor and filth abominable. I had lived in the Red Indians' greasy and musty-smelling wigwams, but I was not prepared for what I saw here. The dim light of a begrimed lamp, which hung from the ceiling, lit up a variety of insolent faces, and a strong odour of aguardiente and pulque filled the atmosphere, which, mixed with the thick fumes of tobacco floating in the air, was enough to intoxicate anybody who breathed it.

Some of the ruffianly fellows stared at us as we entered, and listened and hovered about us while Pikavu parleyed and negotiated with the padrone for our accommodation. There were certainly some fellows amongst them with those types of heads which denote scoundrelism; their jowls were vast and their evil black eyes looked venomous under their lowering brows. I was not at all sorry when, led by the padrone, we made our way to an outhouse where, after a frugal meal, wrapt in our blankets, we stretched ourselves upon the planks. Next morning saw us early under way, and more than six hours of incessant hard riding brought us at noon to the banks of a stream, which crossed the road. There we took our usual *siesta* in a cool and sequestered nook among bushes. Whilst Pikavu was busying himself with unsaddling the horses, I descended the bank to lave my face in one of the pools of water at the bottom of the stream. I was just on the very point of doing so, when I happened to look up and caught sight of a man on the further side of the creek, but he dropped and vanished as suddenly as he appeared. Shortly after this I heard a loud tussle, and Pikavu's repeated shouts and yells. In an instant a vague dread of danger possessed me, and forcing myself up between the bushes and over the loose soil of the overhanging bank, I hurried to the spot, when suddenly a tall man sprang up before me, barring the way. This, however, did not sap my courage yet, and I rushed past him and right on towards Pikavu, whom I saw only a few paces farther on struggling on the ground with all his might with another ruffian for the possession of my rifle, which was lying by his side. Before I reached them, however, a third scoundrel was in front of me, and elevated the muzzle of his gun towards my head.

A more courageous man might experience a shudder at such a moment of imminent danger, but I had no time for that, and stooping intuitively to escape the aim of that terrible weapon, I made another attempt to reach Pikavu, who still pertinaciously grasped the rifle. My second attempt was again unsuccessful, for in another instant the ladrone whom I had first encountered, was again by my side, and I saw his *machete* in his raised hand. I took a good look at him; his rags fairly fluttered in the wind-breeze. His brown face was dirty; his eyes were red-rimmed; a tobacco-stained moustache was upon his upper lip; and one of his hands was wrapped in a filthy rag. The mortifying comprehension of the impossibility to oppose two armed men, which arose in my mind at that moment, drained away my strength and reduced me to a state of impotent wrath. A dreadful weakness came over me when, looking towards Pikavu, I saw that he too could not hold on much longer. I felt that, defenceless as we were, there was nothing else that we could do but abandon the struggle. Our only chance now was to save, if possible, by compromise as much of our belongings as we could. This, I thought, was preferable to withstanding the brute force of our assailants. I shouted to Pikavu to come to me, and after a few moments more he was standing by my side with paled face, and looking anxiously at me. "It's no use, Pikavu, we must let them have the rifle—ask them to let us pass on." Thereupon Pikavu harangued them, and they in return demanded some ammunition. This insolent request had the effect of making my blood boil up with anger—that was adding insult to injury. Any man might feel some irritation if, after having been robbed of his rifle, it was insinuated by the impudent thief that he should supply him also with ammunition, but to refuse and risk a bullet which might have sent one of us to his last account, or a slash of the *machete* which I saw glitter in the hand of one of the ruffians, would have been courage without judgment. So I lifted up my little valise in which the remnant of my cartridges was stowed away (I had parted with all of my powder and shot before leaving the Indian camp), and handed over the package for which I had now no more use. This action was probably the cause that the loss of my rifle was not the only bad consequence of this adventure, for the sight of papers and various articles of clothing which the valise contained no doubt made them greedy, and without much ado they annexed it with the other plunder, and scampered off in the direction from whence we came. I have no doubt that we had been watched and followed, or preceded all the way from the *paradero* where we stayed over night. It was a pre-arranged job, and the whole pack was evidently in league with each other. However, my wrath passed into a smile of resignation as soon as imminent danger was over, and as I realized how fortunate in misfortune I had been. I had my money in my belt which I wore buckled round my waist, but the sight of my worn-out clothes, on which dust and mud had painted a variegated panorama of the roads along which we had passed, probably impressed upon their minds that there was nothing else worth taking from my person. Thus our jaded ponies, which were such sorry-looking beasts that the scamps evidently did not care to take possession of them, my money, and my paint-box too, were saved; but we were left defenceless for the rest of our journey. There was nothing else to do under these circumstances but to console ourselves with the old proverb : " The wind is tempered to the shorn lamb."

We left this robber-infested place, which for cutting a man's throat, or having his own cut, was as pleasant and convenient a locality as need be, rather in a haste; and Pikavu explained to me whilst we were jogging along the dusty road, what had happened before I arrived on the scene of the scuffle. He told me that after unsaddling, he placed the blankets, valise, and the various bags on the ground, and whilst tethering the horses he heard a rustling among the bushes, and at that moment the ladrone seized the rifle which was lying on the blankets, and then the scuffle for its recovery began, with the result as above stated.

The rest of our journey towards Guaymas passed without any other mishap occurring to us. We observed that there must have been considerable traffic along the road over which we now travelled, although only a few haciendas were to be seen in the neighbourhood. It was a fairly good road, but the dust on it was ankle-deep. Passing one of the numerous corrals (a large and strong enclosure of rough planks and stakes) we witnessed a spectacle exciting enough and wonderful to behold. It was a lassoing scene, and we watched it from the saddles of our horses. The ground was high on that side where we stood, so we could easily look over the fence. The herdsmen drove down the cattle into the corral amid the din of their voices and the cracking of raw-hide whips, with which they welted the frightened animals. Selecting one out of the number, a horseman dashed ahead at full speed, swinging his lariat as he moved along, till suddenly, and with unerring aim, the rope uncoiled to its full length, the noose falling over the horns of the infuriated animal, which, now fairly mad with excitement, in turn became the pursuer. The brute, fuming and bristling with rage, bellowed fiercely whilst careering over the ground, and its eyes were fixed upon its tormentor with a glare of extraordinary ferocity. The horse, admirably trained, and apparently delighted with the sport, ran as if the evil one himself were riding it. It leapt ahead, its eyes flashing and its flanks heaving from violent exertion, till it felt the lariat draw, when it suddenly stopped and faced its formidable antagonist, bracing its feet to oppose his motions. Maddened to desperation, the beast almost immediately resumed its attack, but a second horseman meanwhile galloped up and with his lasso deftly caught up one of its hind-legs, when both horses drew in opposite directions. The animal, overpowered and exhausted, sank bellowing to the ground, and another horseman, the *caballero*, quickly drew his keen *machete* athwart the poor beast's neck, whose agonized bellowings, starting eye-balls and dilated nostrils gave evidence of his death-struggle. One of the operators in the meanwhile caught a quantity of the blood in a wooden bowl, and the sickening butchery was complete—sickening, because the faint bleats and the suffering of the dying brute were simply heartrending. One of the bullocks bolted and took to the road, with the dogs in full cry after him, and we scampered off in the opposite direction. He was not allowed to proceed far, a lariat stopped him very soon.

The following day we perceived straight before us in the West some mountains, the tops of which were clearly defined in the distance, and in the afternoon as we ascended the spur of a steep hill, the sea burst almost on a sudden on our view. As I beheld the Pacific again, flooded with brilliant sunshine and overarched by a cloudless sky, I felt like Xenophon's soldiers when at sight of the Euxine they burst out with Thalatta ! Thalatta !

Guaymas was reached that same evening. My intention when I arrived at Tucson, was to push my way to Santa Fé in New Mexico, and to continue my further progress towards Colorado—it had been ordained otherwise ; I stood again on the shore of the Pacific. If there is a chance of going wrong in my calculations, I never neglect that chance. This has invariably been my experience.

CHAPTER XVIII.

Along the West Coast of Mexico—Southward Bound—A Motley Company—Mazatlan—A Fight amongst Steerage Passengers—Manzanilla—Diving for Coins—A Curious Sight—An Alarming Incident—Acapulco—Bay of Panama.

GUAYMAS is a considerable seaport town at the mouth of the Rio San José, yet hardly one person in ten thousand knows more of it than the name. It is located on an elevated site and presents a fine view of the lofty hills and mountains around. Its harbour, which is considered to be the best on the West coast of Mexico, is sheltered from winds by rugged headlands and steeps surrounding it, and the island of Paxaro forms a natural breakwater before its inlet. The town contains some large, well-built and comfortable-looking dwelling houses with balconies and verandas, which strongly contrast with the rude, flat-roofed mud-hovels in their immediate vicinity, but the country around is very arid and destitute of water, which has to be conveyed to the town from a distance of several miles. Rainwater is also carefully preserved in tanks, as it is scarce and consequently valuable. To protect their tanks the residents put padlocks on the taps.

At Guaymas I enjoyed a rest of several days, and one of the first things I did was to buy another rifle to replace the one that was stolen from me a few days ago. The air was very hot whilst I was in that town, and only in the evenings when a breeze sprung up from the sea, which felt like gentle wooings of zephyrs, I sallied forth from the *paradero*, where

I enjoyed the luxury of coolness and shade during the days, and wandered through the narrow and crooked streets. There was not, however, much to be seen. A few belated, rough-looking men, some mounted, some on foot, stole noiselessly through the streets, and here and there small groups of people were gathered together in front of a *posada*, from which occasionally the faint sounds of a guitar and the tinkle of a cymbal, accompanied by the rattling of castanets and tambourines resounded, which testified to an innocent merry-making. By the time I came back to my *paradero*, which was in the centre of the town, I was generally covered with the light brown dust which gives its tint to everything and everybody at Guaymas. Yet I was told that I was fortunate in not being there on a dusty day, or when there is a wind to raise it in clouds.

At last the day came when I had to leave faithful Pikavu. I took passage in the steamer *City of Merida* bound southward, whilst he was awaiting his chance to proceed northward in one of the coasting vessels which ply up and down, and call at the different ports along the Gulf of California. Late one afternoon the steamer, on board of which I embarked, set out, followed by many good wishes from Pikavu; and steaming slowly through the still waters of the harbour, I caught a last glimpse of him, standing on the pier and waving a kindly adieu to me. I was sorry to part from Pikavu; he was very much attached to me, and I was highly pleased with his services. In fact he had only one really disagreeable peculiarity, which occasionally made it a matter of some difficulty for him to find his way to his night-quarters, and this was a propensity to a too liberal indulgence in pulque or maskal.

The ship was sheering swiftly and giddily through a long cresting swell, and the sound of the waves which fretted and chafed against the hull of the steamer, and the monotonous grinding of her screw as it worked its way through the water, were the only sounds heard. The decks were almost deserted, save by a few seasoned hands who came up to smoke ; but the following morning they were crammed with jostling lines of pale but cheerful people. There was a motley assemblage in the steerage, wedged in and compressed like herrings or sardines in a barrel. I wandered among the company with much curiosity. There were half-breed natives on board homeward bound ; Chinamen ; a few Mexican gamblers who plied their nefarious business in playing *monté* in various corners on and below deck ; a few doubtful Mexican beauties who carried their charms to another market ; and a troup of sturdy, weather-beaten gold-diggers and prospectors in rude garments, who, leaving Sonora, were also *en route* to some other place to seek for good luck. The last-named were the most interesting among the passengers, and eager questioners surrounded them wherever they stood or sat, and listened to the accounts of their experiences and incidents in the diggings.

Our sail along the coast would have been very enjoyable but for the heat and the overcrowding, for there was a pretty tight fit in the cabins too. The sun had been burning with terrific fury, and awnings were stretched fore and aft, but they could give but little comfort, for the sun's beams, reflected from the waves, were nearly as hot as those directly from above. We made a short stoppage at the port of Mazatlan, where our steamer replenished her supply of coals ; discharged part of her human freight, and in return took several French and Mexican labourers with their families on board, who came from a neighbouring sugar-cane plantation. The delay thus occasioned was not unwelcome, for it enabled us to go ashore and pay a short visit to the town. We had only a few hours there, and had not time to see much of that place, yet Guaymas' port seems to be far more important than that of Mazatlan. The latter town consists of a handful of huts and sheds around the landing place, and a few better class houses lying on the slopes of low hills farther inland—there is little else to attract the eyes of visitors. The great heat that prevailed during our visit to the town made it, no doubt, that everybody seemed bent upon the mission of procuring in the easiest way and at the earliest possible moment a cool drink. But this was by no means an easy task. As there was no ice in the town, the temperature of the liquids imbibed was only a question of degree, and thus the gamut was run of the more respectable places of refreshment. How this plan succeeded amongst my fellow-passengers who visited the lower-class liquor saloons, I am not prepared to say, but that there was a large amount of conviviality throughout the town around the landing place I can certainly vouch for. A few cattle were chewing the cud in dreamy idleness on the neighbouring meadows, but poultry seemed to be most numerous, with the exception of insects, of which I saw a more than sufficient stock in a horchateria, where I took advantage of the opportunity to feast on roast chicken.

In the evening, after my experience of the dusty and dirty town, I returned with renewed pleasure to the ship, and soon after—the gear of the steamer having meanwhile been overhauled, and her bunks refilled with coal—we started off once more. Some sail was set, and on we went with wind and steam. We were still favoured with smiling skies, and a heat which was like the blast from a furnace. Hamlet, who wanted his "solid flesh to melt," should have been with us. However, we walked about nearly bared to the skin, and all went gaily on. The water was glassy in its stillness, the only ripple being when the steamer with her ponderous movements disturbed the smoothness of its surface. There was plenty of music, dancing, and singing going on, and not a frowning face was to be seen until one day a bustle arose on the afterdeck amongst the steerage passengers. The scrimmage opened with threatening overtures and volleys of oaths, but after a while it grew into a severe hand-to-hand fight. The combatants wrestled and belaboured each other with sticks and fists, using them both very freely. They were fighting together like the proverbial Kilkenny cats, until two or three Mexicans, in fact two or three united Mexican families, kicked one of their adversaries, a French labourer, down the steps. He stretched himself nobly on the ground like an ancient Roman, then he jumped up, shook his head, and swore savagely at his antagonists. I think the French inferior in the science of swearing. How absurdly they swear, and how odd it is to hear them roar out in passion words which are more funny than anything else. Meanwhile the Mexicans on their part turned a sluice of profanity on the poor Frenchman that washed him nearly overboard, and then the fight opened up with savage earnestness, and the demon of discord was dancing a wild dance in their neighbourhood. The Frenchman was put to flight, but being joined by several friends to give aid and help if necessary, he turned, drew a revolver out of his pocket, and pointed it at the head of one of his foes, threatening to blow that ornament from its place. He was so carried away by excitement that, despite the remonstrances of his friends, and all the exertions of those pulling at his arms, he would have suited his actions to his words. For a while longer the horrors of the last Franco-Mexican war were repeating themselves *en miniature* in the steerage. So furious was the combat that they appeared quite oblivious of immediate surroundings, and the lively scene was only now and then interrupted by the operation of digging screaming and fainting women out of the midst of the crowd. We watched from the upper deck the fight that was ahead of any boxing-match for a real live show, until at last the captain made his appearance and marched up—followed by a retinue of sailors—to mediate with a club. The disturbance was soon quelled by the captain's persuasive means, not however until several persons were injured, amongst whom there was one who had done his best to restrain the fury of the combatants; seeing which, I remembered the old saying which is well worth repeating.

"Those who in quarrels interpose must often wipe a bloody nose." And a very good proverb it is to my thinking. In the absence of any other amusement, the intervals between the singing and dancing were enlivened in this fashion; half-a-dozen encounters at least of this sort taking place during the voyage.

We had a long run before we shaped our course inshore again, and then the town of Manzanilla hove in sight. As we approached it, our attention was soon attracted by numbers of children of both sexes, who plunged and dashed with a remarkable swiftness through the water, and swam towards our steamer, which meanwhile had dropped anchor, and was lying about half a mile off the beach, overhauling her rigging. Reaching us, they held out their little nut-brown hands for alms, and nimbly dived into the transparent water, which our eyes could penetrate to a great depth, for the small coins which were thrown to them from board of our ship. These fished-out coins they put into their mouths whilst they swam about, and some of the youngsters must have had a considerable number of them before we hauled up our anchor to resume our voyage. Long knives, stuck in halters and suspended by leather straps from their necks, or fastened around their nude bodies, had to serve them in case of need as a weapon against sharks, which are generally skulking around ships. Occasionally a large fish could be seen swimming in the clear water as plainly as if it had been in the air, and if some one drew their attention to their possible danger, they only laughed and shook their heads, intimating that they had no fear.

Another somewhat alarming incident happened on our further progress, for soon after we had got under way again, a loud and vibrating report was heard, coming from the lower deck. Nobody could mistake it for anything else than an explosion, and most of the passengers turned pale. It was a terrible scare, and only a few succeeded in looking unconcerned. Our anxiety, however, was soon removed when the black cook appeared. Serious as was the occasion only a minute ago, we could not refrain from bursting into a roar of laughter. His eyes and wool were streaming with tomato-juice, and his ears were filled with boiled frijoles. "Good heavens! Pete," the captain cried, "what on earth are you so grave about? Was it a keg o' powder?" "No, sah," the cook replied; "a can o' tomaterses is busted. I put it on de stove to melt the top off, sah, and it done gone busted, sah."

"Oh, good Lord!" the captain said amidst a general outburst of laughter, "don't you know nothing, Pete? A can of water would burst if you put it on the stove, and heat it, didn't you know that? (Despairingly) Oh, you fellows haven't got any judgment! You want somebody a-watching you all the time. No judgment, no judgment! (Turning to the grinning passengers.) It is incredible, but there are no limits to the height of stupidity and careless- ness to which a nigger can attain by constant perseverance and earnest endeavours. I speak from experience. Such a fellow would put a can of powder on the stove to melt the top off." Pete scratched the tomato-juice from his wool, dug the boiled beans from his ears, and shook his head as he disappeared. All the passengers were convulsed with laughter at the ludicrous scene, and even the captain, who was a gray-headed Yankee veteran, and had spent his whole life on the sea, shook from heel to crown, and his good- humoured face beamed with merriment.

To proceed, however. The sun dipped behind the waves as we arrived at Acapulco, where the miners and a good many of the other passengers left our steamer. They were a noisy set, and it was next to impossible to induce them to leave in some sort of order. We were detained at Acapulco for a considerable time, and I stayed on deck till after midnight, but as it was dark I cannot say what the town looks like. Its climate is said to be hot and pestilential. The steamer had been cast from her moorings towards morning, and slowly got into motion again, whilst the shrill screams of her engine-whistle continued at intervals of several minutes.

Steadily making our way towards the glowing South, and passing in due course in full view of the shores of Costa Rica, we finally steamed into the Bay of Panama. We had a fine spell of sunshine during the whole of our voyage, though it was not always a "sea of glass," and occasionally there was quite enough motion to fill one or other of the passengers with a strong desire to be left alone.

BAY OF PANAMA.

CHAPTER XIX.

The City of Panama—Isthmus of Darien—A Stroll along the Coast—A Tropical Sunset—The Panama Railroad—Chagres River Scenery—Aspinwall—Voyage up the Chagres River—Alligators—A Hunting Expedition—In the Swamps of Gorgona—Tropical Vegetation—Look out for Alligators—A Capture—Camping out—Dismal Sounds—An Inquisitive and Distrustful Guide—Uncomfortable Night-Quarters—Our Host and his Lady—The Usual Bill of Fare.

IN the sublime glory of a tropical sunset I took my first view of Panama. The approach to the quaint old city from the sea is marked by numerous islands, many of them of considerable size, the principal one being "Taboga." All vessels of any size are compelled to anchor a great distance out in the Bay, the water being very shallow within three or four miles of the shore, and containing many dangerous reefs and rocks among which the sharks lie in waiting for any hapless victim from a boat that may chance to be capsized. The tide has a rise and fall of twenty to thirty feet, and at high water a small boat can almost enter the city gates, but when the tide is out landing must be made about a mile distant. The city is built directly upon the shore of the Bay of Panama, and the hills and mountains, covered by dense tropical vegetation to their summits, with the towers and ruins of the city at their base, present a beautiful appearance.

Panama is, or was, a walled city. It contains buildings of large size, some of which are stuccoed and painted white or yellow. They are mostly three stories in height, and contain terraces and balconies at each story. I am speaking now only of the principal portion of the town. Many of the streets, especially those in the outskirts, contain long rows of adobe hovels, inhabited by the lower classes or, as they are termed, "natives" (negroes and Indians). The streets are narrow, so much so that the upper stories with their projecting balconies almost meet each other. As a consequence, the thoroughfares are gloomy, the sun never penetrating many of them. The principal structure in the city is the Cathedral, which was built in the early days of the Spanish conquest, and is of large dimensions. Its front is ornamented with large statues, representing Christ and the twelve Apostles, each one standing in a niche. They are much disfigured and nearly hidden from view by the moss and ivy creeping over them. The two steeples, one containing a clock and the other chimes, are also covered with clinging vines, and on the whole the building is imposing, both from its picturesque appearance and ancient architecture, but the machinery of the clock and chimes is corroded and rusty, and the massive walls are falling to pieces. Numerous other churches, all possessing claims to antiquity, are scattered about the town, while remnants of others meet the eye in almost every street. In fact, ruins of religious edifices and Jesuit colleges form a considerable portion of the city, the structures having been torn down or burned during popular outbreaks against the Jesuits.

The old walls surrounding the city possess peculiar interest. Those old conquerors of Pizarro's and Morgan's time were great hewers of stone. Where undisturbed by man, their work remains intact to the present day. Their forts and castles everywhere stand to-day as perfect as though hewn out of the solid rocks themselves on which they are built. The Panama walls on the land side have been pulled down in part, and masses of detached masonry have been rolled down the bank; but to the seaward they rise up, and bid defiance to the angry waves which surge against them. They have withstood the earthquakes and storms of two centuries, and for two centuries the turbulent surf has beaten against them, yet there they stand, apparently growing firmer with age. They are about twenty feet wide, and the ramparts are favourite promenades for all classes of the inhabitants. Walking along them one cannot help wondering whether it is only a legend that the spot where people are now peacefully sauntering once resounded with the tramp of armed men, the clash of weapons, the cries of the victors and the groans of the wounded, that the sturdy walls, now mantled with brambles and overhung with ivy-tod, once were astir with watchful buccaneers, ready to defend the town and property of the conquerors against all comers. At high water the wild breakers toss handfuls of spray high in the air, up to the old walls in amity and greeting, and nothing is more conducive to pensiveness than strolling along, or lying within this half-ruined yet firm and compact enclosure, to watch the waving in the wind of the long grasses on its walls, and listen to the surge of the sea on the shore, but a few steps distant.

The Isthmus of Panama, despite its beauty, is one of the most unhealthy countries in the world, yet the same circumstances which render it unwholesome, make it the gardener's paradise. The gardens in and around the town are brilliant with flowers, and the orchards are a sea of blossoms and overburdened with fruit. Of sweet-smelling flowers there is a great variety altogether unknown in Europe, but the most abundant article of vegetable luxury is the fruit, and the quantity that is consumed must be very large. The town is well supplied, and the best fruit may be bought at the cheapest rate. The sight of the fruit market is very entertaining to a European. The quantity of the vegetable products is astonishing; it is not uncommon to see twenty to thirty cartloads of pine-apples, bananas or melons packed as carelessly as turnips or potatoes in Europe, and other fruits in the same proportion. The different kinds of fruits are almost without number. Mangoes, tamarinds, pine-apples, guava, lemons, grapes, oranges, bananas, melons, cocoa-nuts, jamboos, pomegranates, custard-apples, granadillas, jambolans, nam-nams, limes, mangostan, pomeloes (a near relative of the pompelmoose of the West Indies), persimmons, chestnuts, walnuts, almonds, pecans, pumpkins, and many others which do not merit to be particularly mentioned. There are several Spanish and English newspapers published in the city. One of the latter, the *Panama Star*, bears the well-known motto on its heading—

> "For the cause that lacks assistance,
> For the wrong that needs resistance,
> For the future in the distance,
> And the good that we can do."

A day or two after my arrival at Panama, I took a ride along the coast, scrambling up a steep and rugged path on my wearied mule, and verily the eyes of Morgan, the most renowned of the English buccaneers, could hardly have feasted upon this land of sunbeams and lovely valleys with greater delight than mine. The sea expanded in its full magnificence before my amazed eyes, and the view along the coast and out to land grew in extent and beauty at every step and turn. Had I lived in a dusty, sun-dried town all my life, and one bright beautiful morning had opened my eyes, and for the first time looked down upon a fresh, charming landscape, I could not have been more delighted than I was when the soft splendours of the surrounding coast burst upon my view. Never did I see the earth arrayed in such exquisite beauty, and I wish my pen could do justice to the splendour of the scenery. It is not the grand, the magnificent; there is no great rush and roar of gigantic water-falls as at Niagara, no colossal trees as in the grand primeval forests of California, but the inexpressible wealth and eloquence of flowers, to which all else seems to contribute. In this lovely country one is baffled by a nameless beauty which one cannot analyse or describe. It is the very poetry of nature, beautiful beyond expression—beautiful enough to create a desire to dream away existence in such a place of delight. At every step I took, my ears were greeted with the shrill cry of frightened birds, and now and then finding my way up some steep acclivity, a view would burst upon my eyes so charming that I could but pause and regard it in speechless admiration.

I remained to see the gathering splendours of the departing day. The sun, lighting up the heaven, was setting amid a golden haze, and sank gradually behind the waves. From the horizon to zenith all was within the wondrous influence of its rays. The beautiful light in the sky was brilliant and bright, as bright as brightness can be, and when I turned my eyes from that endless space and looked downwards to this or that side, I saw that below as well as above, beauty and fitness were gloriously visible throughout. The effect on sea and land of the colouring, presented by the reflected hues of the sky, was perfectly magical. The whole valley was flushed by the radiance diffusing itself everywhere. The graceful palms, the huge cacti, the large-leafed shrubs, and the different kinds of trees that grow here in luxuriant profusion, had caught the passing glory, and looked like transformed images of beauty, and the ocean in its gentlest swell stood still with all its rounded billows, as if fixed and motionless for ever.

Looking towards the setting sun, what a flood of beauty filled my view! There seemed to be no boundary along the direction of my vision; it was sight that tired of the vastness, not creation that failed. Clouds of all shapes were visible. Some, heaped and piled up in great irregular masses which took the most fantastic forms, sailed slowly by. They were like floating mountain ranges, soft alps of air; others, higher up, scattered straight above in loose, vapourous flakes were tinged with a delicate pink colour and chased each other across the boundless sapphire arch; whilst low on the horizon a number of fleecy cloudlets, which were aglow with a rich golden saffron light, floated swan-like as on a tranquil sea. Some of these drifted right across the face of the great luminary, who slowly descended in a blaze of golden light to meet his fair image in the Pacific wave. There was a superb blending of colours in that sublime display as if it were a crowning effort of the

Divine spirit. My eyes dwelt enraptured upon the sparkling ocean that danced in the light, stirred now with life by a gentle breeze, and illumined by the sun, which made the water itself seem aflame. This brilliancy of colouring lasted until the fiery ball had disappeared under the horizon, then an ever-deepening crimson took the place of the glowing tints and hues, the shadows grew and multiplied over sea and land, the light faded down the sky, and the gorgeous sunset glory was waning. The evening was mild, warm and full of mystic softness, just such an evening as one would like to pass with some dear friend, mingling past memories with shadowy dreams, and straying along from bygones to futurity. I was loath to leave the shore even when the pageant of the evening had dissolved. The short twilight settled down upon the sea and lent an additional charm to the placid, solemn stillness of the scene. Not a living or moving thing could I see as far as my eyes reached; all was silent and solitary around. I found myself quite alone. Then soft mists began to rise, and night had come. Suddenly the bright moon passed from behind a cloud, and straightway from me to the far-off horizon spread a track of pure and tremulous light over the sea. The moon was almost at its full, and shone brilliantly in a dark azure sky, and its dancing ripples on the waves, striding one after the other, were like molten silver. Long, long I stood and gazed with wondering admiration, very much impressed by the radiance of the night and the tranquillity which reigned supreme. The faint odour of the seaweed floated up from the sands, the pale moon looked down, throwing her silvery light to my feet, and the stars grew in brilliancy, sparkling in their nocturnal vigils like signal fires on the firmament.

I had a long ride back to town, and as I jolted along the path through the sheltering hollow of a palmetto hummock, some horned owls were hooting, and as I approached nearer they took wing and fluttered overhead, sending forth such sounds as seemed scarcely to belong to this world. Night-hawks and night-jars flitted to and fro, uttering their hoarse, melancholy

A HUMMOCK OF PALMETTO TREES.

cries, then remaining motionless for a short time they suddenly swept up with great speed and soared high in the air, describing large circles. They whirled round and round, gradually drawing nearer; turn succeeded turn, but no beat of wings or flutter was perceptible which might have assisted them in their floating and wheeling about. They followed me screaming overhead, and so dismally sounded their cries that I was glad when the click of my animal's hoofs disturbed now and then the gruesome noises of that solitude. Lizards rustled through the grass; the shrill cries of the cicada, the grasshoppers and the frogs made an incessant hum, and here and there lonely fire-flies glinted and glittered among the boughs and on the leaves like solitary bright sparks. The dark crowns of the surrounding trees stood motionless, a delicate transparent mist was spread over the landscape, and only sometimes a soft wind arose which made the leaves of the bushes and trees rustle. Vague dreams filled my drowsy senses, not however to efface from my memory the ethereal glory of the evening nor the hallowed impressions which this grand lesson of nature imparted.

My next move was by railroad to Aspinwall. The day on which I started off was overpoweringly hot, but there was no time to think about that. The railroad winds its way in some parts across unwholesome-looking morasses, and sometimes along the serpentine banks of the river Chagres, then again plunging into the sombre depths of noble palmetto-hummocks, it passes under arbours and grottoes of flowery vines in all the hues of the rainbow, which shield from the hot rays of the tropical sun. The rushing cars, as they flew through this mass of festooned spray, seemed like intruders upon the realms of beauty and peace. That ride on the cars along the gliding river, which is bordered by a fascinating foliage, was a revelation to me; and never shall I forget the pleasing emotion on my mind as I beheld this tropical wilderness expanded before my eyes. Sensations entirely different from those experienced in other countries, almost overwhelmed me. The river was interwoven in a perfect maze of wonderful marshes and lagoons, where weeds throve in rank profusion. Its current was sluggish, and its waters were as yellow as liquorice juice, a drifting froth danced upon its surface, and islands of vegetable matter floated upon its bosom, driven hither and thither by every change of the wind. No signs of cultivation were to be seen, nothing but jungle. Occasionally rich palmetto-hummocks studded the marshes, grey moss from twenty to thirty inches long drooped from the boughs of the cypress-trees, and enormous lily-pads reefed the shores, their great leaves green and wavy, and their blossoms as large as sunflowers.

Dangerous reptiles lie in wait for their prey in these swamps, the margins of which, covered with a dense vegetation ever damp, are inhabited by vast numbers of water-fowl. Various kinds of prowling beasts, stalking the birds, lurk in the thickets, and the grim alligators on the same fell purpose bent are hidden in the water or amongst the high rushes, and many an unwary animal seeking to quench its thirst, is maimed by the blows of their scaly tails. Monkeys are quite numerous, and deer and other game rove about the woods, which are also shady retreats for wild turkeys and the trysting place for green paroquets and red-headed wood-peckers; whilst the flies and mosquitoes also have their "try-sting" place in the surrounding swamps.

The Panama railroad which connects the Atlantic with the Pacific is only forty-seven miles long, yet a great deal of human suffering was associated with its construction. We stopped at the station of Gatun (generally dubbed "Monkey-hill," a rather enigmatical appellation), where there is a large enclosure which is known as the burial place for thousands of white labourers who died of the malarious fever during the building of the road. Funerals to it are even now of frequent occurrence; and skulls and bones are often thrown to the surface. Carts of a very primitive construction are hauled to the common trench, and shoot their gruesome loads into the open pit. For a time after arriving in this country, the foreigner must devote all his energies toward acclimatisation, for no other precautions prevent the attack of the fever, and it is not to be wondered at that the railroad labourers, going to work immediately after landing, fell easy victims to the disease. The number who died has been variously estimated, but it seems to be impossible to arrive at the correct figures, which run up far among thousands. A story is current on the Isthmus which will bear repetition, that each tie, or sleeper, beneath the rails, marks the death of one of the builders. Will the same appalling mortality prevail during the construction of the Panama Canal? Fever, indeed, breeds prodigally, and numbers of persons died since the opening of the railroad who only passed through this pestilential focus.

Aspinwall or Colon stands on a small island called Manzanilla. The highlands of Puerto Bello are on one side of the Bay, whilst on the other several high peaks tower in the distance, their deep blue colour contrasting finely with the tropical verdure of the shore. The swampy nature of the island causes the town to be very unhealthy. The air is close and malarious, and the badness of the water is also supposed to have some share in producing sickness and death to the unacclimatised. The hotel, where I lodged during my short visit, looked dingy, and showed no windows from the outside—nothing but a dilapidated door on the lower story, on the panels of which the boys had evidently often tried their knives. The door swung creaking on its rusty hinges, and the boys delighted in knocking and tapping with its massive knocker and chain, to the great annoyance of the landlady. The whole inside of the house was dark, with an odour of fish and onions permanently in the dingy little dining-room and gloomy hall. I remember there were two or three steps down to it, and old-fashioned small panes of glass in the windows. Several game-cocks were tied by their legs to the door-steps leading to the *patio*, or inner court, where a few creepers clung rotting to the crumbling walls. In its deep recesses, the whole day through, dark skinned men struck matches on the mouldings and lounged and smoked. Great spiders' webs, reflecting all the colours of the rainbow, swung from the ceiling of my bedroom, and to sit upon one of the cane-bottomed chairs—at least it was cane when the bottoms were there—without smashing it, required the dexterity of a juggler. There were more distinct varieties of snoring to be heard at night than in the pigsty of a big farm. The nights that I passed were, in consequence of the swarms of mosquitoes, indescribable. Such a face as I carried to the breakfast-table every morning should have moved the heart of the buxom hostess, but she generally made no other remark than that she "hoped I had slept well."

I proceeded up the Chagres river in a boat. Its banks for nearly the entire distance were completely hidden by a dense and beautiful foliage. On either side were walls of twisted boughs of cocoa-nut trees, cypress, mango, plantain, vines and tropical creepers and streamers of many-coloured blossoms. Large water lilies obstructed in some places our passage, the boat forcing its way slowly through them. In such rough parts the boatmen steered the boat in shore as far as they could, and some of them clambered up to and walked along the bank, and dragged the boat by means of a line, while one or two remained to steer. This was sometimes hard work, for the banks in places were very steep and covered so thickly with bushes and creepers that it was almost impossible to force a path through them. As the day was drawing to its close, not a breath of air was felt, and the heat brought out the alligators. Several times we saw one or two of these ugly creatures swimming along in the river, with their eyes and noses above the water. More than a third of their length was visible, but the height above water was not more than three or four inches. It was the first time that I ever had seen these big saurians in their native waters, and the very idea of seeing them was indeed a treat. I would have liked to try a shot, but I could have had only a small chance of success, as alligators afloat are

TROPICAL SWAMP VEGETATION.

very wary, and a rifle-bullet will glance off unless it strikes a vital part.

The sun was gradually disappearing behind the trees, filling their tops with a glow and warmth that contrasted strangely with their sombre appearance an hour later, when twilight had succeeded the sunset. In a wider sweep beyond, a purple haze, as a subtle drapery, hung over the summits of far-off mountains like a misty gauze, and threw back a mellow light, such as is nowhere else to be seen save in the marvellous glory of a summer's sunset. As we glided along on the tawny water, herons, cranes and flamingoes, spreading their wings wide, rose up in the air, and lent a weirdness to the hour and scene by the strange sound of their wings, their glinting plumage, and their cries as they disappeared in the gloom—

> "And far away in the twilight sky
> We heard them singing a lessening cry—
> Farther and farther till out of sight,
> And we stood alone in the silent night."

I disembarked at Cruces; this place being at the base of the mountains, I made it my head-quarters for some time. One day I started in company of a guide, whom I had hired in Gorgona, on an expedition, the objective point of which was to see alligators. "Come with me," said my grey-headed conductor, "and I'll show you a heap of 'gators and snakes." So we went. My friend carried a shot-gun, which was a formidable weapon, loading in the breech, and resembling a double-barrelled howitzer. I was equipped with my rifle. The morning was bright, the sky blue and cloudless, and the atmosphere full of that delicious spirit which nature seems to breathe in these tropical latitudes. After a march of several miles we crawled into a sea of marshes, the lily-pads and smart-weed, with roots many feet long, clogging the way. We forced a passage into the swaying mass, trying to strike across the marsh and save several miles of travel. But it took us hours to get through, for obstacles were numerous and our progress therefore slow. Great soggy bunches of slippery moss struggled in the depth ; the ground was covered with dead trees, but the tropical suckers and vines were so luxuriant that the trees were hidden. We kept a bright look-out for alligators, but saw none. Marsh hens clucked in the rushes, the plaintive cry of the snipe floated in the air, and a number of white cranes, with their heads under their wings, were standing on one foot among the reeds that closed around us. Once we came upon a flock of wild ducks so suddenly that they had no time to take wing, so they dived instead, and thus got out of the way. We frightened a great many birds with most brilliant plumage out of their reedy home, which flew screeching in all directions at our approach, and large flocks of white curlew sailed off in the blue sky like pieces of white paper. Monkeys in the trees chattered defiance at our encroachment upon their lawful and hereditary domains, and at times dozens of butterflies fluttered around.

At 3 P.M. we had travelled about fifteen miles. The weather was very hot, and the exertion, as may be supposed, made me perspire. As far as the eye could reach nothing was to be seen but cane-swamps, which stretched north, south, east, and west; they were many miles wide, and scarcely divided from the horizon by a rim of pines and palmettoes. It was hard to give it up without even seeing an alligator; prudence, however, prevailed. I thought we ought to retrace our steps, as I was anxious for dinner. A council was held, I reasoned that we should probably suffer if night overtook us in the swamp; moreover, that starvation stared us in the face unless we killed something within the next few hours, but my companion declared that if it took another day to work our way up, we should make the attempt. He had been up as far as we could go only a few weeks before, and therefore knew what he was talking about. He strengthened his argument by adding that alligators are thereabouts as sure as the "wringing of his nose brings forth blood." This last settled the question. After another hour's hard work of plodding and struggling we came to a small piece of sluggish water, surrounded by tall canes and lilies, and partly covered with rushes from fifteen to twenty feet high. The moss-dripping boughs of the funereal cypress overhung its waters, and large beds of smart-weed and rank vegetation stretched across it. We had as much as we could do to breast the rushes and canes, but we entered into them right gallantly, and waded into the black mud. My companion was ahead with his blunderbuss, and suddenly turning round he gave me a sign to stop. The cause was soon apparent in the presence of a great water-snake which lay coiled in the rushes. He peppered at the old fellow and filled him with shot, and shortly afterwards we saw underneath a cypress our first alligator, about six feet long. A bullet was sent after him, but the ball glanced from his back, and the wary fellow paddled for the water. Another monster was soon sighted, and almost at the same moment there was a shout from my man to look out. Look out I did, and what a sight was presented! Several of the armoured reptiles were lying on the bank, and some we could hear were breaking down the canes and rushes. We opened a murderous fire at once, but such a waste of powder and lead I never saw; bullets whistled in every direction, my rifle and my companion's howitzer dealt destruction truly, but it was to the surrounding rushes and trees. My companion could not use his blunderbuss much before, and seemed eager to show that he was in a position to use it now, and to some purpose, for its terrible cracking was making the woods ring. Several alligators were saluted, but the bullets glanced from their backs without doing them the slightest injury; they shed the shots as a duck sheds water.

A big monster was lying lazily on the edge of the marsh. Nothing daunted at our approach, he did nôt even wink until we sprinkled his hide with bullets. Then he turned to crawl from the bank into the water, while his little eyes gleamed with a baleful light. There was little fascination about these orbs, and no mistaking the malignant intentions of their owner. One ball at least took effect, for he slothed around for a few moments and made an effort to work himself down through a mass of weeds. We counted one, two, three, and fired both together. That double discharge had hit again, there was no doubt about it. I heard a distinct groan as the scaly monster received his death wound. With eyes flashing like balls of fire, he threw up his claws, lashed furiously with his tail, and clutched the tall reeds as if trying to drag himself into the water. But the effort was too much; he was fast becoming exhausted by the loss of blood. I felt greatly relieved to see him topple over and take to flopping and thrashing around on the ground. His struggles gradually diminished, and at last he lay motionless, his fearful jaws open, and his yellowish belly turned up to the sun. He was more than eleven feet long, and we found as we skinned him that one of the bullets had penetrated the abdomen, and another the region of the heart. Whilst my companion occupied himself in dissecting the captured animal, in order to cut some steaks from his body to serve us for supper, he found several half-digested ducks in his stomach. Meanwhile I tried to make a hole in a redheaded turkey-buzzard, but he skinned his eye at the marksman, and winged his way through the air. My friend, like a true follower of Nimrod, pursued his murderous vocation with wonderful success, for a twelve-inch lizard was his next victim. Then I knocked an eye out of a large bird; its head drooped, but before we could approach, it was gone. It had either been lost in the dense growth which covered the water with a network of rushes and parasitical plants, or it was devoured by an alligator. Five or six more of these beasts we saw in the distance, but they made for the swamp, and we could hear them hopping into it, and raising a violent splashing, plunging and pounding of the water, in the midst of which they disappeared as we passed by. Many singular birds and reptiles were to be seen, hundreds of white and blue cranes stalked over the marshes or winged their way through the air, and once, when we broke through the cane, a thousand jack-daws flooded into the sky, almost deafening us with their complaints.

A PANAMA SWAMP.

After a long search for an outlet we came at last to a clearing, and as it was getting pretty late, and the shadows were fast deepening, we prepared at once for camping. The preparation of our supper did not cost much trouble. The fire was built, the camp-kettle unpacked, and, as the sun went down and lit up with golden radiance the trunks of the surrounding trees, we sat down to supper. The meat of the alligator-steaks was white as chicken, and we could have eaten it under the supposition that it was fish; but there was something wrong about it—it was very tough, and we concluded the alligator must have been an aged individual. Afterwards we used the fat for greasing our soaked boots.

The broad moon rose undimmed in the sky, and the atmosphere was so clear that the stars sparkled like diamonds. A gentle breeze was blowing, making the tall, yellow reeds dance in the moonlight, while the palmetto trees stood around us like a row of sentinels, their bark glimmering pale and ghostly in the moonlight. We were a considerable distance from the swamps, and deep silence reigned through the forest. The stillness seemed unnatural. Nothing was heard but the occasional faint chug-chug-chug cry of the cranes and herons in the reeds and the soughing of the wind in the trees. In the distance we could see the lagoon, and the moon standing up from the clear sky like a disc of pure silver. Falling stars shot from the zenith, and in the smooth, unrippled surface of the lagoon they were vividly reflected. A thin trail of smoke from our fire rose to the soft mellow sky, and seated on a log, with my eyes fixed on the place where the embers of the fire were glowing, I enjoyed to the fullest extent the cool evening air, fragrant from the forest, thinking over the events of the day, and listening at intervals to the quaint prattle of my companion, resting near me. Although his limbs rested, his tongue kept going, talking and questioning me. Sleep weighed down my eyelids before he ceased talking, and we both resigned ourselves to slumber in order to recruit our strength for to-morrow's march before us. We had been lying down perhaps a couple of hours when I awoke. I was roused by some slight noises as if of creeping bodies, or the snapping of small twigs, but I could distinguish nothing in the gloominess around. The dying embers of our fire cast a red glare on the neighbouring vegetation, causing the darkness beyond to appear all the more profound, and to throw out in greater distinctness the little insect lights which glittered like sparks. The scream of some animal near by startled me. I bounded at once to my feet and pricked up my ears to the suspicious noise. I was greatly alarmed, and even the tips of my hair seemed to have ears as I listened with a beating heart and in agonized suspense, for I thought that some grim alligator was croaking near by. Most dismal and unearthly sounds were to be heard on all sides, which became instantly productive of all sorts of conjectures. The plants and trees all appeared imbued with spirit and to speak a language of their own, and even the shadows seemed to move about as if endowed with life. The strange sounds appeared to come from every point of the compass—first in front, then in the rear, next on the right, and again on the left. Now it was like the silvery tinkle of a little bell, or a plaintive voice calling in the distance; then a rustling noise, and next a sob from the interior of the forest. Then again a sudden breath of wind would cause the tall trees to tremble, and make our fire blaze up more brightly. I listened and waited, full of that kind of nervous suspense which accompanies the expectation of something to come, one knows not what. I could not close my eyes again; I saw in the darkness all kinds of strange, gaunt shapes creeping about, with hollow eyes and wide mouths all agape, and monsters with a baleful, stern presence seemed everywhere. At last the suspense became too tantalising for enduring alone, so I tried to awake my sleeping companion, but calling him up was impossible; he would not move. The fearful sounds seemed to be only sweet lullabies to his slumber. With joyful heart, indeed, did I welcome the first faint rays of the returning daylight, and after a frugal breakfast we again got on our legs, and continued forcing our way through the forest for about an hour, when we observed smoke in the distance rising up between the trees. As we had no doubt that somebody was in the vicinity of the fire or smoke, we turned immediately towards it, but when we came to the place it was deserted. We found the fire still burning, and several branches of surrounding trees newly broken down; we also noticed other indications that some one had recently been camping upon the spot. After some vain regrets as to our disappointment, we proceeded on our march through the magnificent woods of palmettoes, and through thickets where wild vines grew luxuriantly. How delicious was the sunlight glinting through the forest glades! How delicate the green mosses clothing the trunks of fallen trees!

At this juncture we stopped, and I proceeded to unpack my portfolio to make a sketch. Such a mysterious array of artist-traps my companion's wondering eyes had never beheld. He controlled, however, his curiosity until the tin box containing the painting materials was produced, when he gave a prolonged whistle and forthwith proceeded to make all sorts of inquiries.

"You ain't a show, be ye?" asked the old man. Visions of travelling quacks and mountebanks danced probably before his imagination as he put this question. I answered in the negative.

"If it ain't a show, it's a butterfly-hunter, I reckon," he murmured to himself, viewing my proceedings with awe. After a while came another question—

"Are ye rock or plant huntin'?"

Assuring him that I was not looking for plants or minerals or butterflies, and before I had time to explain and give him the desired information, I was assailed with quite a volley of questions.

"Whar be ye from? What mout be your name? What do ye want hyar?" &c.

I did not answer at once, but soon it became evident to me that unless I stopped him to explain, he would smother me with his wild guesses. With, I trust, commendable patience, I at last answered the inquiries of his heated imagination, and proceeded in comparative peace to hurry through with my sketch. My explanation pleased him mightily, he shouted with merriment at the idea of my strange employment. In return I was amused exceedingly by his description of a naturalist, with whom he had roamed through the forests a few years ago, collecting butterflies and insects. After I had finished my sketch I walked to a pool near by, the water of which seemed sweet and clear like crystal, and I stooped down to take a drink. "Stranger, wait a minnit," said my companion, pulling from his pocket at the same time a flask of spirits and inviting me to drink. I poured some of the blistering fluid into my calabash-cup, mixed it with water, and drank it. He resumed his inquiries again, and finished with the somewhat more pointed and less complimentary question: "Reckon ye don't want to take my flask?" By dint of much parleying I demonstrated that I meant no harm. "A man wants to keep his eyes open in these regions; ye can't always tell!"

The remark was pardonable, for certainly there was little gentility in my appearance. With a flabby slouch hat, dirty boots, trousers bedraggled with mud, and carrying mysterious packages of various sizes along with a roll of blankets, I could not have been a common traveller in his mind. However, I assured him that I would do him no harm, and he asked me no more questions, but seemed to regard me as a strange being.

Resuming our walk through the forest, after several hours' hard clambering over hidden rocks and fallen trees, we gained once more the open country, an orange grove being sighted about a mile from us in straight line. Beyond a marsh we observed several men, and as it was more than a day since we had seen a human being, and we were nearly out of provisions, having shot nothing fit to eat, we steered at once towards the orange-mound. A wretched little cabin soon hove in sight.

A knock-kneed darkey stood in front with his hands in his pockets, and a naked little boy gazed at us in astonishment. We hailed the darkey and he piloted us to his cabin. Its occupants had made a feeble attempt to start an orange-grove, but the trees looked sickly and showed a lack of attention. The man, whose face was as black as ink, and whose teeth stood out from his mouth like a row of grave-stones, offered us his flask, out of which my companion took a very hearty draught. Soon a fish and a wild duck lay in a saucepan over the fire; but the duck was rank, and I took but one mouthful. The fish, however, was good, and I took possession of it, leaving my friend to wash down the duck with spirits.

During our dinner I heard a very remarkable alligator story —one of those tales of ridiculous superstition and ignorance which are characteristic of the negroes and Indians thereabouts. The squaw of our host related that her father when he was dying informed her that one of his nearest relatives was an alligator, and in pursuance of her father's instructions and command she often went to the river, and standing upon the bank, called out his name, upon which an alligator always came to her out of the water, and ate from her hands the meat which she had brought. She described the reptile as much handsomer, and not like other alligators, but that his body was spotted, and his nose red.

"Yes, sah," added our host, " there are such critters; they are not like udder or'nary alligators; dey have a large tongue dat fills their mouths, an' are kinder whinin' and wheezin', jest like an ole woman."

"And is your alligator uncle still living?" I asked of the old woman.

"Now, hiar," fell in the old man. "You think dat she is falsifying undoubtedly."

"Oh, no! I beg your pardon, by no means," I said.

"It is more'n forty years ago," continued the squaw—"long afore your time dat was, sah—an' one day the alligator neber came, and I waited all the next day, but he neber come back again, an' nobody eber seed him again."

"Is that the truth you told me?" I asked.

"Not'in' but the trufe, sah," she answered. "I would not tell you a lie, sah."

"I am sure of that," I remarked, "and as it is so very seldom we meet with so much modesty along with so much zeal for truth, when met, it is right encouragement should be forthcoming;" and herewith I offered them three plugs of tobacco for the *true* story, one for the old man, and two for the old lady. They were very much pleased, and I bought some venison for our supper before we parted. The old master wanted me afterwards to buy some deer and otter skins as well, but we did not drive a bargain.

After a weary march of several hours, we approached, towards evening, the village of Buena Vista, and asked a brown fellow, who lay in the long grass near his hut, for shelter; but he scarcely lifted his head to look at the wayfarers, and not till after an eloquent address of my guide, the meaning of which hardly penetrated his skull, the fellow entered into more friendly relations with us, and took us to his hut. Quite a number of mules that were browsing near by brayed their welcome to us in their best and most approved style. We found the accommodation of the cabin to consist of a single apartment, whose staple commodity was dirt, and which could only be entered through a filthy sty. Upon a plank sat a stolid squaw in a dirty calico-frock, consuming tobacco enough to unsettle the nerves of a rhinoceros, and nursing a little papoose, who greeted me with an infantile whoop. The squaw treated us with perfect indifference as we entered, and indeed seemed to be quite deaf to my affable greetings; however, that supreme wisdom that teaches the little boy to wipe his nose on his shirt sleeve had fitted her out with a pair of ears that counteracted her deafness, so that she could hear—as I afterwards had occasion to notice—as readily as any other person.

Mine host was a burly, reticent fellow, but after I had inquired about his better half, be became more communicative, and a conversation began somewhat in this fashion :—

Host—" Umph, how ? "

Guest—" How ? Very tired. Do you know the country around ? How long have you lived here ? "

Host—." Umph, three years."

Guest—" Do you like the place ? "

Host—" Yas—umph—not 'xactly."

Guest—" Have you married into the tribe ? "

Host—" Umph, not partic'larly ; I jes stay hiar. When a feller likes a squaw he jes' gives her ole man a mule, or sometimes a pig an' some money, an' takes de gal. Dey live together as long as dey like, an' then trade off wif somebody else."

The tone in which he said the last words struck me as if this monster would have liked me to drive a bargain with him. Meanwhile my soul yearned for an unknown something which broiled in a large pot on the open fire. At last supper came. It consisted of the usual fare—fat pork, corn-bread and coffee. My bed that night was of plank, and through the whole night I had a dreamy consciousness of shivering. When daylight appeared I noticed the absence of a log in the cabin-wall beside me—a generous style of ventilation for which I was not adequately grateful ; besides, my couch of straw was deluged with rain, and preoccupied by vermin. The cabin was filled in the morning with myriads of healthy-looking flies, which refused to move, no matter how persistently they were urged to do so. They apparently came to flavour the soup and to improve the coffee. Our quarters were far from comfortable, and altogether the whole village looked as if an earthquake had recently been fooling around its vicinity.

Early in the morning we indulged in a repetition of the evening bill of fare, whilst the squaw began a vigorous scrutiny of the child's head, which, judging from her frequent ejaculations, was not altogether barren of results. It so disgusted me that I turned almost sick, for which I was heartily laughed at by my companion. I set the case down as an additional evidence of the filthiness of the people, which is generally regarded as their characteristic trait, and departed with unspoken maledictions upon our host. Dead tired, covered with mud, and craving for rest, we got back without mishap to Cruces, having been absent three days.

CHAPTER XX.

On the Way to Mount Ancon—The Natives and their Homes—A Weary Night—Birds and Insects—The Land and the People—Camping out—Mosquitoes and other Nuisances—Deadliness of the Climate—The Panama Fever.

SHORTLY after our return from the excursion, the description of which fills the preceding pages, I set off early one morning with my man—the venerable boy, who had again undertaken to be my guide—to Ancon. We passed out of Cruces among all the idle people that were assembled there watching our departure, and soon after leaving, the path led through a very rough piece of country. We had to ride through a rocky gorge which was in some places scarcely more than wide enough for our mules to squeeze through in single file. It seemed to have been the bed of a brook which during the rainy season threaded this pass, but at the present time its course was dry. There were deep foot-holes at regular distances, which appeared to have been worn out by the hoofs of passing animals. It was a wearisome, trippling hobble. My mule, backing and rearing, declined occasionally to proceed, and I had to thwack him until he made a brave struggle to behave properly. At times, however, he stopped suddenly, and no amount of whacking and prodding would make him move from the spot. Thereupon my guide screwed his thin scraggy tail till the miserable beast started again, giving forth sounds like those of a wheezy bagpipe in the last agony. To be able fully to appreciate a mule, one should listen to his voice, for one can never really know whether he likes a mule or not until he has heard him bray. Coming out of the narrow gorge, we rode over a stretch of low and swampy country. The ground was broken with bogs and peaty pools, the margins of which were full of water-lilies, and the clear spaces of the water reflected the distant mountains like mirrors. Then we made a steep ascent over a lofty knoll, which was crowned with tall trees. The ascent became very tedious and fatiguing, for the path ran zig-zag along the edge of a rocky bank, and we had to dodge with our heads the overhanging boughs; but passing over this, the highest point of our route, we had a beautiful view. High on the horizon lay a wavy line of hills, sharply outlined in the strong glare of the sunlight; their delicate blue colour springing so suddenly upon our vision against the rich and deep tints of the surrounding trees, that I was delighted with the effect.

Descending again into the valley we passed through several villages, snugly nestled amid orange and cocoa-nut trees, and the dusky inhabitants, most of them attired in paradisiacal simplicity, gazed agape with open-eyed astonishment, and their dogs ran out of the huts snarling and barking at us as we passed by. Every mixture of Spanish, negro and Indian, every shade of complexion, was represented, and a good deal of said complexions was visible on account of the conspicuous scarcity of clothes. Men and women were lounging about the places in happy idleness, some mainly occupied in examining their rags, looking for—well, never mind what; others in minding the innumerable pigs; whilst troops of infants in all the guileless indecency of childhood were playing about the cabins. The dwellings, with few exceptions, were the wretchedest hovels of sticks and grass. Some of them were mere sheds without walls, open to wind and rain; only a roof of matting and grass supported on a few poles stuck in the ground. The archi-

THE NATIVES AND THEIR HOMES: A PANAMA VILLAGE.

tecture of the others of these repulsive dens was scarcely less primitive. They were conical in shape, and in their rugged, grass-thatched roofs, inclining down to the ground, were little holes which served as chimney, window and door in one. These huts were foul as pigsties, and not as good as average chicken-coops, yet a good many people of both sexes, besides a great number of pigs, dogs and fowls, were within or around them. The lanes along which we had to pass were a depository of a heterogeneous mass of rubbish and refuse, and everywhere dilapidation, poverty and pestilential squalor was visible, obtruding themselves in the most offensive way. The water in a neighbouring ditch was covered with a green scum, bearing on its surface dead cats and dogs, surrounded with weeds like eggs in a dish of spinach. This abominable cesspool exhaled in the hot weather a poisonous stench, yet we saw women and children draw the turbid liquid from it in bowls and jugs, which the natives make out of the fruit-shells of the calabash trees. At the intersection of two roads we asked of an old man the way to Ancon. There was no answer. "Which is the way to Ancon?" repeated my companion in Spanish. The taciturn man neither stirred nor opened his mouth. A third time the question was asked; the old man was dumb again, but pointing with his thumb to one side he thus answered our question. That was all the information we could elicit from him.

At last the summit of Mount Ancon, whose southern base is laved by the waves of the Pacific Ocean, hove in sight on our right hand. On the left we could see plainly the "Cerro de los Buccaneros" (hill of the buccaneers), from the summit of which the terrible Morgan first looked upon Panama in the year 1670. Bold men, indeed, were these old buccaneers, and the romance, adventure and daring to be found in the records of their exploits on sea and land are scarcely surpassed in history. In their frail, wooden ships they dared to steer for continents which they only could guess of, and struggled against tempests, and hazarded their lives on seas where fable was their only chart.

The view from the summit of the hill over the broad, rich valley was beautiful. The eternal summer of this land paints earth in all its choicest colouring. There lay outspread, like the longed-for land of promise, the *tierra calliente*, intersected by rivers and swamps rippling in the sunshine, and far in the distance—as far as eye could reach to right and left—stood a long line of uplifted mountains. Turning eastward I saw my old friend, the Chagres river, winding along dark forests, and displaying here and there its bright gleaming water; northward and southward ravines, and beyond them uncounted mountains which the very sky seemed tenderly to bend over and kiss. On the eastern horizon lay a great bank of hazy, purple-grey clouds, and the broad valley was dotted over with the sombre shadow of forests, above which here and there a few tall, graceful cocoa-palms waved their feathery crowns, enhancing by contrast the picturesque beauty of the scene. The intense colouring of the rich foliage of the trees round us, through the openings of which a sky of the most brilliant blue was visible, was perfectly bewildering; and the trees themselves formed beautiful groups, creating a foreground on which my eyes—hungry for sketches—lingered with delight. Everywhere was the wonted display of flowers, whose gorgeous hues, combined with the overabundant greenery, formed a very feast of colour. The ground was covered thickly with them, and even amongst the trees and bushes a fresh growth of plants and herbs flourished in luxuriance.

Evening drew on; the sun, touching with an indefinably rich carmine glow the rank herbage around, was sinking low on the western horizon. Dusk settled swiftly down upon the hills. The evenings of this land have but little twilight; the sun, like a globe of fire, seems to drop from out the sky behind the earth, and night rushes up. The grasshoppers sang merrily round us as we took up our quarters for the night under the shelter of a rock, which was covered with a dense growth of delicate plants, and overhung with lace-like lianas and large creepers. Some dry branches were collected, and soon we had a good fire; but nevertheless the creatures of darkness immediately began to appear, and after the glorious enjoyment of the day I felt a mortifying kind of contrast. I was nearly devoured alive by insects. Clouds on clouds of mosquitoes swarmed down and furiously attacked me with their envenomed stings. They seemed to come from all quarters of the heavens to make a prey of me, for my companion did not suffer half as much from them. I struggled in vain, strove to knock them down, smacked my face with frantic violence—on they came in myriads, and maddened me almost to despair. Hot as the night, and almost unendurable as the stifling sultriness of the atmosphere was, I stretched my weary legs as near as possible to the blazing fire in the hope of repelling these bloodthirsty tormentors; but all was to no purpose, for they followed me into the smoke, and, inflicting their stings with incessant pertinacity, made even this place quite untenable. Another scarcely less painful bother were the ants. The moment I lay down on the plantain leaves and grass with which we covered the ground, thousands of these pests swarmed from innumerable holes, and tormented me in an equal if not a greater degree than the mosquitoes. Legions of them crawled over me and took possession of my neck, hands, and every assailable part of my body. The tickling, itching, and prickling sensation was more intolerable than pain. The heat and the thousands of active creatures on my body rendered the night extremely uncomfortable, and effectually banished sleep. If ever an unfortunate mortal underwent slow torture, I did that night.

In the early morning, as soon as the first streak of dawn was visible in the eastern sky, the early risers among the birds and insects sounded their clear notes, and began to chirp and scream, and whistle their morning song. The winged inhabitants of the air seem to awaken to active life in those latitudes as suddenly as day succeeds the night, and night the day. First a few faint notes are heard, then comes a low twittering—a mere suggestion of a song—then gradually the tone increases in volume, stronger and stronger, until it bursts forth in all its rich plenitude. As the sun rises and the sky becomes decked in purple the call of thousands of birds, and the hum of millions of insects, combine to make a melodious din; and all the bright day long, with the exception of an hour or two at noon, there is a radiant quiver of sound and airy life, the buzz of countless flies and beetles, and a rush and whiz of their wings. Birds and insects keep on with their chirruping and carolling, and the ground, too, is literally swarming with inhabitants. Bumble-bees with a hum come through the world of grass; ear-wigs scuttle up and down with pitchforks at their tails; beetles stagger about with heavy loads; ladybirds come and "fly away home," and all around is busy and replete with life. The deep-sounding whoops of cranes, the clang of herons, and boom of bitterns, the gobbles of wild turkeys, the chattering of green paroquets and many others of the woodpecker tribe, and the voices of ivory-bills, red-birds, and mocking-birds fill the marshes and woods with music; whilst among the boughs of the trees troops of monkeys pursue their merry sport, and mingle their screams with the various notes of the birds. What a noisy set they are! At midday, however, everything becomes silent and motionless for a short time, all animation seems suspended beneath the ardour of the solar rays. It is the hour of silence and rest. The water-fowl are concealed among the sedges, the wild rabbit and timid doe slumber under the shrubs. Only the grasshoppers chirp faintly amongst the grass, and now and then the far-away notes of a bird, invisible in the trees, can be heard. Those must be halcyon days for all the different kinds of animals, and I should say that they have a good time of it thereabouts.

Thus for several weeks I roamed at large, whistled away dull care, and "stumped it" at the rate of a few miles every day. Bohió, Obisbo, San Pablo, Emperador, Paraiso, Barbacoas, Rio Grande, Matachin, Gorgona, Gatun, Cruces, and other places I visited in turn, and when night set in I often slept under "heaven's starry canopy" in preference to the miserable accommodation of the dirty hovels of the natives, with their unfailing accompaniment of cockroaches and bugs. I can hardly express my disgust with which I often chased these offensive insects, creeping in gathering shoals from every corner of the wretched huts. Besides this, I hated to sleep in these human kennels for some other reasons. The air in them was never free from a nauseous stench, for everywhere the lanes and thoroughfares of the villages were littered with garbage, and bones of animals lay scattered about, picked clean by the flocks of vultures and turkey-buzzards, which alone performed the office of scavengers. But the scenery of the country when once seen can scarcely be forgotten. The strongest effort of imagination cannot picture anything so heavenly, and as for trying to describe it—that would be a vain attempt; the brush of a painter can alone convey to those who never have beheld it an apprehension of its beauty. Yet when I state that the hills as well as the valleys are covered with a sheet of blossoms, a faint idea may perhaps be formed of its loveliness and fragrance; but when I aver in contrast that, on entering a hut or speaking with some of the inhabitants, I almost regretted that I had an organ of smell, I give no idea of the filthiness of the villages and the slovenly character of the people who occupy them. If cleanliness be next to godliness, as the saying goes, then are they the least divine of human creatures. The population of their scanty garments is beyond census, and all the different kinds of the active nocturnal parasites seem to attain to a condition of complete, material well-being among them. These people possess other remarkable characteristics. The indolence which seems to control everybody is incredible; it matches their disgusting filthiness. They seem to have a constitutional incapacity for any kind of effort, and it cannot but be expected that there are no bounds to their ignorance. They are as ignorant as the cattle which they tend, and one cannot have any conception of their credulity, and the silly absurdities which they believe. There are still people to be found who believe that there are families among them which are related to alligators, and that women are sometimes delivered of young alligators instead of children. Such absurd and extravagant notions verify the assertion that they are as ignorant and credulous as they are dirty and lazy.

Their inordinate love of gambling is also remarkable. All these qualifications, indeed, go hand in hand in this country. Laziness constitutes a powerful incentive to the practice of gambling, and these people, apparently not knowing what else to do with their time, gamble one way or another. They gamble with dice, with cards, or even with fruit-stones, as I had occasion to observe. Once I chanced to look into one of the huts, and was surprised to find at least half a dozen women and men squatting on the earth floor busily engaged in this active pastime. My sudden appearance on the scene did not discountenance and restrain them at all, for they continued gambling without putting themselves to much trouble about answering my request. They are true lotus-eaters, these natives, but they need not sail away to distant isles to eat and dream. Their country is productive beyond all example, and nature supplies all their wants in abundance. The soil on which they live yields its treasures without compelling them to hard labour, and their principal food—frijoles, chillis, tamales, and some other vegetables, beside fruit—costs them very little trouble. They have scarcely more to do than to stoop and pick them up, or climb and shake a tree. This makes them lazy, and they pass their time, when not asleep, in gambling and cock-fighting. Their recreations number but these; they don't seem to know of any others. Cock-fights are a favourite amusement, and nearly every hut has a game-cock tied by one leg to the front of the cabin by means of a long cord, while in many cases alongside of the rooster, and tied in the same manner, is a pig or a child—sometimes both.

Prolific nature has blessed their women with innumerable dusky babies. I had seen nothing like it before. Families of eight, ten, and more, seem by no means uncommon. Children play about in swarms; indeed, the most conspicuous objects in the villages, that meet the eye of the traveller, are the number of dirty black urchins piled in heaps in every corner about the huts, who appear to vie with the buzzards in picking up what they can find in the filth and dust of the place. I might continue *ad infinitum* to enumerate the unpleasant qualities of these peculiar people, but I refrain.

Of the food eaten by the natives, the greater part is vegetable, as domesticated animals, with the exception of hogs, are by no means plentiful. Flesh-pots often haunted my dreams, but seldom my repasts; bananas, oranges, saltless frijoles, and sometimes fat bacon, had to be washed down with thick, black coffee. These hardships and privations, however, held but a small place in my mind. The grandeur of the views from the summits of the mountains, and the picturesque bits of scenery in the valleys, recurred to me rather than the hideous repasts, or the weary marches and the toilsome climbing. I thought oftenest of the amusing incidents; the comical side of the picture was more frequently looked at than the dismal or disagreeable one. Each time I traversed some new scenes, new wonders revealed themselves. Wild forests, lofty flower-covered hills, rich valleys, meandering streams, offered a never-ending and incessantly changing variety of landscapes. When I camped in the open air during my adventurous tramp I spread some plantain or mango-leaves upon the ground, my blankets served me for covering, and my paint-box for a pillow. Thus I lay down and watched the monkeys' funny somersaults. Their acrobatic performances of hanging down by their long tails and swinging from the boughs of the trees, which drooped under the weight of their burdens, were sometimes very ludicrous to look at. What a bliss to lie on such a couch of moss and gaze through the green roof above! I was stared at and chattered at by monkeys and paroquets, but unfortunately this fun was rather too often alloyed with unpleasant sensations, and the greatest drawback to my enjoyment of sleep were the biting insects and snakes. The country is infested with an endless variety of noisome vermin, and abounds in snakes, which swarm through the bushes during the hot nights. Under my very blanket one evening I caught a large hairy tarantula. Being disturbed in its comfortable *siesta*, the villainous-looking brute, with a devilish wriggle, seemed ready to venture offensive war. Thereupon I was a wrathful man, and thrust a piece of wire through its loathsome body; but though pinned to the ground, I found it the next morning still alive and kicking. Worst of all these nuisances, however, were the mosquitoes and ants. Their sociability was sometimes—to say the least—very disagreeable. Mosquitoes and ants are generally found associated in partnership, and such multitudes of them collected in some localities at night that, in order to escape their attacks, I was often compelled to light fires and envelop myself in dense smoke. But even by raising clouds of smoke there was little protection to be found, and sleep was sometimes impossible. Thousands upon thousands of these bloodsuckers came, so that sometimes I had to rise in despair, and, overpowered as I was by fatigue and sleepiness, had to walk about during the remaining hours of the night, flourishing branches and leaves for fear that my bleaching bones would alone remain to indicate my fate. The omnipresent insect-life is at first rather startling to a new comer. The hum of unseen insects is everywhere heard, even at night; but one's prejudice against the non-biting species soon dies out. One is soon indifferent to cockroaches and wood-lice running distractedly over one's body; they after a time become familiar and lose their effect upon the mind, and one reserves his active enmity for the troublesome mosquitoes and ants.

As soon as evening draws on, and the sun sinks below the horizon, the numerous flies disappear, mosquitoes take their place, and the savage cries and screams of some otherwise harmless animals disturb the stillness and make night hideous. One can hear them nightly howl and croak. Presently we hear the owls hooting, and the night-jars (*Caprimulgus vociferus*) wheeling about make a screeching noise. The horned owls often gave me a fright when weirdly and ghostlike they swept down and circled around my fire, flapping with their wings and uttering nocturnal solos, which often very strikingly resembled the wailing or groaning of some wretch being throttled. The sound of their cries is very harsh and piercing, and has the nearest earthly resemblance to the howling of the detested coyote that shrills at night. The frogs, squatted on the margin of the marshes, croak the music they like best; and the grasshoppers, and crickets too, cannot go to rest without their grinding chirrup; especially the pale-green *Plataphyllum concavum*, by means of the membranes of its wingsheaths, makes a peculiar sound which floats unceasingly through the air; but, to be truthful and just, even the hideous noises were sweet in my ears when compared to the tormenting stings of the impudent mosquitoes and ants.

The luxuriance of the vegetation and the profusion of nature is lavish beyond imagination. Everything appears to grow to the utmost extent and ripeness. Plants which in Europe are reared at great expense in hot-houses, and obtain under the best care but a puny and uncharacteristic form, flourish around in all the vigour and exuberance of their perfect being. What a gorgeous blending of all that is beautiful and picturesque in nature is to be found there! Truly a paradise on earth is the Isthmus of Panama, everything fascinatingly and exquisitely beautiful! everything so perfectly enchanting that one could worship at this shrine of loveliness, but for the deadliness of the climate, where it is almost impossible for a foreigner to live, so fatal are the swamp-fevers. The poisonous vapours emanating from the rank and decaying vegetation are the cause of it. Yet, in spite of this, there are homes there where the natives love, and sorrow, and rejoice, and where children are born and old people die. Human nature is, after all, pretty much the same all over the world, wherever one finds it, and life repeats the same old story in the malarious swamps of Panama, and runs in much the same grooves as anywhere else.

I tasted of almost every kind of native fruit; some of it is very curious to look at, and some of it is very good to the palate. The grape-fruit has the flavour and taste of an orange, and is a rich and juicy fruit for a hot day, but the skin and pulp must be avoided. Guavas and granadillas are fragrant and luscious. The sappadillo is a small round fruit, the colour of a potato on the outside, and as sweet as honey inside. Custard-apples are covered with a rough skin, but their inside is a mass of sweet custard almost too rich in taste. Mangoes are delicious; lemons are enormous in size and very fine, so are limes and tamarinds. But the fruits I liked best were those to which I had been accustomed—oranges, pine-apples, and bananas, although the taste of a pine-apple ripened in its native soil and under its native sun was a joy before unknown to me. Fed upon that delicate food, my passion for it grew, but, alas! it was the fatal lure which led me into a wretched state of misery, for in due course the fever came and rattled with my bones as if a funeral had been going on inside of me. Suffering a pain in my head, fit to crack it—worlds, to say nothing of oranges and pine-apples, would not have induced me to stretch forth my hands for them. Vain now were all their fascinations, and with the spirit of a hero I advanced upon my stock of quinine, and courageously swallowed large quantities of this nasty stuff.

Strangers are most certain to catch the Panama, or Chagres fever, as it is called there—a sort of cross between ordinary and yellow fever. The native inhabitants, and those who remain there a longer time, and by dint of careful living become somewhat accustomed to the climate, are not so subject to this serious malady as foreigners, all of whom are liable to infection, and having contracted the disease, the chances are greatly in favour of the undertaker. These are the distinctive beauties and inconveniences of this land of gorgeous skies; with its indolent and slovenly inhabitants, its sweet-scented flowers succulent fruits, and fever-breathing swamps.

CHAPTER XXI.

A Terrible Experience at Sea—The Lull before the Storm—Caught in a Cyclone—Man Overboard—The Steamer comes to Grief—Sad Incidents—We Arrive at Vera Cruz—Mexican Festivities and National Dances.

I LEFT Colon in the small steamship *Tampico*, bound for New Orleans. I heard, after paying for my berth, that the steamers on this route are far from pleasant; yet rumours seldom trouble a man who can better afford to lose his head than his passage-money. Never before had I been so tossed backwards and forwards in coming to a resolution as to what I should do; but having been through all the agonies of the Panama fever, my health had rendered it imperative to make a change. I wanted to go to Brazil, but after turning the question about in all the aspects which it seemed to present, I thought it better to remove my penates and shift further north, little thinking that fate, or my unlucky star, or whatever be the name of that mysterious power that shapes our ends, had still some terrible days reserved for me—" whilst we strain at the gnat we swallow a camel." A shrill whistle, and we started. The sun was shining brightly; the sky was one pure dome of blue, unflecked by even the tiniest fleecy cloud, and the air was mild even to balminess. My cabin was neat and clean, but was close to the smoke-stack, and very hot. As the dismal and disagreeable feelings wear off connected with a sea-voyage, the mind reverts most naturally to its pleasures. The sunsets on the sea in the southern latitudes are most glorious for beauty of colour, and no word-painting can properly depict the endless variety of the glowing tints presented, especially as the pure blue fades into shades of a faint green tinge, and mixes with the golden hue of the horizon. The most extraordinary and exquisite effect is often seen after the sun has set below the horizon ; then a warm roseate glow is thrown over the entire sky, and at once the sunset, the twilight, and the night absolutely following the day is presented. The evening star creeps out overhead. and moonlight gives additional sublimity to the scene. The remembrance of these sunsets, rendered the more remarkable by the almost total absence of twilight, is the most unalloyed of all the pleasures of a voyage in these seas ; and he who has not witnessed sunrise and sunset in the tropics cannot form the least idea of their magnificence and splendour.

A strange display of ruddy colouring in the sky was seen the first night after we left Colon. It lasted a considerable time, until towards midnight it slowly disappeared. The sight, though very beautiful, caused a little uneasiness and anxiety among the passengers, as it was alleged by some of the crew to be the herald of destructive gales. A firmament wrapped in a robe of crimson is no unfit emblem of disaster, and in a past age would have been looked upon as a disagreeable omen, but at present, after a few cursory remarks and allusions to its foreboding a serious storm, no more attention was paid its warnings, and the passengers were as jolly as could be, singing and dancing on deck till the midnight hours. And with reason, for everything went on as merrily as marriage bells up to the third day. We had a good run and were clear off the coast of Yucatan, and calculated we would reach New Orleans on the third day. However, certain atmospherical indications soon led us to expect a change ; nor was it long before it was realized.

The morning of the third day was lowering. The air was moist and heavy, and masses of leaden-coloured clouds floated low over the sea. We seemed to be shut in all round with a heavy pall of ominous darkness. It almost looked like night. The heavens appeared to have contracted, and all betokened the approach of a gale. The air was unnaturally still, as if nature was holding its breath previous to a violent effort or a fierce onslaught. The sails flapped heavily against the masts, and the low, moaning sound of the long ground-swell created an uneasy feeling, which was not allayed by an observation from the captain that we should ": catch it pretty soon." The lowering of the lighter spars, the furling of the sails, and all the work usually made in anticipation of an approaching gale, betokened that the crew were preparing for a heavy sea. Soon we felt that the captain's prognostication was about to be realized. The signs of bad weather thickened. The wind, which had lulled for a brief time previous, now sprang up, and the waves fretted and chafed against the hull of the little steamer with a peculiar, sharp, chirping sound. Then a hollow noise, like distant thunder, was heard approaching nearer and nearer, and at last the artillery of the skies played an overture. First, there shot forth a blinding dart of lightning, rapidly followed by a rattling peal of thunder; then the wind began to whistle through the rigging, the swell of the sea gradually increased until the crests of the waves rose in foam, which the wind whirled off in clouds of spray. The billows, forming on the horizon, moved down like phantoms on the ship, which began to heave, and roll, and pitch until she heaved all the poetry out of my head, and I had to retire to my berth. At last Jupiter Pluvius descended in all his majesty, bespattering the deck with spots as big as halfpence. A tremendous shower of rain came down, then it thundered, and the lightning lit up at intervals the scene; hail followed, and the surging sound of the billows rang through the air. Heavy gusts of wind came with terrific violence, causing the waves to race madly around us with foam-curds upon their crests. At times when a wave struck the ship it would be buried in foam and spray, rolling heavily at the same time. I could not stay in my cabin, not so much from positive apprehension as from that feeling of doubt which is even more distressing. I tried to make my way to where one of the sailors was clinging to the wheel rather than controlling it; but ere I could reach that place my feet developed suddenly a desire for the dissolution of partnership and became inspired with an individuality which, much as I deprecated it, I could not for the moment subdue. Clinging with great difficulty to the davits, I looked out on the wond rful sea. It made me nearly forget my fear to look out upon so grand a scene, though at times the waves rose so alarmingly that I could not bear to look at them. The fierce roaring of the wind, the creaking of the masts, the straining and groaning of the bulkheads, as the ship laboured in the weltering sea, were frightful.

Just then I noticed a squall, blacker and heavier than any we had encountered till then, bearing down upon us. All along the horizon, between the black water and the still blacker heaven, there was a streak of chaotic, tossing foam-crests of luminous whiteness, and with a roar like thunder there advanced a turbid mass of water, foaming and frothing like yeast, and, rushing forward, it hurried on like a perpendicular wall. I shall never forget that sight. Nearer and nearer every moment, it boiled and roared, and gathering strength as it advanced it bounded onward with irresistible power in its track, and then with a crash a mountain-wave lifted our vessel to its summit, only to slide down again into the gulf of boiling and whirling spume. It was the wildest struggle I ever gazed on, and as I watched that awful scene another dense, black precipice of solid water rose before us, seeming to overtop the mainmast. I closed my eyes in horror as the vessel was carried down into the deep trough of the wave; and as the water broke over her, she heaved over so fearfully, staggering and quivering, that I thought she would shoot us all overboard; but the gallant little steamer regained her balance.

Clambering with difficulty over the wet and slippery deck, I returned to the dining saloon, where all the cabin passengers were huddled together—a breathless stillness brooding over all. While thus standing in their midst, we were startled by the unmistakable crash of timber, that shook the vessel from bow to stern, and the cries of despair that arose from the deck. Every soul in the ship was on the alert in a moment, and the excitement prevailing was intense. We had scarcely time to turn and ask each other "What was that?" when we heard that most terrific of all cries at sea—"Man overboard!" The cry flew like lightning through the ship, and in an instant all was commotion. Then rose to the skies another terrible crash and a withering shriek—a loud and long-protracted note of woe—

> "Such as when tempests roar and timbers creak,
> And over the side the masts in thunder go,
> While on the deck resistless billows break,
> Dragging their victims to the gulf below."

Such was the crash. A thrill of horror followed, and the women and children, of whom there were a good many amongst the passengers, uttered piercing shrieks, adding to the general confusion.

With one or two others I rushed upon deck, and I shall never forget the fearful spectacle that was revealed to my eyes. In endeavouring to describe the scene I can be guilty of no exaggeration, for all that the imagination can picture or the mind conceive must fail to convey any adequate idea of the grandeur and sublimity on the one hand, and the misery on the other, presented by the fearful spectacle. Language utterly fails to paint the horror. The scene was indescribably grand, if one could conceive the idea of grandeur in the midst of so much destruction and ruin.

The noise of the wind blended with the thunder's awful hymn, and a black rolling sea, with a strange, sullen sound, was rushing fast upon us from afar, bearing death in its train. The vivid flashes of lightning, breaking forth from almost every point in the firmament, followed one another in rapid succession and illuminated the wild waste of waters; the thunder pealed its loudest, and its roar, re-echoed and prolonged, seemed the agonies of the expiring clouds as they dissolved into rain. The ship was every now and then struck by tremendous seas, and the hissing and seething billows, rushing on in the rear, reaching higher and higher, and hindered by no obstruction, were leaping with unrelenting fury over the deck, tearing away all the fixtures, and annihilating everything that came within their reach. All the moveable effects were washed off the decks; the bulwarks were stove in; the wheel dashed to pieces, leaving a mere fragment in its place; one of the boats was gone; several sails were blown into shreds, and the decks almost completely cleared. But the saddest part is yet to be told. The man at the wheel had been knocked down and carried overboard with resistless force. We had a glimpse or two of the wretched being just as with frantic gestures for help and shrieks of terror, he sped past, riding on the top of a billow. Plank after plank was cast over for him to seize and try to sustain himself till a boat could be lowered and the ship put about. But it was useless; a boat could not live a moment in the terrific sea that was running. As soon as the lashings were cut and the boat fell, it was swamped immediately; the sea was too wild, it was impossible to send the boat off. All the efforts of the crew were unavailing, and nothing could be done to save the poor sailor, whom we saw through the whirling clouds of spray struggling for his life in the seething water. I can never forget the sight. Horror-struck we looked on, and his gaze met ours with an expression in it of such anxiety and despair as I have never seen before, and hope never to see again. At last his head drooped, he sank, and we saw him no more; the wailing wind chanted over his grave the burial-rites. He was hurled into eternity without a moment's preparation, and before anything could be done to save him. The sad incident cast a gloom over all the passengers. Death had been among us, filling our minds with sadness.

During all this time the captain, wet to the skin, stood gallantly on the bridge, calling and shouting amidst the roar of the elements and giving orders with cool self-possession to his men at their perilous work, though the noise of the storm often drowned his voice, and his words were inaudible at a distance of several feet. The heaviest gusts were between three and four P.M., then there was a sudden calm, but it lasted only for a few hours, and then it began to blow again in heavy squalls, the storm increasing with the growing darkness.

It would be futile to attempt a description of the night that followed. It was a night of storm and hurricane in which every one was kept awake solely from fear. Those were hours of terrible and painful suspense; the seconds seemed lengthened into hours, and the general excitement amounted to perfect agony. Towards midnight the gale was raging with fearful fury; the steamer became unmanageable, and was driven by the roaring wind at a frightful velocity. Heavy seas were washing over the vessel fore and aft, and the rain fell in great showers, increasing the darkness and mingling its hissing noise with the crash of the waves as they beat furiously against the hull of the steamer. It seemed as if death were raging round our floating prison, seeking entrance to engulf his prey. The water poured along the passage into the saloon, tossing the harmonium from end to end, while plates, cruet-stands, and wine-glasses seemed imbued with animation, and rushed recklessly to destruction. At each roll the chairs, tables, and other furniture of the saloon were upset with frightful clatter; the hull of the ship groaned with straining and the timbers creaked. The sea pouring down the hatchway over all, drowned out the fires, and the vast streams of water, which collected on the lower deck, discharged themselves into the steerage, and left no dry spot to lie upon, perch upon, or cling to. The wretched passengers ran wildly from one place to another, vainly seeking for a place of refuge, but the surging and raging element drenched them wherever they went. The crew spoke lightly of the storm at first, and joked at it, but ultimately they altered their tone and said we had got into a cyclone; then many of the passengers took their money and watches and valuables out of their trunks and lockers, and fastening them around their waists with handkerchiefs, prepared for the worst. A regular panic prevailed, although the captain did all he could to allay the alarm and to re-establish confidence and hope.

About that time another accident occurred which heightened the horror of the scene. A man had his arm and leg broken by a falling spar, and was so much wounded in the head that the top of his skull was nearly carried away. He was extricated from beneath the smashed lumber, and carried down into a cabin. Kind hands did all that was possible to relieve his sufferings, and he received all the attention that could be given to him; but the dread tyrant Death had marked him for his own. It was a piteous spectacle. His look as he lay dying, his nerves all unstrung because of the fearful shock and the pain he had to endure, his teeth broken, and the perspiration in beads upon his livid face, and the deadly collapse which came over him as death approached, were awe-inspiring, and for the time made the roaring of the storm pass unnoticed. The poor man lingered on for about an hour before he died. His sufferings had been dreadful. I don't know what unspoken horrors may yet be in store for me, but I think this sight will haunt me to my grave. The accident occurred about half-past eleven o'clock, and the scenes that followed can hardly be described. All was seemingly lost, and the cries of anguish from women and children were sufficient to appal the most stout-hearted. Attempts were again made to launch the boats, but they could not be lowered, and the utter horror and despair that now seemed to seize upon all can only be realised by those who have passed through a similar scene. Men stand erect, and look towards heaven, with some pride and consciousness still left that they have a right to the succour of the God who made them—lifting their hands, their eyes, their hearts towards the heavens they cannot see, and calling through the storm for help and mercy. One takes his babe from its mother's arms, and with a wistful glance into that mother's tearful but brave eyes, imprints a kiss on its dimpled face, and is then ready to die. The terrified woman, who has lost almost her reason with fright, can do nothing but cling to her husband; and the last feeling in her rending human heart is love for her babe. Yet for all these things what could my heart care? I sat and listened to the incessant discharges of the thunder, and eyed the tempest shake the lightnings overhead and the resistless billows break over the deck and mock at the fruitless efforts of the vessel against them. I could not well do more. Yet hark! what meant the sounds we now heard? The ship-bell tolled, and so thrilling and strange were the tinkling sounds that it seemed to those who heard them to be the ringing of our death-knell. But we all assembled in the large saloon—it was then after midnight. A lady sat at the harmonium, and began to sing with a trembling voice and in a manner that touched us all. The words were strangely sweet. It was the hymn:

> "Amid the roaring of the sea
> My soul still hangs her hope on Thee,
> My constant love, Thy faithful care,
> Is all that saves me from despair."

We were all spellbound, and listened breathlessly; and as, in a voice of surpassing softness, she began again to sing, one after another chimed in; the wild wind swelled the notes, and thrilling and strange was the power these sacred melodies exerted—

> "Here we all may meet no more,
> But there is a happier shore;
> There, released from toil and pain,
> Brethren, we shall meet again."

It was a solemn moment, as amongst the general sobs and weeping of the trembling crowd and the turmoil of the furious elements was heard:

> "God of mercy, God of love!
> Hear our sad, repentant song,
> Sorrow dwells on every face,
> Penitence on every tongue."

Such a feeling of sadness then overpowered all that no one could master his feelings. So we went through that awful night, and as daylight was making its first faint appearance we looked about, but saw nothing except a sombre sky with thick rain, and immense waves striding one after the other. The morning was intensely dark and gloomy; day and night seemed struggling against each other in the heavens. An oppressive stillness was in the atmosphere, and the clouds, pressing heavily downward, caused an insufferable heat. In spite of the great storm of thunder, lightning, and rain, the air seemed hotter than ever. The rain-squalls continued the whole day, and we were struck occasionally by heavy seas, but towards evening the wind veered and held the clouds in check. The gale slowly abated, the sea became a little less agitated, and its swell gradually decreased, but the sky continued dark and cloudy even after that. The next morning, however, the weather took a more favourable turn; the clouds began to separate, and the fitful glimpses of the sun gave sufficient light to see that we were fairly out of the cyclone. It was two days before the storm blew itself entirely out, and the sea went down. And now there was revealed to us the full extent of the fearful havoc caused by the violent tornado. Our ship was in a very battered condition. One of the masts had been broken off, and all its canvas carried away; the life-boats were more or less wrecked; the bulwarks, deck-house, and skylight smashed to pieces; several of the lighter spars were swept away; and much other damage was done to the ship. The cabins, saloon, and steerage were flooded, and it was for some time a matter of doubt as to whether the vessel had not sprung a leak. When at last the sun broke thoroughly through the clouds, the spirits of the passengers rose simultaneously, and we began to speak of the horrors of the night, and of our narrow escape. There had been death in the air, and the chance was one to a thousand for us all. One sailor was carried overboard, another had been crushed by the falling spars, and a third was badly injured. We were exposed to the drenching seas for two days and it wanted little to make the vessel go in pieces, as it was driven at the mercy of the hurricane for many hours. For myself, I had always longed to see a great storm on the ocean—I had now seen it. I was fully satisfied. I do not wish to see it again.

After the dead man had been buried, we made sail; the vessel was trimmed, and everything made as snug as possible under the circumstances. There were a number of mules and horses on board (rather ugly customers, by-the-by, for the occasion) many of which had been killed by the terrible rolling of the vessel. Their carcases were hauled up from the hold, and thrown overboard. Steering westward, and shaping our course so as to reach Vera Cruz to repair damages, we went bounding along now under close-reefed topsails, and but for the help of a powerful current which caught the steamer, not a man of us would have lived to tell the story. All our hopes rested in two narrow strips of straining and bulging sails; if these had split, farewell to life, for the waters would have crushed us to atoms without leaving a whole plank to tell of our fate. Fortunately wind and sea moderated at last, and we arrived at Vera Cruz in safety. Our dilapidated little steamer threaded her way cautiously through the narrow and crowded harbour, where she was going to be refitted before proceeding on her voyage to New Orleans.

She reached her anchorage late at night, and before the steam-whistle had even ceased to emit its discordant sounds, the passengers hustled and crowded each other on the gangway, and the landing stage in their eagerness and anxiety to set foot again on firm land. They were like a pack of frightened sheep after this most eventful voyage. I must, however, not omit to mention that before dispersing, a meeting of the passengers was held in the saloon, and the following resolutions were adopted: "Whereas during our voyage two distressing accidents have occurred, and two human beings have been suddenly hurried into eternity; and whereas both who were lost have left families dependent on them, it is therefore resolved that we, the passengers on the ss. *Tampico*, pay to the captain of the said steamer the sums set opposite to our names, to be used as the captain may best select for the benefit of the afflicted by this sad calamity; and that we bow in devout thanksgiving to God for the support vouchsafed to us during the terrible hours of suspense regarding the safety of the ship, and for our deliverance through a merciful Providence from threatening death. Resolved, that we deeply sympathize with the captain, officers, and the crew of the ss. *Tampico* in the trying position in which these distressing scenes have placed them, and that we desire most earnestly to testify our high appreciation of their prompt and efficient action during so many of the terrible scenes as passed under our immediate observation.".

In the ordinary course of things we should have been in New Orleans by the time we arrived at Vera Cruz, but we did not count upon so disastrous a voyage through the Caribbean Sea. I had thus been thrown involuntarily into a curious place and society, and saw many interesting things which otherwise I might never have witnessed. Vera Cruz is nicely situated, and its towers, cupolas, and battlements give it an imposing appearance from the sea. There are some beautiful gardens and plantations in and near the town, which are studded with snug villas; farther on, however, the place is surrounded by barren sandhills and ponds of stagnant water, which make it very unhealthy, and all strangers are liable to the attack of yellow fever. The town has the unenviable notoriety of being a perfect hot-bed of this scourge, and one of its principal seats. Yet its smiling gardens seem ever rejoicing in the balmy breezes of summer, and the gay-coloured flowers delight the senses with their perfume. Here the people come and go, and lounge, and gossip, as if there were no such malady or sickness in all the world. The bowers of mimosas, and the neighbouring orange groves fill at intervals the air with their odours, whilst the crowns of the feathery palms throw their cool shade over the houses, and wave slowly above their silent roofs, which they overhang like symbols of peace and tranquillity.

The houses of Vera Cruz are mostly large, some of them being three stories high, and though many of them look rough and falling into decay, the outside appearance of dilapidation is the worst of them, and is more than compensated for by the internal comfort and luxury which is seen on entering, and which the Mexicans know so well how to enjoy. They are built in the old Spanish or Moorish style, with flat roofs and wooden balconies in front, where the dark-eyed señoritas are lying languidly in their hammocks during the mid-day heat. The houses enclose generally a square *patio* or courtyard with covered galleries, and the footpaths in front of them are also frequently under arcades. There is a good number of religious buildings with spires and domes in the town; many of them, however, are closed and neglected, and only a few are now in use. On a small island, not far from the shore, stands the Castle of St. Juan de Ulloa, frowning with heavy guns from its battlements. This curious old stronghold, in which the military element is quite conspicuous, commands the town as well as the harbour. In the evenings one may almost always see soldiers, in any kind of dress over military trousers, loitering on its ramparts, or in the neighbouring streets. The Castle contains also a lighthouse from which the approach of any vessel is signalled, and in the thick walls surrounding it, are huge iron rings fixed, to which the vessels are made fast—for the anchorage of the harbour, which is a mere passage between the town and the island on which the citadel is built, is very bad and unsafe. Vera Cruz is connected by railway with the City of Mexico, from which it is about one hundred and ninety miles distant. It was the first Mexican town which was occupied by the French in 1861; and their war operations were carried from there into the interior of the country. After the establishment of the Mexican empire, the ill-starred Austrian Archduke Maximilian landed there on the 29th of May, 1864. The remembrance of this terrible struggle of the republic is still kept alive by various observances and festivities; as for example, the "cinco de Mayo" (5th of May) the anniversary of a military victory over the French at Puebla in 1862, is honoured with the pomp of fireworks, music, and public rejoicings at Vera Cruz as well as other Mexican towns.

During the heat of the day only few pedestrians are to be seen on the streets and thoroughfares, but in the cool of the evenings, under skies of intensest blue, all is˙activity, and the plazas and promenades are full of life, music, noise, bustle, and laughter until late at night. The evenings are charming, for when the sun had gone down, the heat is replaced by a fresh and agreeable coolness, which renders the evening hours the most delightful of all during the day. The Mexicans then resign themselves to enjoyment; tinkling guitars are everywhere heard; parties bent on pleasure or for short excursions or picnics are met; and everything possible seems to be done to pass the time pleasantly. In the magic twilight, when the air is still and scarce a breath is stirring, beautiful, dark-eyed women in picturesque attire can be observed thronging the smooth, dusty streets. They are peculiar in dress and manner, lively and chatty, with an elegance of carriage and contour that are almost matchless. In their large scarlet-faced cloaks, their coloured dresses of pink, white, yellow or green, and with their gilded combs in the black hair, they are sure to excite the admiration of strangers. They are reared under the solemn shadow of Catholicism; their culture, it is said, is narrow, but one can see many a face marked by that lofty stoicism and quick sensibility; that fiery passion and princely pride combined, which, as is known, are the qualities of their brothers and husbands, whose burdens they help to bear.

On the green of the market-place of any Mexican town, or in the "Alameda," whose broad, smooth and shady walks are crowded with people in the long summer evenings—the rich to show their finery, the poor to ventilate their rags—the traveller knows where the "horchaterias" are by the sound of a soft, ceaseless blending of music and singing, which comes floating on the fragrant air from every "paradero" and "posada." He may mingle with the crowd, and sip a glass of "mascal" or "pulque" or a cup of chocolate at one of the booths, bedecked with gay flags. At these booths, full facilities for gambling are given, and he will generally find there several groups, all absorbed in this favourite pastime. Outside on every hand are seen waving scarfs and the undulating forms of dancers; the air is filled with song and laughter, while the music of the guitar is heard right on till midnight, when the revellers retire to rest.

Like every part of South and Central America, Mexico has its peculiar dances, which, though differing from the national dances of Spain in some details, possess all their principal characteristics, just as the various dialects of these countries resemble the rich old mother tongue of Spain. They are mostly accompanied by the guitar and the click of castanets, and are full of grace. Every ball or "tertullo" winds up with the national dance, when all the exuberance of the occasion culminates in a brief abandonment to the intoxication of the "fandango" or the "yamacueca" before the festivity comes to an end.

The Mexicans have some customs devoted to feasting and dancing—a kind of thanksgiving—when the ears of the new corn fill and it becomes fit for use. These festivities last several days, during which the "resbaloscas" (national dances) succeed each other without any apparent interval of repose. As a festivity of this kind happened to fall while we were lying at Vera Cruz, I went to see the fun. All classes were represented —the rich and fashionable were to be seen in elegant carriages; well-dressed planters with their families; smiling girls with their gallant attendants; ranchmen; Indians—even some Chinamen were observed gliding about in their silent way, with their mild, melancholy faces; while rosy and chubby, and dirty and happy children were everywhere perceptible. Mexicans on horseback, with wild, yet sleepy, dark faces, costumed roughly yet picturesquely in their classic drapery, were puffing away at pipes, cigars and cigarettes. Beautifully formed women, with melting dark eyes, could be seen twirling pretty little "cigarillos," stuffed with a fragrant wax-coloured tobacco, while others did not disdain to roll a cheaper and coarser tobacco with their nicotine-besmeared fingers. It seemed as if time had gone backwards; it was an old-world scene, reminding of the time when noble dames and valiant knights and troubadours assembled to admire the feats of prowess and bravery at the tournament of some hospitable duke. The dance took place inside an open space, which was surrounded by rows of benches and seats; countless fires lighting up the scene and revealing many weird and fantastic figures, enraptured with the fervour of the "fandango." No man can desire a better partner for a dance than a Mexican girl. The fair ones of Mexico take to dancing as naturally as a duck takes to water, and throw into it the whole spirit of their joyous nature. Here were young señoritas with their shapely shoulders and rounded arms all bare, with eyes like meteors and teeth as dazzling as pure snow, flirting with their "amigos," while the happy fellows, with a proud look as if to say "What do you think of us?" were pacing up and down in the arena. The swagger peculiar to the young gallants of this country has certain graces of its own, which are inimitable and could not be copied. The young men had donned white shirts embroidered in front, buckskin pantaloons with rows of silver buttons and black embroidery down the leg, short buckskin jackets, rainbow-coloured *zarapas*, black belts and *sombreros*, while some had linen jackets and high boots over linen pantaloons. Most of them were armed, and wore ostentatious bracelets on their wrists.

After the preliminary parade they cast aside the "catenas" and the serapes, and as soon as the noisy music of drums, tambourines, guitars, cymbals, and castanets was heard, they rushed with a pleasant and smiling "buenas tardes" (good evening) to their fair partners, and at once began the "fandango." And then, to look at the blazing eyes flashing like fire, the nervous hands, the flirting and sighing, whirling and swerving, the swinging and stooping ! To fully take in the scene, the reader must imagine how, through the black hair of the ladies, their marvellous eyes, wild-wide, beam full on their partners' faces with a mystical stare; how they constantly coquet with their partners, now permitting them to hover around and then suddenly retreat with a swift twirl and all sorts of bewitching postures and gestures ; how they seemingly strive to resist the impulse to fall into their lovers' arms with a voluptuous, reinviting languor of movement hardly capable of description. Meanwhile the spectators, keeping time with their hands and feet, urge on the suitors with such cries as "Buscalo ! buscalo !" until the dance suddenly stops. Then partners are changed, the music recommences, and the dance goes on again, and thus it continues for hours at a stretch.

On this occasion they danced till the red fire-light died away, and darkness began to cover the place, but still they danced on and on for some time. Sometimes the festivity is kept up through the entire night, but the "fandango," so merry at its opening, often closes in a wild debauch, and not infrequently in bloodshed and death. The "yamacueca" is danced by two persons only, and when the guitars strike up, accompanied with the click of castanets, a crowd soon collects around the figures, swaying and bending like willows in the wind, and enters into all the spirit and excitement of the dance. A song, whose words and melody are full of love, passion and entreaty, is generally sung, which the two dancers forcibly express in their attitudes, and which increase in fervour as the song progresses. This dance must be seen to be appreciated; more than that I cannot say—it bewilders the brain. When I witnessed it, there was especially one charming young girl, with delicate features of a voluptuous cast, conspicuous through her bewitching attitudes. Her beautiful face, whose dimpled loveliness the fire-light speckled, attracted general attention. The young hidalgo that was deemed worthy of her favour, after the dance was over, presented her with a bunch of beautiful flowers, dropping at the same time a fragrant shower of snow-white blossoms over her, and—" all ye sighs wrung from his heart, go lull her when she lays herself down, and falls asleep!" As it is just possible the reader may be anxious to hear who this " masher" was, I may mention that he was only a barber, the very same who did me the honour the next morning to remove my beard.

CHAPTER XXII.

Our Interrupted Voyage continued—We Enter the Mouth of the Mississippi —Voyage up the River—Arrival at New Orleans—Its Sights—The Creole Women—I Engage Passage to Havana—Our Sail Down Stream —Disappointments—Nervous Forebodings—Sickness on Board—Quarantine—An Iliad of Woes—Yellow Fever—Its Horrors—Free Again —City of Havana.

AFTER a delay of more than a week, our steamer—refitted and repaired—set out again on her interrupted voyage to New Orleans. Once more was I ensconced in a cabin, once more on board the *Tampico*. As the ship left her moorings and steamed slowly towards the entrance of the harbour under the batteries of the Castle of St. Juan de Ulloa, their guns flashed out their parting salute to us, and when at last we were fairly out to sea, the dim outlines of the coast of Mexico faded in the distance. Being sandwiched again for several days between the sky and the pathless sea, I dawdled away the time as well as I could, principally with watching the transparent shadows flit across the waters, or scanning the vast compass of the open sky. In spite of there being nothing to do, the time passed quickly and pleasantly, for to a landscape painter the great, simple line of the glorious sweep of the horizon, and the magnificent expanse of water offer an endless variety of effects. Thus our steamer was making her way, and the waves, exhibiting the most perfect transparency of a delicate, cold-looking blue, chased us now from behind, but did not shake us about as roughly as on our preceding voyage. At night we crossed the bar, and early the following morning we entered the mouth of the Mississippi. The grey dawn had not yet blushed in the East, and the rayless heaven sent no beams, not even those of the stars, to light up the darkness, as we entered the river. So dark was it that nothing could be seen unless quite near, and our fog-bell was going almost all the time, as boats and fishing smacks floated past us—mysterious boats that came like phantoms out of the shadow and resolved their shapes into shadow again, but not until we had hailed several of them, and learned how the changeable bars lay among the currents and labyrinthlike channels above us. Sometimes an animated conversation was continued long after the passing boats had faded away in the distance, and the voices returned to us out of the darkness, growing gradually fainter and fainter like oft-repeated echoes, until they too were lost. Daylight broke at last through the clouds and allowed us to gaze upon the broad and very dirty river, which glides along with a languid stream. In some places the river spreads to an enormous breadth, and shows to its best advantage where widest. Truly, this is a river on a mighty scale, and quite fulfilled all my expectations. How dark and deep, how sullen this immense current rolls and sweeps along, through the broad extent of marshy plains, which for a long distance meet one's sight! Miles to the East and miles to the West there is one unbroken reach of level tracts, and at a glance one takes in wide sweeps of the stream, fringed with low banks; and the eye roves still farther to a background of rolling plains, diversified with farms, orchards, hamlets, and villages. The river derives an ever-shifting beauty and grace from the constant transit of canvased sea-craft, reeking steamers, boats and barges, some of which are rigged out with gay streamers fluttering from the tops of masts or poles. Proceeding up the stream, we continually passed scores of them, laden with human freight as well as with the produce of various climes. Occasionally we could see a string of barges ascending the river. They were lashed together in one long line and towed by one or more steam-tugs. When the river is in flood it overflows vast stretches of land, and the low-lying quarters of many villages and towns along its shores are submerged. Its passage is then beset with unusual difficulties, as dead trees, torn away from its banks and hurled into the current by storms or inundations, and weeds and other marshy vegetation, float in its turbid waters. Collisions with these obstructions, which are carried along with great velocity until they are caught on a sandbank, are a source of great danger in the navigation of this river. Ships are often damaged by a snag and sometimes even sunk. We saw a half-sunken boat near one of these treacherous sandbanks, which became a total wreck.

Our steamer reached at last the goal of her voyage, and as she drew along the river-side, we were met by the usual number of hotel-touts and porters who, as is the custom in America, crowd the railway-stations, landings, and piers on the arrival of trains and steamers, trying to inveigle passengers to the hotels by which they are respectively employed. I avoided all intercourse with these fellows, and snubbed every individual that betrayed the least disposition to assist me in any way, or the slightest symptoms of calling a hack, and thus managed to escape. When I had walked with my portmanteau a short distance, a number of jehus drove in great haste after me, offering me their services. I hailed one and asked his fare. He wanted two dollars for driving me up-town, but as it was not convenient to pay it just then—having made up my mind to practise the strictest economy —I told him to let it lie over till morning, and in the meantime he might think of something that he would like to add to it. He saw the soundness of my advice, and went on his way extorting, whilst I, "humping my swags," made my way to a little inn, not far from where we landed, and there put up for the nights, though that part of the city looked rather dingy with its long rows of unsightly warehouses along the river's bank.

For several days I spent hours every morning and evening trudging through the streets, and my chief occupation during these peregrinations was to look at the quaint brick houses and to stare in at the show-windows, until I sometimes began to fear that the occupier might appear on the doorstep and order me to move on. "Jackson Square" and several others of the public places are ornamented with bronze statues, and in some of the gardens are groups and groves of beautiful trees among which shrubbery and flowers abound. One of the things that most strikes the stranger is the large number of lottery offices, billiard, and refreshment-rooms, and the bustle and gay life along Carondelet Street, while the other thoroughfares looked comparatively deserted. Whilst walking about the town the day after my arrival, I suddenly came upon this fine broad street, which is a very pretty promenade where, late in the afternoon, and especially on Sundays and holidays, all the "swells" and fashionable people turn out for a stroll. Most of the white inhabitants are of Spanish or French descent (New Orleans was founded by the French in 1717), but such numbers of negroes and mulattoes, and such a mixture of coloured races commingle together that one hears a jargon of tongues in which French, English, and Spanish have the better in turns. New Orleans has its genus "masher" as well as other cities, and they sit in groups in front of the numerous cafés and refreshment saloons enjoying their *dolce far niente*, and watch the ceaseless flow of elegant carriages and the crowds of people of all sorts and conditions who are continually passing.

There is much to be seen in the streets of New Orleans; there are plenty of elegant conveyances, and some good horse-flesh, too, and a large amount of reckless driving; but in my own opinion the beauty of the Creole women impresses one most of all. They are probably the handsomest women in the United States. Their figures are of matchless grace and beauty, slight and lithe, with finely-moulded limbs. The majority of them are brunettes, with clear complexions, flowing black hair, heavy eyelids, drooping as if in pensive melancholy, and large, dark, lustrous eyes, as it were bright with tears like the partially closed petals of a flower filled with pearly dew. Their carriage is so easy and natural as to be almost the poetry of motion. With a proud expression that rests upon their finely arched lips, they walk like empresses, carrying the grandeur of the Spanish *noblesse*, or sit in the saddle in an attitude that is the perfection of graceful ease. Wherever Nature is in the habit of ornamenting her favourites with dimples they are to be found on them, and the loveliness of their features is scarcely anywhere surpassed. Some of them look like figures chiselled out of marble. Carondelet Street, which seems to be their favourite resort, is the best place to see them, and surveying the lively scene on a lovely evening I received the impression that, like their countrymen from over the water, the French portion of the male inhabitants of this city are great admirers of female beauty. "Elle est belle et impérieuse à donner le délire ; sa vue seule est tout un poème," said a young " swell " to his companion with whom he conversed in an undertone at my side, as one of these superb-looking creatures, the fire of whose eyes seemed to burn into his heart, was passing by on horseback. " Oui, elle est tout à la fois ange et houri, et je parierais la tête de ma femme à couper qu'elle va tourner la vôtre," answered the other gentleman as coolly as if he had gone through this hazardous operation several times before.

The steamer *Great Republic*, one of those big monster boats which combine the comforts and luxuries of well-ordered hotels and form so characteristic a feature of American river navigation, was moored off one of the quays in the river, preparing for her return voyage to St. Louis. I was in a very undecided state of mind as to what route I should take next in my journey to the North, and visited the steamer with the intention of making inquiries as to the time of her starting. Whilst doing so I noticed a small brig lying near, her name, *Jennie Lee*, being painted astern in large white letters. I was told that she was bound for Havana. Ruminating over all that I have read and heard of the beauties of the city of Havana and the island of Cuba, I naturally felt at that moment a keen desire to view them. I suppose it must have been these glowing descriptions that induced me to inquire whether there was any accommodation for a passenger on board, and having received an affirmative answer, I decided, though not without some hesitation, to engage a passage in this vessel. I scarcely could believe that it, lay within my power to do it, until I embarked the following day, and we set out on our voyage.

Passing down the mighty river, we caught favouring winds and with flowing sails sped on our way under the escort of innumerable gulls. No sooner, however, had we fairly got clear of the land and entered the Gulf of Mexico when the wind failed us in the most unexpected manner, and later on we were at the mercy of a foul wind, and made but little progress. Our voyage was characterized by a more than usual degree of tediousness, however, after several days, a light breeze coming at last enabled us to average between forty and fifty miles a day, and so creep at a snail's pace towards our destination. But we had then still to undergo a day or two more of changeable weather before we picked up a favourable wind, which brought us in sight of "Dry Tortugas," one of the Florida reefs. During days and nights, the sea being calm, I remained on deck, and had waking dreams, or else lay in the cabin and had other dreams, some waking some sleeping, there being but little difference between them. For some days I was in a very desponding mood, and weighed down with a feeling of depression and languor which I could not throw off. A strange mixture of nervous foreboding and a hundred other emotions in turns possessed me—there being behind them all, like a dark shadow, the vague dread of approaching danger. I had stretched myself on the deck one morning to enjoy the coolness of the breeze, and to deliver myself over to gloom and loneliness, in the growing conviction that I was getting ill. My head ached as if it were going to burst. I was neither dreaming nor thinking; I was too wretched to do either, so I lay letting my mind wander lazily off into vacuity, while almost without consciousness I gradually fixed my attention upon the fragmentary talk of two sailors who were standing near, and joining in careless conversation, but I was suddenly startled from my apathy by hearing the words " yellow fever." I was seized with horror at the thought, and springing to my feet, asked the astonished sailors what was the matter, and they told me that two of the

x

crew lay sick in the galleys with yellow fever. Towards evening I grew worse, and how shall I describe my feelings as the dreadful conviction dawned upon me that I too had been infected with this loathsome malady! It seemed to me as if I were in a horrid dream, and were trying in vain to awake from it. We were by this time not far from land; in fact the next morning I was told that the faint outlines of the two castles and the citadel of Havana could be already descried in the far distance, but as the fever was raging in me I had to keep in my berth, and so can give but a meagre description of our approach thither. As there were now three cases of sickness on board, the master of the vessel spread more canvas and headed steadily towards the coast. Finally we entered the narrow inlet to the harbour, passed the Punta and Morro castles situated to right and left of it, and sailing a long distance into the broad bay which expands beyond, we reached the quarantine quarter, where we came to anchor. A steam-launch came puffing towards us, and I was removed at once with my two companions in misfortune to one of those pesthouses, called quarantine-ships, on board of which I was received by a fellow in a sort of tawdry uniform with patches of gilding, who strutted about like a turkey-cock blown out with personal conceit, and roused my indignation by ordering me to one of the cells in a gruff tone of voice, and looking at me with a savage leer in his morose and surly eyes. It was an ugly boat, manned by an ugly crew of thick-lipped, coarse and woolly-headed ruffians. They were a rough lot indeed, and utter strangers to the softer side of life— apparently incapable of a kindly word or thought for one in distress, and devoid of that fellow-feeling which seems to belong by nature to even the meanest wretch. Even now as I pen these lines, the remembrance of their brutality makes my blood surge wildly through my veins. That the reader may not be taken in by the high-sounding words " Quarantine ship," I must say that it was the hulk of an old, worm-eaten and disused vessel of some sort or other, which had been converted into a hospital-ship by being divided below deck into a number of small and

THE QUARANTINE SHIP (HAVANA).

almost air-tight compartments, each with a separate door. Of all the abominations that ever took the shape or form of a ship for the occupancy of human beings, this was certainly the most abominable. No one seemed to think of ventilation. The heat was distressing in this slough of despond, and there were even notices posted on the walls of the cells and passages forbidding the opening of the portholes, so there was no outlet for the foul air, nor any means of introducing fresh air into this pesthouse, and a pesthouse it was in the full sense of the term, with all the pestilential effluvia of diverse diseases corked up and preserved for the benefit of succeeding victims.

And now farewell—a long farewell to happiness; farewell to peace of mind, farewell to tranquil dreams and to the blessed consolations of sleep. I have now to record an Iliad of woes—the pains and horrors of the yellow fever. Far from home and kindred, and vainly hungering for words of sympathy, nothing was left to me within these dark and doleful walls but the blankness of gloomy, silent desolation. I am one upon whom trouble works inwardly, making me outwardly silent, yet the sudden transition from the sight of so much that was beautiful in nature to a lonely berth in a prison, with nobody to soothe or administer to my helplessness, stirred the sluggish blood within me, and drove me almost to madness. It was the gloomiest time I ever spent, and no outlook for the future could have been more depressing. To languish in sickness in a foreign land, with death's breath fluttering on one's cheeks, to wrestle dumbly with dumb fate, before whose power one must bow, or rather whose power bows one down, and to endure from day to day the dull monotony of hope deferred, is certainly the most disheartening vicissitude one can encounter during one's travels. I had indeed cause to rue that day when I was removed on board this forbidding and ill-omened ship. Most of my time 1 lay there in a half-dazed condition in which the memories of past joys and pleasures soothed to some extent my sufferings. It seemed as if they, like flickering shadows, had anxiously fluttered about my narrow prison-cell to solace and cheer my sinking spirits, and sometimes I became almost stupefied by long reflection; and would sit to a late hour at night, unconscious of everything round me until the rising dawn glistened dimly through the portholes. My mournful meditations were sometimes interrupted by a heavy-winged crow flapping its solitary homeward way overhead, or by the sharp twit-twit of the glancing swallow, and occasionally my attention was attracted to the white seagulls and cormorants which circled now and then round the ship darting on floating fragments, and rising again. Their cries sound so very melancholy when one's mind is depressed, yet how I envied them their freedom! They were in their element—free, whilst I lay there sick and abandoned. With the exception of the birds, however, I saw no other living or moving thing during the greater portion of the days which I spent there. I did indeed see one of the attendants who brought my food to the window which had been let into the door of my cabin, and the doctor I saw occasionally too—and he saw me—but it was through the glass of the window. Behind this protection he glanced at me, shouted a few questions, left a few directions, which I had to carry out myself, and went away.

Now and again I heard the distant church-bells chiming to service, the sounds of which, softened and mellowed by distance fell on my ears as pleasantly as sweet music; and the tinkle of the vesper-bell, carried sometimes over the bay by the breath of the wind, brought involuntarily into my mind thoughts of all fair and beautiful things. I thought of home with all its mild and social endearments, and of the sunny past, the happy time when my heart was lighter. What a blissful halo hovers over one's home when looked back upon through the telescope of memory across the ocean! It may be that "absence makes the heart grow fonder," or it may be that the yearnings for the associations of early life foster these feelings, but the fact remains that to a dweller in a foreign land his home, and all that belongs to it, seems agonizingly beautiful. Its solemn influences breathed their balm over my mind, they were my solace and support when my fate was at the darkest.

At other moments my imagination took its unimpeded flight and created a fairy-land in which the charming landscapes through which I lately had wandered, with their fragrant forests and mystical lakes, rose up like a tender dream before my enraptured senses, and I lived over again the joyous hours of my recent rambles—those bygone days which seemed then so sweet, so fair and so ravishing, until I returned reluctantly to the present, and was left again not so much in terror as in hatred and abomination of myself.

Often I sat down to write, trying to disentangle myself from the labyrinth of mournful thoughts, and it was then, paralyzed as I was in my artist-life by this accumulation of disappointment and trouble that—to combat the sense of the distracting dullness and languor—the idea came into my mind of writing down what I saw scattered on my track, the troubles as well as the happiness I had enjoyed during my travels.

And now for the dismal imaginings that haunt the bed of yellow fever. No one can speak upon this subject who has not been a victim of this dreadful visitation. It was not so much the physical suffering as the moral and spiritual horror of appearing to oneself an outcast, shunned and despised by everybody, that weighed so heavily and crushingly on my mind. Over everything brooded a sense of loneliness and desolation until all the lights of hope, which flamed up occasionally at the beginning of my prison-life, had gradually gone out, one after the other, and I relapsed into .sheer, stupid melancholy, caring for nothing—a mental wreck. My fate seemed to be sealed, and as hope for human help was apparently in vain, the misery of my dull wretchedness made me wish that the end might come soon—it will be only a short struggle, I thought, but to lie helpless and to be tortured day and night by hopes and doubts, was worse than death. These maddening thoughts kept obtruding themselves on my overwrought imagination in spite of all endeavours to chase them away, and even when wearied nature asserted herself and I fell asleep, my sufferings were not at all mitigated. On the contrary, I was troubled by the activity of my brain even more at nights. Broken, incoherent incidents crossed my sleeping imagination, and restless, quickly-changing dreams haunted me, which were accompanied by fits of perspiration and oppression such as I shall not attempt to describe. They were so powerfully and truthfully depicted on my mind when I awoke, and filled me with such amazement that fear seemed absorbed for a while in sheer astonishment, for I had but to close my eyes to see the gaunt visions cross my imagination again with every dreary adjunct they possessed in my dreams. I can in fact give no adequate description of the horrors of these nights. Rats swarmed and scampered through the echoing passages and along the deserted deck, and as I lay I heard the gnawing of their teeth behind the wainscoting in the dead of the night. There is such a weirdness and uncanniness attaching to these beasts that no tale of horror seems to be complete without them. And I realized this to the full as I lay awake listening to their scurrying and scampering about in every direction.

And when at last old buried hopes awoke again in my heart and revived the feebly flickering spark of my life, the wearisome postponement and delay from day to day of my release made me so low-spirited that I often sat up in bed until my mind became exhausted. My pen runs on by fits and starts, and I am quite unable and shall not therefore attempt to convey my doleful impressions in words.

Thus time wore on, and for the space of more than five weeks I was a close prisoner in this foul den, and had even to bribe my attendant, who brought my food to the window which I have mentioned before, to leave the port-hole in the passage so that I could open it at nights to let in the fresh air. Creatures with lungs need air, and no kind of dwellings, and hospitals least of all, should be constructed on the principle of an oyster-can, wherefrom people carry with them the seeds of disease and death. But enough of these wretched days—why conjure up all their dire associations? A confused recollection of misery and dull discomfort is all that I shall ever retain of them, and may I never see the like again.

At last I was free, my terrible ordeal was over; again I breathed the pure air. The doctor whom I consulted after my release, advised a calm, unexciting mode of life with freedom from worry and anxiety. Such advice it was very easy to give, but very difficult to follow in my circumstances. For a long time after I left the ship, an undefinable feeling of horror clung to my heart, and I was abstracted from everything by a dreamy, thankful amazement at my own existence. I had such a lassitude of body and mind that I could scarcely realize that I' had been so providentially saved from this peril, and although accustomed to sudden changes, I could not get rid of a sense of intense loneliness, such as comes sometimes over a stranger in a foreign land. I was still too giddy and weak and had to keep too much indoors, to receive more than a dreamlike impression of the city of Havana; however, I doubt whether I should feel inclined to live long in it. The city stands upon level ground along the entrance to, and on the west side of the bay, and is strongly fortified. The suburbs of Guadelupe, Jesus-Maria, Salud, Cerro, and Harcon surround the city proper, whereas Regla, another suburb, lies opposite on the east side of the bay. The streets within the fortification walls are narrow, crooked, partly ill-paved, partly unpaved, and I can hardly venture to assert that the people whom I met during my peregrinations were dressed in their holiday attire. The streets appeared to be frequented by none but shabby, seedy passengers; the women, mostly negresses, wearing worn-out calico dresses, and, drearier still, unworthy shoes, or none at all. As for the men, I saw none, I saw only males. I went to see the Cathedral which contains the ashes of Columbus, and walked for a few days amongst that faded mob, and felt as if I were a dismasted ship in the middle of the sea. The streets in some of the suburbs, especially Salud, are wider and better laid out, but except the few public buildings, there is nothing to look at, nothing to cling to.

Thankful that these weary days were ended which were the most helpless of any that I had lived, I boarded a steamer, and as she carried me away from the harbour, past the Morro and the Punta castles, I beheld for the last time the spires and domes of the city, and the grey walls of the citadel, and even the quarantine-ship anchored far off the shore where as a captive I had lain so long. The sight will not soon fade from my memory. Long did my eyes rest on the receding coast whose outlines grew every moment weaker, and how vividly came back to my mind, even as we stood out to sea, the sufferings I had endured on the quiet waters of its bay. But I will eschew these mournful reminiscences which recur in such sombre guise to me, and leave to another chapter the description of my further movements.

CHAPTER XXIII.

The Keys of Florida—Harpooning Turtles—City of Charleston, S.C.—Arrival at Jacksonville, Florida—An Excursion to St. Augustine—The Last of the Seminoles and Modocs—A Turtle Breeding Establishment—A Sail on the St. John River—Lake Santa Fee—A Taciturn Lady Artist—The Journey Continued Northward—Lake Memphremagog—Its Scenery in Autumn.

THE shore and the city of Havana were soon altogether lost to view, and the following night passed without any incident worth relating. At daybreak we found ourselves near one of the "Keys of Florida," a group of small islands and sundry coral reefs which raise their jagged tops above the surface of the water. Here I had the opportunity of observing how turtles are caught. The shores of Florida and the Gulf of Mexico are favourite haunts of these animals, and the females, accompanied by the males, frequently traverse, as I was told, hundreds of miles of sea in order to deposit their eggs there. As we approached two boats were seen in the distance, with several men in each, who were harpooning these poor animals, whilst farther off lay a steamer, riding at anchor, to which the boats belonged. The larger species (some of which weigh from 1,000 to 1,200 pounds) are harpooned as they float asleep on the surface of the water. One of the crew deftly guides the boat, the oarsmen promptly respond to his directions, and approaching silently, the harpooner, standing in the bows, lowers his terrible weapon close to the water and darts it with great precision at the animal. The harpoon consists of a two-pronged, or sometimes of a single-pronged iron barb, about ten inches in length. This barb is attached to a long rope and loosely slipped into a socket at the end of a staff about twelve or more feet long. As soon as the deadly weapon flies from the hand of the harpooner and strikes the animal, the barbed head slips off at once from the staff and remains sticking in the shell. The animal dives immediately it has been pierced, but, after being allowed to struggle so as to exhaust its strength, it is soon, by means of the line, brought to the surface of the water and dragged on board. The larger sized turtles are also sometimes, when within easy reach, by a sudden twist overturned on their backs, in which position they are helpless for the moment, and easily hauled on board the craft. On the shores, which these valuable animals regularly visit in the breeding season to deposit their eggs, their pursuers follow them by their track on the sand, cut off their retreat, and throw them on their backs. Iron spikes are sometimes even necessary to accomplish this, owing to their great size and heavy weight. Their large shells or carapaces, besides being largely exported for manufacturing purposes, are used by the natives of some of the countries around the Gulf of Mexico for drinking troughs for cattle, or as cribs for little children, and the Indians of Yucatan even roof their huts with them.

But to return to our subject. The remainder of our voyage to Charleston, S. C., was devoid of interest. The city of Charleston is built on a tongue of land between the rivers Ashley and Cooper. Fully half of the residents are black or coloured. The great Civil War of 1860–65 began here with the passage of the ordinance of secession in December, 1860. "Meeting and King Streets" are the principal thoroughfares; they run parallel to each other the entire length of the city. The steeple of St. Michael's church in Meeting Street (whether it still exists or not I am unable to say, as the last terrible earthquake destroyed nearly half of the buildings in the town) affords a fine view of the city and the harbour, with the many ships riding at anchor on its quiet waters. A more beautiful and inspiring sight it would be difficult to imagine. As one looks forward Fort Sumter, Castle Pinkney, Fort Moultrie on Sullivan's Island, Morris' and James' Islands, all appear in view. They are spots of great interest, as they were the scene of some of the most stirring incidents in the memorable four years' struggle of the Southern Confederacy. The harbour is one of the largest on the American coast, and beyond stretches, as far as eye can reach, the deep blue sea.

I was a wanderer on the face of the earth like the legendary Jew. Leaving Charleston I went south again by rail to Savannah, visited Port Royal, and arrived at Jacksonville, Florida, in a steamer. Rich with natural verdure, and beautified by the hands of labour, this little town brings every moment some new beauty to sight, and cannot but charm the senses of the visitor. It is a lovely resting-place; dreamy, hazy nature is here in a gentle mood, and living seems but breathing. Bowery gardens with crimson and rich purpled flowers of every shade in brilliant bloom surround the neat cottages and houses, and afford sheltered spots for rest in the soft air and life-giving sunshine. The holly winds its rich leaves among the branches and climbs up the stems of the trees; oranges and bananas yield their luscious fruit; the magnolias and plantains lift their plumed crowns to the blue sky, and all day long the air is tremulous with the song of birds and balmy with the rich odour of flowers. Wreaths, bouquets, and nosegays of different shapes are sold about the streets, and principally on the public promenades every evening at sunset. Some people even indulge in the luxury of strewing flower-leaves on their beds, so that the rooms in which they sleep breathe the richest and purest of odours. There are several good, though dear hotels at Jacksonville, which are crowded during the season. Many northern families spend the winter months there, and then "stylish" young ladies may be seen contending here and there at lawn-tennis, or they stroll at their own sweet will among the country-lanes, picking roses and handfuls of wild, fragrant violets. Occasionally one falls in with family or social parties picnicing in sheltered spots, whilst some of the fair belles are flirting with their smiling cavaliers in some shady nook where the cuckoo calls and the wood-pigeons coo. During the whole season there is a rustling of muslin flounces, and dainty young damsels, as beautiful and fascinating as the houris of Paradise, flit hither and thither in the evenings, whilst the older folks, bathed in the soft moonlight, sit in front of the hotels, or on the verandas, engaged in conversation. Or when—as it sometimes happens—the fickle thermometer falls to the shivering point so that fires are in use, the guests assemble in the saloons of the hotels, and elegant women can be seen seated around the tables, planning, designing, creating, or whatever one may be pleased to term the calling into existence of those wondrous articles that are intended to adorn the female form divine; whilst others chat, laugh, sing, play or dance, changing toilets almost every hour.

For some weeks I had been as isolated as a separate planet— the world forgetting, by the world forgot—and felt as snug as the proverbial bug in a rug. In the mornings and evenings I roamed along the banks of the river, strolled through the daisied fields and found dreamy enjoyment in sun and air, in shining waters and clear skies. The meadows bloomed green; the river glided gently by; the air was laden with the scent of flowers; birds were darting among the boughs of the trees, and everything was charming, everything was bright, beautiful and gay. How refreshing I found this lively little town after the gloomy days at Havana, can easily be imagined. The icicles of dismay that had gathered there around my heart soon began to thaw, and I smelt gratefully the scent of the flowers, and revelled in a bed unrocked by billows with the fullest appreciation after the abominable cabin-life on board the quarantine-ship.

In the grey of an early morning I went on board a little steamer which was preparing to start on one of her usual trips to St. Augustine. After leaving the mouth of the St. John river, we rounded the "Hazard Lighthouse" and steered southward. It was late in the evening, and darkness had already set in by the time we reached there. St. Augustine is not only the oldest town in Florida, but the most ancient built by Europeans on the whole continent of North America, for it was founded by the Spaniards long before the Puritan fathers came over from England in the *Mayflower* and settled on the coast of New England. The town stands on a narrow peninsula formed by the St. Sebastian and Matanzas rivers. One feels there as though one has gone back centuries in time's calendar; everything is so quaint and old, that it is hard for the visitor to believe that he is in the nineteenth century and upon the American continent. The town, in spite of its quaintness, is very lovely. Scattered around are houses, huts and hovels of all shapes, sorts and sizes, many of mud only, others of rough stones, the crevices filled or not filled, as it might happen, with coarse mortar or mud. Grass grows between the big cobble stones with which the odd-looking narrow streets are paved, and its old houses built centuries ago, and its singular-looking people are interesting subjects for study. The lover of the picturesque can here be abundantly gratified. The old Fort Marion is now inhabited by Indian prisoners, the remnants of the refractory Seminoles and Modocs.

I gladly availed myself of an invitation whilst at St. Augustine to visit a green turtle breeding establishment in the neighbourhood. Proceeding there, I was kindly shown over the whole place, and everything was explained to me. The eggs of the smaller but most valuable of all the species—the green turtle, from which the well-known turtle soup is made—are buried in sand and exposed to the heat of the sun. From the high temperature communicated by the solar rays to the sand, the process of hatching is completed in about two weeks' time. The mothers lay frequently as many as one hundred eggs, which are round and slightly depressed at both ends. When the young turtles are hatched, their instinct leads them at once to the large ponds. During the first days of their life they are very feeble, white in colour, and about the size of frogs, but they grow rapidly and soon attain to their usual size. The eggs of nearly all the turtles, as well as their flesh, are excellent for human food, and their fat is a good substitute for oil and butter. The green turtles are captured by the hundreds in the open sea when they are sleeping on the surface of the water. They are easily approached in a boat and caught by a noose being placed over their heads. They, as well as the other species, resort year after year with the greatest punctuality to the same favoured locality, where they drag themselves ashore sufficiently inland to be safe from the tide. There, using their hind flippers as a shovel, they excavate deep holes in the sand, into which the females deposit the eggs, and having covered them carefully, and levelled the surface, they return to sea, leaving them to be hatched by the heat of the sun.

The St. John river is only a few miles distant from St. Augustine, across a flat country with a few orange groves and groups of palmetto trees scattered here and there. This river is said (though scarcely correctly) to be the only river in America flowing from south to north. I took a pleasant sail down the river on my way back to Jacksonville. For a good distance the marshes along its shores appear like a prairie dotted over on either side with cypress and other trees, though various points along the river lying high, present beautiful views of distant hills and high land, which is generally marked by a rim of purplish woods. The air was alive with waterfowl. Hundreds of broad-billed ducks were pouring into the marshes as our little steamer was passing by; and several times we saw flocks of wild geese floating peacefully among the sedges with their heads under their wings, but at our approach they flew off with a tremendous splutter. Storks, herons and cranes stretched their long necks in alarm, and many lubberly buzzards balanced themselves on the dead limbs of fallen trees, and assisted their ascent by flapping and striking the air with their wings.

Rounding a bluff point we saw an alligator paddling smoothly across the river, with his snout above water as far back as his evil little eyes. It was an animating sight, and a volley of shots was sent after him, but they caused only an upheaval of the water as they struck it in the rear of the animal, and before the passengers had time to reload, the alligator disappeared with a violent plunge, lashing the water into foaming spray. A great deal of lead has been uselessly scattered and wasted by passengers shooting alligators from board the steamers, for duty to their families, no doubt, compels these wary beasts to dash forward and dive under water before the shots reach them. Only in the eye or in the depression behind it, will a ball take effect on the upper surface of their bodies, but a larger mark to aim at, and a far better chance to hit the vulnerable parts behind its claws, or in the abdomen, is offered when the animal is snoozing, or sunning itself on one of the numerous sandbanks which abound in the river. Here and there the sand and the vegetable matter, which are carried by the force of the water, accumulate along the shore or in midstream, forming banks, some of which assume the dimensions of islands along which the tide is slackened and the river shallowed. Some of these islets appear above the surface only at low water.

After my return to Jacksonville, where I spent another week or two—half the time on foot, and the other half walking—I resumed my journey one day, and made my way to Lake Santa Fee. I felt pretty much like a stray leaf, borne hither and thither as wind and currents directed; for a few days I was here, for a few weeks there, and sometimes I knew very little where I should be the next day. Lake Santa Fee is lovely, and I liked it at its first sight. The beautiful mirror of water stretches itself over a considerable space—a smooth surface reflecting the surrounding verdant slopes, the fine trees, and the sky above so pure and blue. The soft murmur of the lake is heard, and its glistening waters can be seen from the windows of the hotel. How solemnly calm it sometimes appeared when gold-bordered clouds were sailing swiftly through the blue, and the setting sun caused the waters to glow like molten gold! Then the bright sky next to the horizon became almost transparent, and the luminous hue spread gradually over the whole heavenly vault, while a hazy tinge was shed over land and water which gave to the landscape a peculiar charm and colouring. Later in the evenings, when only the tops of the distant hills were gilt by the rays of the setting sun, and twilight set in, and all around began to be steeped in gloom, then one by one the stars crept out overhead, glistening and glittering in the dreamy welkin, and the birds ceased their low, faint song, until nothing was heard in the dead silence of the night except the gentle hum of the leaves and the sound of the water breaking on the pebbly shore. How calm and holy were these still evenings! There was a delightful sense of repose over everything. Such scenes touch and quicken the inner nature of man; a soothing influence seems to creep over him, and he longs for a closer intimacy with that spirit which seems to pervade everything, and creates so much that is wonderful and beautiful.

I often used a boat on the lake, and my diversion was to steal up a bayou among the reeds, into which the sparkling water of a babbling brook discharged itself, and where scores of blackbirds were twittering in the rushes. There I watched the reflection of the trees in the amber-like water, which was as clear as crystal, while butterflies fluttered around, and crossbills turned their heads archly to look at me as I sat sketching. The banks were covered with a luxuriant growth of live oak, cypress and palmettos, and delightfully shaded by madrona trees, which dotted and lined the margin of the lake, and strained themselves in leaning over to peer into the water. Trees, bushes, and reeds were crowded with birds, and wild flowers breathed rich perfume to the air.

One day as I was sketching in a boat a group of handsome madronas and live oaks with spreading branches, and thick, dark foliage, I espied a lady, separated from me by but a few yards of reeds. Seated on a log near the water's edge, she was occupied like myself in trying to catch and portray the passing glory of the radiant landscape. My eyes were attracted by the outline of her figure, but all I could see was a mass of light hair, which fell over and shaded her face. At her side was a little girl clad in pink. I rowed to the shore out of pure joy at seeing a fellow artist, and my curiosity was on tiptoe to see her painting. We compared our work and exchanged compliments. Her voice sounded soft and sweet like that of a bird in the forest, so of course I praised her painting, although she made a sad daub of it. She amended, however, the insufficiency of her artistic endowment with a great deal of conceit and highly enlarged self-esteem. Happy creature! there is no greater blessing in the world than to possess a contented mind. She told me with just the *soupçon* of a smile curling her upper lip, that my sketch was "as pretty" as hers. How soothing and comforting these words were! She could make a handsome picture if she could have such a comfortable seat as I had in my boat, she added, with an expression of yearning in her eyes which I should never have supposed the human countenance capable of. Of course I offered her courteously a seat in the boat, thinking that it would be rather pleasant and amusing were there two to paint together, and she of the yearning eyes went on yearning and painting for several hours, and did not speak at all. Looking dreamily before her as if I were taking her to a funeral, she sat at my side enshrouded in silent melancholy and deeply absorbed in her work. Ladies, like ghosts, never speak till spoken to, I thought, and so I tried to cheer up her sinking spirits by talking to her, but my several attempts at conversation were all to no purpose, and only answered by that stereotyped yearning look—just what she was yearning for I did not know. Our talk, which was entirely done by myself, could hardly have been classed under the head of pastimes, so after another attack on her reservedness and taciturnity, which proved again a failure, I saw the force at last of giving in. The bottom having thus been completely knocked out of what

Y

had promised to be an enjoyment, I consoled myself by listening to the frivolous chatter of her little sister. I do not claim paternity, nor even is pretence made to originality for the mild pun, if I aver that she—being always a-musing—was one of the pleasantest companions I ever had. At last she finished her work, and wrote "Lily," her name, in a very prominent place on her sketch. This pet name has always seemed to me emblematic and suggestive of a girl with a big white head on a thin stalk, and this time at all events the name did not belie the owner. When she stopped painting, and I was asked to take her ashore, I remarked by way of another trial how beautifully her little hands were shaped. This trite observation seemed to gladden her heart, for she turned, and the grateful look she gave me was almost enough to melt my coat buttons. Having reached the shore, she smiled, and— *mirabile dictu!*—whispered a few words of thanks in generous acknowledgment—whether of the service and help I had given her, or of the compliment, I do not know. Thoughtless young men! You could do ever so much good in this sorrow-stricken world if you only would. You can always bring a flush of pleasure to the most melancholy girl by saying, if only in her hearing, some such innocent but pleasing flattery, free from harm. You ought not to begrudge her the gladness she feels, and she would always remember you as kind and sympathetic. I stood looking after her as she started from my side, but before I finished my meditation she faded in silence like a vision away.

But I must resume my description. In my erratic way I did what, according to the notion generally entertained, the comets are said to do in theirs—I moved again. Having returned to Charleston, I proceeded northward by rail *viâ* Washington, Baltimore, New York and Boston, Mass., on my way to Canada. I made short stoppages at several of the cities through which I passed, and finally went from Boston to Lake Memphremagog, where I spent the last few weeks of a beautiful autumn. I had reached another calm, quiet resting-place, just such as I could wish it to be, and had the opportunity of seeing the scenery of the lake, which presents many attractions in its peculiar loveliness. No language can describe the beauty of its rockbound shores in autumn. They are then clothed with rich and glorious tints, and the verdure of their woods is changed into every possible variety of hues—brilliant scarlet, vivid violet, with shades of brown and glittering yellow. The green leaves of the maples, elms, and oaks have faded and turned into bright crimson, brown and gold, and the whole of the woodlands are decked in the gayest and most brilliant colours.

The lake, the name of which is of Indian origin, and signifies "beautiful water," is about thirty miles long, and from one to two miles in width. It lies on the borders of Vermont and Canada, in the great basin between the White and Green Mountains, but fully two-thirds of it are in Canada. The lake contains a number of beautiful islands which impart to it some resemblance to Scotch loch scenery, and the tourist may easily in his fancy feel himself transported to Loch Lomond, or Loch Katrine, of both of which the lake put me in mind. These islands vary considerably in size. Some of them are mere islets of naked cliffs, covering only a few square yards, whilst others are many acres in circumference. Most of these, being overgrown with forest trees, combine all kinds of beauty man can witness. A steamer, starting on its course from Newport, makes two trips daily during seasonable weather, touching at various points along the shores. Each run from one end of the lake to the other takes about three hours' time, and as he glides over the cold and clear water, the eye of the tourist takes in the scenery of the mountains, the most prominent of which is Owl's Head, a huge cone which rises quite abruptly from the shore. The mountain looks from a distance like a great haystack. Its summit, which is one mass of jagged rocks as if broken up by some volcanic agency, is nearly 3,000 feet above the level of the lake, and the view which is obtained from it is very beautiful as well as extensive over the great Canadian forests, while on either hand and behind are the wide, fertile plains that stretch away to the river St. Lawrence. On a bright day even the spires of the city of Montreal are said to be visible with the aid of a glass.

On the western shore of the lake are the highest mountains, and as the steamer skirts their base, the scenery becomes wilder. One receives manifold views of fantastic cliffs, and brown, moss-covered rocks, which peep here and there through the foliage of the trees, or rise high above them, adding variety to the landscape. "Jay Peak" may be seen, which stands prominently in the foreground, whereas on the east "Mount Washington" reaches above its neighbours. Northward of Owl's Head is "Mount Orford" and "Mount Elephantis" which, when viewed from a certain point, resembles a huge elephant in repose. Newport village, where I took up my quarters during the time I was at the lake, lies at its southern shore. It is a pleasant country village of a neat and thrifty appearance; its fine hotels being much frequented by townspeople during the summer months.

A few feathery flakes of snow, the first instalment of the approaching winter, were dancing through the air, reminding me to hurry up and shorten my stay if I did not wish to be snowed in. Nevertheless I lingered a few days more at lovely Memphremagog, and when at last I was leaving the cold weather gave unmistakeable signs of its presence.

Continuing my journey by rail, I arrived in a couple of hours at the Victoria Bridge, spanning the St. Lawrence river, and as we emerged from the dark passage of the tubular structure, we were in full view of the city of Montreal.

CHAPTER XXIV.

Arrival in Canada—Montreal—Christmas at Toronto—Niagara Falls in Winter—A Voyage Down the St. Lawrence River—The Thousand Islands—Shooting the Rapids—Quebec—The Montmorency Falls—An Excursion to the Saguenay River—Gulf of St. Lawrence—Island of Anticosti—The Shores of Labrador—Homeward Bound—Conclusion.

THE change from sunny Florida to Canada in the month of November, and the transition from a temperature of spring-like mildness to frost and snow was the reverse of cheerful. The blue, genial sky of Florida was replaced by one of gray and dull colour. It struck me the more as I was greeted the morning after my arrival at Montreal by sleet and snow, which was falling in a very persistent manner and was dolefully depressing to me. I shrunk from going into the streets for fear of sinking over my boots in the slush. It is not very often that the weather in Canada provokes complaints on account of its muddiness, but at the time of which I speak it was very far from presenting the uniformly snowy and frozen aspect with which the winter months are credited in that country. During the succeeding days too the weather had been as bad as bad can be. However, I braved the downpour and went into the gloomy streets, and as I was walking through one of the avenues on the lower slopes of the noble mountain which gives to the city its name, I found myself at one of those numerous points which disclose such charming views of the city, the broad, gleaming river, and the rolling plains and woodlands beyond, with the green mountains of Vermont as a fit background.

I had lived in and roamed over Canada before, and now I trod the same paths again. I was fond of the recollections of those bygone days, for I was revelling then in the delights of scenery and adventure, and perhaps the memory of that time, which was undimmed by troubles and unvexed by storms, was one reason why I wished to retread the same way. The contrast, however, which the scene offered that day! The trees, clothed in desolation, stood woeful in the drizzling rain. I could not see much more in the bleak, dull light than the two towers of the church of Notre Dame—the most prominent objects in the city—rising as dark silhouettes to a great height over the house-tops.

The misty rains were followed by heavy falls of snow as I arrived at Toronto. It was the day before Christmas, and a gloomy Christmas-eve it was. The snow lay thick upon the ground, the sky was a level slate overhead, and a cold, piercing wind was blowing. Sitting by a warm fire in the large sitting-room of the "Revere House," and writing to the music of clinking shovels on the pavement and to the cries of "Clean your door-steps!" from the street arabs, I naturally fell into a reverie as I watched the heavy flakes of snow settling down with a persistency that added incessantly to the accumulated drifts, which lay already to the depth of a good many inches on the ground and side-walks, causing delays, and interfering with the foot-traffic. A busy hum of voices, mingled with the tinkling of glasses, filled the adjoining bar-room, where the thirsty were indulging in hot and cold drinks. They seemed to have no other object of so much importance at heart as keeping their blood in circulation. The wind whirled around the corners, blowing great gusts into the eyes of the few passers-by, and tall, rough-booted men came stamping into the room where I was sitting, and gathered around the roaring fire, which caused their shaggy coats to steam and smell of scorching.

"I heard the church bells moaning
A weary lament to the skies,
Like my own notes, faint and broken,
They sank into sobbings and sighs."

My heart fondly turns to the old, good Christmas customs. To me they speak of home with all its memories of childhood's joys and youthful hopes. The friends I had made in America did not efface from my mind the friends I had left behind me in the old world, and whether I stood amid the snows of Canada, by the mighty Falls of Niagara, the waters of the Mississippi, or in the burning sands of Mexico, the tender strains of *Home, Sweet Home*—as if wafted by the breeze over the waves of the vast Atlantic—often recalled to my memory the many friends of my native land.—Well, cheer up old fellow, brace up! you may howl forth your sentiments and write pathetic complaints—what's the good of it? Well, merry Christmas! You may say that, but merry Christmases don't travel; they stay indoors, and only people at home enjoy them. They don't get on steamers and railroad-cars and go a-bumpin' around the world, they don't! Merry Christmas! no fun, no merriment, and nothing in my stocking—but a hole.

The city of Toronto is built on and fronts a wide bay which is separated from the main body of Lake Ontario by a narrow, semi-circular, sandy beach, whose south-western extremity, guarding the entrance, is called Gibraltar Point. Comfortable boats run from Toronto across the lake to the mouth of the river Niagara, a distance of thirty-six miles, and up the Lower Niagara, to Lewiston, from whence visitors may proceed to the whirlpool; General Brock's monument on the heights of Queenston; and to the Falls.

I had seen the Falls several times during my previous stay in Canada. They are no doubt sublime, and the scenery around is wild and grand, but the land in the vicinity of and including the Falls, was then private property, and thrown open to the public at such ridiculously high charges that the cost of seeing all around and below the Falls was very expensive. I could hardly divest my mind of the idea that I was not "doing" Niagara, but that Niagara was "doing" me. The latter conjecture was ever present in my thoughts, for after I had been there for a few minutes during my first visit, I began to lose money, and after a couple of days I was almost beggared in trying to get near the cataract. There were so many fees and gratuities to be paid at the various "entrances" to the Falls, under the Falls, to the caves, and over the bridges, that after all the worry and expense one could have readily sympathized with the man who, on being politely requested by his cicerone to come again at some future time, asked to be thrown in rather than return to see them. One gets accustomed, however, to everything. I walked and paid almost mechanically until I went about with my pockets inside out. Although I refused the aid of several guides who followed at my heels, as is the custom of that fraternity, I paid in less than two days more than eight dollars in admission fees, including those at every bridge.

Let us imagine a *pater-familias* going to see the Falls accompanied by his better half, and say half a dozen of children. Arrived there, he would read : Entrance to the Falls, twenty-five cents each person ; further on : Entrance to the Cave of the Winds, fifty cents ; &c., &c. Seeing that he would have to pay such a heavy ransom, he would most naturally explain to his wife and offspring how much grander the Falls look when seen from a distance. All this, however, is changed now, as all the land adjoining the Falls on the American side has been bought by the State in which they are situated. I had seen the famous whirlpool and the much-vaunted Falls in spring, within a few days of the snow's disappearance ; had seen them in summer when they were embowered in a leafy paradise, and no wonder that I desired to see them in the glittering garb of ice and snow. I therefore tempted the gods and took another run to the Falls in the depth of winter. I had a little money— having by this time recovered from the financially crippled condition in which my former visits to the same place had left me—and a great deal of time which, as Mark Twain remarks, is not money, as I took my departure by a train which left Toronto on the morning of a bitterly cold day. Snow covered the ground already to the depth of several inches, and, borne on the wings of a biting east wind, it still came whirling down in blinding flakes. The hoary rocks, which have been hewn into their present shape by the thundering blows of the cataract, and have withstood the ice-crush of so many winters, were hung with long glittering icicles, and the forest-trees presented an almost magical appearance. The frost coated their trunks and branches with transparent ice, and all around seemed sprinkled over with diamonds from the myriads of sparkling crystals. The Falls undoubtedly surpass all expectations, and thrill and impress the visitor. Never resting and never conquered by any obstacle, they are the realized idea of active power and irresistible strength ; and all that has been written about them fails to give an adequate idea of their grandeur. They are too stupendous to be described. The sublime entirely overwhelms one's sight, and it is not possible by words to describe the sensation of vastness which is experienced on approaching them. Unbroken by any obstacle, in simple majesty the enormous mass of water, which has never paused since it began to exist, and will never pause until time shall cease to be, descends with a single bound on the huge boulders that are washed down from the sides of the rocks around, and stuns one with its thundering sound. Water, vapour, foam and atmosphere are all mixed up together in sublime confusion, shutting out the entire sky from view. A steady, deafening roar thunders incessantly in one's ears, under which the very ground perceptibly quails and vibrates. On several occasions I remained till after sunset and watched the parting light as it gradually faded from the upper part of the unbroken mass of emerald water, and felt overwhelmed by the beauty of the scene. It is little more than a hundred years since the Falls were first seen by a white man, a Jesuit missionary. They were then surrounded by dark and gloomy forests, and unknown save to the Indians; but to-day their various points of vantage are invaded by young couples enjoying their honeymoons, and by people of the *grand tour;* and thousands of the curious will, no doubt, in future come to admire their magnitude and splendour. So much for the Niagara.

Spring came at last; the winter's icy shroud had disappeared as I boarded one of the steamers that run down the lake and the river St. Lawrence. About six miles below the town of Kingston begins that remarkable chain of islands which, with the Gallop, Long Sault, and Lachine rapids, constitute the big sights of the St. Lawrence river. They are called the "Thousand Islands," but their actual number belies their name, for there are no less than 1,800 of them. They are of all sizes, and being mostly wooded to the water's brink, they present a rich succession of picturesque landscapes. The water is studded with them. We came to the first rapid, and over it we went like a shot. There is such a fascination in the sliding, down-hill motion in a steamer that I wished, whilst we sped through the calm reach below, the next rapid might be longer. The second, the Long Sault, is a continuous rapid of nine miles, rushing along at the rate of about twenty miles an hour. Its channel is divided in the centre by an island which is passed quite close by the steamers, but such is the velocity of the current that the rocks and trees displayed themselves only in blurred outlines as we flew wildly past them. The Coteau, Cedar, Split Rock, and Cascade rapids followed successively, but they are of smaller extent than either of the preceding ones, though their passage is also very exciting. The last are the Lachine rapids, which begin nine miles above Montreal, opposite the Indian village of Caughnawaga, which boasts of a famous team of La Crosse players. These rapids are considered the most difficult for navigation, and a canal has been built for the purpose of avoiding them, the current being so swift and wild. Our steamer, however, not being deeply laden, kept to the river the whole distance, and descending the rapids in safety we reached at last that *chef-d'œuvre* of engineering—the Victoria Bridge; and darkness fell as we drew alongside the wharves of Montreal.

The next step in my journey was by the Grand Trunk railway to Quebec. The appearance of this town, with its fortress on a high rock, bears in its general conformation some resemblance to the old town of Edinburgh. Mounting the steep streets I came to the entrance of the fort, and passing through a series of gates I soon reached the highest point of Cape Diamond, upon which the citadel stands, with its guns of very large calibre. Surveying the scenery from the ramparts of the old French fortifications, I was delighted with the view obtained over the entire town and the river, Point Levi on the opposite shore; the Isle of Orleans, where the English army under General Wolfe landed in June, 1759; and the low ground adjoining the St. Lawrence stretching away for several miles with woods, mountains, pastures and fields in great diversity. The whole expanse of the river beneath one's eye swarms with steamers and every kind of river-craft darting hither and thither in incessant activity. It is one of the finest sights in Canada, and the eyes become almost bewildered when they wander over the whole wide panorama. In the far distance the Falls of the Montmorency river are just discernible. They are too far off to see them distinctly, but their thin shades and the dimly glittering lights on the tumbling water enable one to guess where they are. On the neighbouring Plains of Abraham was fought the memorable battle which resulted in the defeat of the French army and the death of General Wolfe. The spot where the hero expired is marked by a rock, and pointed out to visitors.

I took a ride to the Montmorency Falls, seven miles below Quebec, on my way to that most wonderful of rivers—the Saguenay. The road passes through the French village of Beauport, and the scenery around is very pleasing. The stream descends over a rocky wall two hundred and forty feet in height, from which the visitor in favourable weather enjoys a fine panoramic view of a wide hill-girt sweep of the basin of the St. Lawrence. In winter the spray of the tumbling stream freezes very often to a cone of ice, and numbers of people resort there for the purpose of enjoying the favourite pastime of tobogganing from the top of the cone down the steep incline.

I continued my excursion by steamer. The banks of the St. Lawrence are partly overgrown with wood, partly bare or pasture-land, with spaces of cultivated land between. The landscape for some distance has few striking beauties of its own, and presents rather a sameness of undulating surfaces which are only here and there relieved by villages, decidedly French in character, amongst which the lovely Cacouna—famous as a summer resort of families from Quebec and Montreal—chiefly attracts the eye of the stranger. Further on, however, the broad surface of the river is interspersed with rugged, solitary islets, some covered with trees to the water's edge, whilst others are nothing more than bald, bleak rocks, serving as a foreground to intricate masses of stern heights, which rise to the clouds beyond, and recede in the distance into fleecy mountains of bright and silvery snow. They afford a prospect so charming that if there were nothing else to be seen the tourist would be well repaid; but in addition to this the contrast of the broad St Lawrence with the narrow Saguenay is in the highest degree astounding. How sudden and how wonderful the change is! On gliding into this gloomy river, wild nature stares one in the face in naked majesty and primitive grandeur. The river is flanked on either side by mountains which almost shut out the very light of heaven, and pile on pile of massive cliffs, varying in perpendicular height from 1,200 to 1,600 feet, rise precipitately out of the clear, deep water, whose ceaseless music is heard as it laves their jagged sides. How the swift river scourges the rocky walls! The scene at every turn is one of untamed wildness. Ever and anon glens widen down upon us, and forest glades lead our hearts away into the gloom of their recesses; rugged and stupendous rocks, beaten and torn by the storms of centuries, look sullenly down—here an overhanging ledge with stunted shrubs

THE "BRANDY-POTS" IN THE RIVER ST. LAWRENCE.

—there a towering precipice, from whose summit ages of frost have broken masses of rocks, which lie here and there in shattered fragments on the strand. This is the character of the Saguenay from its mouth to its source. It seems one huge mountain rent asunder at some remote age by some great convulsion of nature. Grey clouds were brooding over the river, and the heavy rains which had prevailed for several days in the mountains, had swollen the rivulets, which poured down from the hillsides and rocks into the river as we steamed by. Under the dark shadow of the overhanging mountains the steamer seemed like a floating toy launched on the unfathomable depth—a diminutive but bold intruder into the mysteries of the rock-bound and precipitous mountain-gorge. The distant breaking crash of the water, as it beat against the rugged shore, was heard from afar as we approached Ha-ha Bay, which is sixty miles from the mouth of the river, and affords the first landing. The name "Ha-ha" Bay is said to have arisen from the circumstance of early navigators who were proceeding in sailing vessels up the river, through what was apparently an endless succession of stern and high rocks, without hope of landing or finding bottom for their anchors, breaking out at last into laughing "ha-ha" when they reached this landing and anchorage. The distance from Quebec to Ha-ha Bay is about 200 miles.

Re-entering and passing down the St. Lawrence river Bic Island came prominently into view. Several other rocky shoals, amongst which the dangerous "Brandy Pots" stem the mighty current of the stream, and a string of snug villages and hamlets extend along the shore, of which the quaint little white-washed houses with red roofs, and the tin or tile-covered church spires, glitter in the sunshine.

I went on board the Allan Line steamer *Hibernian*, bound for Liverpool, at Father Point. The anchor was weighed, and the vessel forged down the St. Lawrence through many interesting objects. Forests, rocks, and mountains, displaying their striking summits, imparted animation and varied beauty to the scenery. It is impossible not to speak with enthusiasm of this river, which flows beyond Father Point with majestic quiet and shows near its mouth the enormous width of forty miles. Vessels of every description throng the river, and the sea-going steamers and tug-drawn ships, rich with various sorts of products and lined with human beings, afford a highly interesting sight as the traveller passes along. The effect of the groups of sailing vessels with all sails spread, which reflect in the clear stream, is very peculiar. They suggest the idea of immense birds floating and skimming on the water, and no wonder that the ships of Cartier, the first discoverer of Canada, when seen by the Delaware Indians, who inhabited then the shores of the river, filled them with amazement and fear. They thought that some huge, dark animals with broad, white wings, spitting out fire and bellowing with the voice of thunder, were passing over the river.

The shades were falling fast, and the faint rays of the evening sun were playing among the ridges of the mountains we had left behind us, as we steamed into the Gulf of St. Lawrence. One night and part of the next day of lonely sea, and then the island of Anticosti relieved the monotony of the scene. We passed near enough to be within tolerably good view of the island, but its entire coast seems marshy and bleak, with only one solitary sign of human habitation visible, what we thought to be a lighthouse on its south-western extremity. The following day the coast of Labrador hove in sight to our left, whilst the gloomy, mysterious mountain-masses of Newfoundland presented an uninviting and indeed menacing appearance to our right. Soon after this the Strait of Belle Isle was fairly entered. Here, the descent of drizzly rain obscured the view to some extent, but occasionally the sun broke through the clouds and allowed us a glimpse or two of the scarred and desolate rocks. Later on, the weather was very rough and changeable; dark clouds gathered like a black curtain, and gave unwelcome augury of a soaking wet night. The swell of the sea was very considerable, so much so that it was difficult to decide which

COAST OF LABRADOR.

was harder, to keep on one's feet during the evening, or to keep in bed during the night, but in the morning the swell had much subsided and the day turned out very bright. We enjoyed genial sunshine, but there along the coast snow was still lying in the deep gulches and water-courses—winter was still lingering there in the lap of spring. Yet bleak and desolate as are the shores of Labrador, they are grand and sometimes strangely beautiful. One need not envy those who can regard such a scene with indifference. The dark cliffs rear their huge forms that have been sculptured by tempests, and moulded by the hands of frost-giants into their present shape, and towards evening it is grand to see their long shadows falling on the surface of the waves. But grander still must be the sight when the Atlantic is lashed into fury, and the wild breakers, like the battalions of an invading host, charge up as if determined to carry the fortress, and fling their spray high in the air over the loftiest summits of the savage rocks. To think of a stormy December night out here, when the shrieking wind seems to be the only thing alive in a great, bleak, starless, snowy world!

The great projection of land, called Labrador, extends between Hudson's Bay and the Atlantic ocean, being separated from the most northern point of Newfoundland by the Straits of Belle Isle, which are but twelve miles in width. The dimensions of this peninsula are enormous, its extreme length is one thousand one hundred miles, its breadth four hundred and seventy miles. The popular idea regarding Labrador is well founded, there is not, perhaps, on the face of the earth a more uninviting region than Labrador. On the greater part of it snow lies from September till June, and in winter the coast is inaccessible for the most part, being blockaded by icefields drifting from Baffin's Bay. In spring and summer thousands of glittering icebergs, stranded or floating, impart a stern beauty to the grim and rocky shores, and storms of a terrific character are very frequent. The whole of this vast wilderness is uninhabited by civilized man, with the exception of a few settlements on the St. Lawrence, several mission stations of the Moravian Brethren on the Atlantic coast, and some widely separated trading posts of the whilom Hudson Bay Company. Otherwise its silence is unbroken save by the cry of wild beasts, and the solemn roar of the ocean. Wandering tribes of Nasquapee and Wistasini Indians are thinly scattered over the interior, while nomadic tribes of Esquimaux occupy the northern coast. During the brief summer the whole coast for hundreds of miles swarms with fishermen from Newfoundland, Nova Scotia, Canada and the United States. They are engaged in the capture and cure of cod, salmon and herring. Fatal disasters are frequent among the small fishing craft, as the bleak coast is often swept by storms, their ships are dashed to pieces, and the poor fishermen shipwrecked and lost. There was one of the Moravian missionaries, from one of the settlements mentioned above, on board of our steamer, and his fellow-passengers did not tire in listening to his stories of storms, wreck and disasters; of how a ship was driven ashore one wild night; how brave men gathered to the rescue; how the crew one after another dropped into the water; how a young mother was washed ashore, dead, clasping a babe in her arms, and other tales of horror. As the shores were fading away from our sight, a detached iceberg, and a multitude of floating ice-flakes, which occupied a large space, were seen in the distance, and a group of Newfoundland whalers headed northward towards the cheerless region where the veil dropped over the hapless *Erebus* and *Terror*, and where Sir John Franklin with his brave crew disappeared into its icy breast. What a wonderful sight it is to see the chaste and stately icebergs, with their fantastic shapes in grandly picturesque arrangement, their glittering pinnacles and dazzling white turrets, sail slowly past, carrying in their bosom fragments from the Arctic mountains to help in the erection of a new continent!

Our steamer proceeded on her trackless path—once more was I rocking in the swell of the Atlantic on my homeward way. The voyage became tedious as we got into the open sea, and any land, it seemed to me, would have appeared beautiful to most of my pining fellow-passengers. Cold, unpleasant days with gusts of wind succeeded each other, the sun peeping occasionally in fitful glances through the clouds. These atmospheric changes continued during the whole voyage, and only a few of the passengers ventured to crawl on deck for a little shivering.

At early dawn of a raw, misty morning we entered the Mersey, and as we were steaming up the river the sailors were busy washing the decks, which seemed to me a very unnecessary proceeding in the dull fog and the drizzly rain which was falling. Shortly afterwards our steamer reached Liverpool, and as we were bowling towards the landing-stage in front of one of the docks, the bells rang out from the spires their merry peal to the air of *Home Again.* "All's well that ends well."

Thus comes to an end the record of my nine years' travels, which, I trust, is not wholly uninteresting. Much more perchance might be said, but I think I can hear the reader exclaim from the recesses of his cozy room, into which these uninvited pages may intrude: "No more of America!" And he shall be obeyed, for there is a limit in everything, which, I fear, I have already much exceeded.

Many of my travels were accompanied by discomfort, some were even full of dangers and privations, but though I have not always steered my course quite successfully through the manifold shallows and breakers that lay ahead in my lot, I have gained at least a rich and varied experience which no money can purchase. Besides this, I have outlived romance indeed, and roused myself from some dreamings. One thinks of all the charms and wonders of a tropical clime, of ever green islands, with groves of palms and golden oranges, but finds out to one's own sorrow that there are two sides to the question. These islands are all very pleasant and beautiful, but their unfailing accompaniment of fevers, heat and biting insects are the reverse of it. I may remark, however, by the way, while reviewing for a moment the unpleasant side of my travels, that I think with saddened feelings only of the few weeks which I spent at Havana in a very perilous position. My visit there I had cause to regret, for there I discovered by painful experience what an entirely new signification the word " travelling " acquires in time of sickness; yet let me add that I have not the slightest doubt of there being much scenery of great beauty on the island of Cuba, which unfortunately I was debarred by my illness from seeing. Of all other places, however, which I visited during my rambles, I retain a grateful memory; every country has left me some agreeable reminiscences to recall. Backwards my memory is often traversing, and when I think of California, it conveys to my mind a vivid idea of the inexhaustible variety of its resources—an idea of fragrant pine-forests, of snow-capped mountains mirrored in quiet, timber-belted lakes; of deep cañons and foaming cataracts; of vine-clad hills with fruit-farms at their feet; and of babbling brooks and streams rippling in the sunshine. On the Sandwich Islands I received a lasting impression of bright, blue skies; the ever-changing sea; the most brilliant moon and glittering stars; but above all, of their awe-inspiring fire-fountains and extinct volcanoes. How many sweet recollections Hilo conjures up in my mind! My enjoyments there were only tinged by regret that I had to leave. Panama recalls a memory of gorgeous flowers on hills, in valleys and dales; of fragrant blossoms which birds and insects seek; and—what wealth of colour and dreaminess of twilight, what noble sunsets I have witnessed there! With what humble adoration I often raised my head and looked up to the glowing skies that roof these tangled forests! Only Havana is an exception, it brings but recollections of dull suffering, and of the saddest episode of my travels, to my mind. Yet even after this trial my love for nature still remains clear and bright, and in spite of toil and trouble, with which some of my rambles were associated, there remains still much happiness to me in remembering the enjoyments of those days when I roamed at large. They well repay me for all I had suffered for them, for "memory no less than sight owes many of its charms to the far away." I am back from the far West, back from the lands of marvels—but my heart lingers there still. Recollections sometimes throng my fancy, and now that these days are over, and I breathe again under the old British flag, my thoughts often go flying back to the cloudless skies of these lands, and to the people I have known there. Even when in bed at night, the places I visited, and from whose haunts I am now so far removed, pass often vividly across my mind, and I live my little adventures over again in my sleep. Much depends in a great measure upon the companionship of one's travels. I must say that I was, on the whole, fortunate in mine. I brought away with me weird stories from the lips of frontiersmen, Indians and trappers, as they told them around their campfires; and when I peruse the lines of my diary, which were jotted down amid the scenes described, my memory recalls the incidents in them, and then my heart sinks from fear that I shall never see the like, nor enjoy such happiness again. An old aphorism says that if a man once becomes a sailor, a soldier, or an artist, it is hard for him to give it up, because there is a dash of vagabondage in either of these occupations which fascinates him; so I hope that, should I again go forth, it may be to visit fresh scenes of beauty, for having for so many years communed with nature proves that I can be held long in the bondage of admiring the Creator's beautiful handiwork. Such is man—always either anticipating or recalling. I have not been long back, and yet I am in thoughts again rambling through beautiful forests and swimming in rippling streams. A rest, however, will prove beneficial to me. And now I must rest my weary pen also, and bid adieu to the reader.

THE END.

www.ingramcontent.com/pod-product-compliance
Lightning Source LLC
Chambersburg PA
CBHW030554300426
44111CB00009B/971